People, Politics, and Child Welfare
in British Columbia

Edited by Leslie T. Foster and Brian Wharf

People, Politics, and Child Welfare in British Columbia

UBCPress · Vancouver · Toronto

16 15 14 13 12 11 10 09 08 07   5 4 3 2 1

Printed in Canada on ancient-forest-free paper (100% post-consumer recycled) that is processed chlorine- and acid-free, with vegetable-based inks.

Library and Archives Canada Cataloguing in Publication

People, politics, and child welfare in British Columbia / edited by Leslie T. Foster and Brian Wharf.

Includes bibliographical references and index.
ISBN 978-0-7748-1372-3 (bound); 978-0-7748-1373-0 (pbk.)

1. Child welfare – Government policy – British Columbia. 2. Child welfare – British Columbia. 3. Poverty – British Columbia. 4. Child welfare – Government policy – British Columbia – History. I. Foster, Leslie T., 1947- II. Wharf, Brian

HV745.B7P45 2007   362.709711   C2007-900459-8

Canadä

UBC Press gratefully acknowledges the financial support for our publishing program of the Government of Canada through the Book Publishing Industry Development Program (BPIDP), and of the Canada Council for the Arts, and the British Columbia Arts Council.

This book has been published with the help of a grant from the Canadian Federation for the Humanities and Social Sciences, through the Aid to Scholarly Publications Programme, using funds provided by the Social Sciences and Humanities Research Council of Canada.

All royalties from sales of this volume will go to the Together Against Poverty Society.

Printed and bound in Canada by Friesens
Set in Stone by Artegraphica Design
Copy editor: Audrey McClellan
Proofreader: Sarah Munro
Indexer: Nora Johnston

UBC Press
The University of British Columbia
2029 West Mall
Vancouver, BC V6T 1Z2
604-822-5959 / Fax: 604-822-6083
www.ubcpress.ca

Contents

Figures and Tables

Foreword

Deryck Thomson

"Two parents can't raise a child any more than one. You need
a whole community – everybody – to raise a child."

– Toni Morrison

"Children are the nation's most precious asset" – so goes an oft-repeated
adage. If it is true, why do we continue to allow one child in every five to
live in poverty among us, even though a motion to eliminate child poverty
by the year 2001 was approved unanimously sixteen years ago in Canada's
House of Commons?

This is, of course, a rhetorical question for which we already have the
answers. Despite public posturing, political pronouncements, and govern-
mental assurances, the care and protection of children hold a low priority
on political agendas. This is particularly true if the children's parents are
poor, trapped in a socio-economic milieu that profoundly affects the care
and nurture of about a million young members of this nation's "most precious asset."

Despite best efforts, families do break down. If there are not sufficient
community resources available to help put them back together, the welfare
of infants and children may be deemed at such risk that the state is required
to intercede.

Just how effectively the British Columbia government has carried out its
statutory obligations is a major theme of this book. As they record the government's successes and failures, the authors provide a compelling account
of child welfare in British Columbia and the evolution of its policies, programs, and practices since its inception in 1901, when the *Children's Protection Act* was passed. The book pays a well-deserved tribute to the hard
slogging of a small but feisty group of female pioneers who were appalled
by the practice of warehousing infants and children in orphanages and

workhouses, rather than placing them in supervised foster homes for their care and protection.

From that early era to the present, the state's responsibility for child welfare has been the subject of sharp philosophical differences, political twists and turns, numerous legislative amendments, bureaucratic tinkering, and a continuing ambivalence about its role in relation to a mixed voluntary and government-funded community-based social services sector focused on preventing family breakdown.

One of the most egregious issues in child welfare, not only in British Columbia but throughout Canada, was the enforced separation of Aboriginal children from their parents and community during their learning years. These children were confined in residential schools funded by the federal government and operated by religious orders whose sole objective was to break all familial and cultural bonds and replace them with the norms and institutions of the predominant white society. Formal public apologies for this treatment have been issued by church and state, but the ill effects continue, the most blatant evident in the disproportionate number of Aboriginal children still being taken into government care. Only in recent years have Aboriginal communities won the legal right to assume responsibility for the welfare of their own children and the preservation of their cultural heritage. (Traditionally, Aboriginal people have used storytellers to preserve family and community histories, passing records orally from one generation to the next. One such story has been included in this book.)

The book was produced by a collective of seasoned observers and participants in the fray (an appropriate word for what follows), consisting of academics, former senior civil servants, First Nations academics and storytellers, and some "boots-on-the-ground" community social work practitioners. All share a common interest in the ongoing development of child welfare policies, programs, and practice within the province's distinctive urban, rural, and Aboriginal communities. Their thoughtful contributions are embedded in solid scholarship, research, and some street-smart experience acquired in the ongoing struggle for effective care and protection of children regardless of race, colour, or creed. What has emerged from this joint endeavour is an ongoing and fascinating saga involving people and personalities, power and politics. Its outcome continues to depend on the rest of us.

Interviews were conducted with former cabinet ministers (including a premier) responsible for enactment of old, and implementation of new, legislation under the aegis of Social Credit, New Democratic, and Liberal governments with notably diverse approaches to ensuring the welfare of children and families, each secure in the belief that its policies were in the best interests of all concerned. Consultations were sought with a variety of others, including former senior civil servants who had weathered the political and media storms in carrying out policies; front-line staff members responsible for all the heavy lifting; and last, but by no means least, parents and their advocates with first-hand experience of the bureaucratic maze.

Among other things, the book focuses on several major issues that have arisen in the last three decades of the twentieth century and the first years of the new millennium. Five events in particular have had profound effects on child welfare in British Columbia. The first was the election of a New Democratic Party (NDP) government in 1972. The NDP premier, Dave Barrett, was a professional social worker, fully grounded in the social democratic principle of active partnership between government and governed. He lost no time in appointing an elected social work colleague to the human resources ministry, and this man, Norm Levi, moved with astonishing speed to clean the ministerial house from top to bottom – mandate, mission, administrative and line staff complement. Within a whirlwind first (and only) term of office, Levi integrated and decentralized a multiplicity of services to be administered under the new *Community Resources Act,* which devolved substantial responsibility for administration and delivery of social services to locally elected community resource boards. This experiment lasted only three years, which was not long enough to allow its potential to be realized. Along with his associates, Levi led a moribund ministry through a sea change unmatched by any previous reorganization, only to have it overturned a few years later by his Social Credit successor, who quickly reined in the community activists by returning control to the central bureaucracy.

Several years later, another swing of the political pendulum returned the NDP to power. Like her NDP predecessor, the new minister, Joan Smallwood, was determined to return democracy to the community marketplace, where decisions regarding social services should reside. In short order she had dispatched two panels of knowledgeable, experienced community participants to travel across the province, seeking proposals for strengthening and improving the child welfare enterprise. She would decide how to proceed based on the proposals and recommendations solicited from hundreds of citizens across the province, including First Nations constituencies. The vast majority recommended that ministry services be community-based, decentralized, and placed under citizen control. Community development was the tool by which these objectives would be achieved.

The speed and passion with which Smallwood approached the task disconcerted a cautious ministry bureaucracy. She was relieved of her cabinet post before she could fully implement her plans. The process stumbled, but carried on at a slower pace. Despite attempts to introduce outcome measurements and related corporate management techniques, there was only a slight variation in numbers of children coming into or moving out of ministry care.

The third event took place in 1992, but did not become public knowledge for quite some time. A five-and-a-half-year-old child had died in horrific circumstances while known to the ministry but not under the ministry's supervision. In 1994, the minister who replaced Smallwood, Joy MacPhail, ordered an independent inquiry, chaired by Justice Thomas Gove, to look into the child's death. After receiving the sworn testimony of 115 witnesses, the inquiry's final report was released in November 1995. The inquiry prefaced its 118 recommendations with the statement that care and protection of the child was to remain paramount in all future deliberations. Many of the recommendations centred on the need for preventive programs and services that were community-based and readily accessible with governance under direction of citizen boards and community councils. Throughout the province the report received widespread public and media attention, which reiterated the need for construction of community-based support services designed to prevent family breakdown and consequent government intervention.

The fourth event took place as the new century dawned. The political pendulum swung once again, this time bringing a Liberal government to power. Another visionary minister, Gordon Hogg, found himself caught in the middle of a growing dilemma: how to do more with less. The governance of programs and management was to be ceded to several appointed regional authorities, whose primary task was to reduce expenditures for children and family services by 30 percent. This directive left many currently proposed and badly needed preventive community initiatives wallowing in the dust. A midterm review restored some of the funding, but still fell far short of requirements.

And the fifth event, one that is still unfolding, relates to the multiplicity of reviews and recommendations following the murder of a young aboriginal child who was being cared for by a relative under a "kith and kin" agreement. In large measure the future of the child welfare enterprise in British Columbia will be determined by the outcome of government response to these reviews.

Child welfare remains a work in progress, with roads to be travelled and songs to be sung before poverty is replaced by health and well-being for all children. Having spent more than fifty years of my professional life on this fascinating journey, I hope you will join me on this journey after reading this book.

Preface

Child welfare is a tough area to work in and to write about. It is also tough for children and their families who end up in the system. It is an area, however, that does not appear to be important to the general public. After all, only 1 to 1.5 percent of British Columbia's children are in the care of the state during any particular year. But when something goes wrong, as it must – it is impossible to protect all of the children all of the time – there is a media furor and public outcry from whomever is the opposition political party at the time, focusing on problems with the system and demands for something new to be done or for someone's head to roll.

It has been difficult to finish this book. We started work on it in early 2004, and since then we have found it challenging to keep up with the almost continuous changes in the child welfare enterprise. For example, since early 2004 there have been numerous leadership changes in the province's child welfare ministry, with four different ministers responsible for child welfare (Tom Christensen replaced Stan Hagen in August 2006) and no fewer than four different deputy ministers or acting deputy ministers. Such is the instability of child welfare leadership and the rapidity of change.

As a result of these changes, we have provided updates for some of the later chapters in the book in an attempt to portray the emerging child welfare story in the province. The first complete draft was finished in October 2005, but since then there have been even more changes. In particular, there have been several reviews of the circumstances surrounding the murder of a young Aboriginal child who was in the child welfare system. One of those reports has not yet been released to the public, even though it is complete, because the Attorney General continues to review it to ensure the privacy of people involved was protected.

Since the beginning of September 2006, there have been several important child welfare–related events that we would like to mention, only because they represent unfinished business in the child welfare enterprise in British Columbia and illustrate the difficulties of completing the "story." At the beginning of September, the number of Aboriginal children in care exceeded the number of non-Aboriginal children in care for the first time in the province's history, as predicted in Chapter 2. This trend continued into October.

On 20 September 2006, the Child and Youth Officer and the Provincial Health Officer released a special joint report, "Health and Well-Being of Children in Care in British Columbia: Report 1 on Health Services Utilization and Mortality." To no one's surprise, the health of children in continuing care, where the government is the sole guardian, is substantially poorer than that of children not in care. Children in continuing care experienced similar common health problems to those not in care, but at rates 1.2 to 1.4 times those of the general child population. In addition, nearly 65 percent of children in continuing care suffered from mental disorders, a rate over four times that of the general child and youth population. The report also noted higher rates of pregnancy among female youth in continuous care, higher rates for intentional and unintentional injuries and poisonings, and higher death rates. For those who leave care, the dismal picture does not end, as the poorer health status persists. Clearly, while government care might be safer in some instances than being in the care of one's family, the prospects for children in state care are not bright.

The attempt to appoint a new Representative for Children and Youth has run into political wrangling between the government and opposition, with each blaming the other for delays in meeting to interview and hire the representative. This is in spite of a plea by Ted Hughes, the author of a major review on child welfare released in April 2006, to depoliticize child welfare. Hughes was also the person who recommended that the Representative position be created, in his report on the child welfare system. Hughes, who had remained silent since delivering his report, publicly admonished the politicians on 2 October, suggesting that they get "on with it." As reporter Les Leyne noted in his column of 3 October 2006, in the *Victoria Times Colonist,* "Hughes said bluntly the month-long delay in picking someone for the new representative for children and youth post that he recommended is 'unacceptable'" (p. A.10).

A recent coroner's report on the murder of another child in care has kept the media spotlight on the child welfare enterprise, although the death occurred five years ago. The story of child welfare in British Columbia continues to evolve.

Leslie T. Foster and Brian Wharf
October 2006

Note to readers: Although most chapters focus on a particular policy, practice, or individual, the antecedents to events are often the same for different chapters. Thus readers will encounter some duplication of material that chapter authors deemed necessary for telling a complete and coherent story.

Acknowledgments

Our thanks go to the many politicians, public servants, and child protection workers who helped shape child welfare policy and practice over the past half century, particularly those who consented to share their views, sometimes with the authors of more than one chapter. We also want to thank the authors, who spent many hours interviewing, discussing, drafting, and redrafting their contributions. We acknowledge the work of Jean Wilson of UBC Press, who supported this project from its beginning, and of Anna Eberhard Friedlander, who helped guide us through the final stages to publication. Thanks also go to the external reviewers of the first draft of the manuscript for their thoughtful comments, and to the UBC Press staff who assisted in the editorial process.

As we developed this book, we received financial support from the Ministry of Children and Family Development and the Ministry of Health. In addition, the two ministries gave us unlimited access to annual and other reports as well as to historical and contemporary data and information, which are presented in several of the chapters and also in the appendices at the end of the book. Special mention should be made of the assistance provided to us by Brian McKee, who took many of the rough figures, tables, and maps and made them presentable and also helped enormously in the final preparation of the manuscript. Colleagues at the University of Victoria in the Human and Social Development Faculty and the International Institute of Child Rights and Development also gave us support.

We pay tribute to our families. Les was helped in many ways, too many to mention, by his wife, Mary Virtue, and also by the patience and encouragement of his children, Noelle, Stefan, Christopher, and Dylan. As always, Brian's chapters benefited from the incisive comments provided by his wife, Marilyn Callahan.

Last, but far from least, we pay tribute to the resilience of the children and families who survived the abuse of poverty over many decades. However, those who survived the assaults on their cultures, communities, and families carried out by the many colonization initiatives introduced by the federal government and supported in part by the province are perhaps the real heroes in this book.

Abbreviations

BA(CYC)	Bachelor of Arts in Child and Youth Care degree
BCGEU	British Columbia Government Employees Union
BSW	Bachelor of Social Work degree
CAS	Children's Aid Society
CELDIC	Commission on Emotional and Learning Disorders in Children
CFCSA	*Child, Family and Community Service Act*
CHHRC	Community health and human resource centre
CIC	Children in care of the state
CRB	Community resource board
HSDA	Health service delivery area
IA	Income assistance
JAMC	Joint Aboriginal Management Committee
MCFD	Ministry of Children and Family Development
MOU	Memorandum of understanding
MSS	Ministry of Social Services
MSW	Master of Social Work degree
NDP	New Democratic Party
OACAS	Ontario Association of Children's Aid Societies
ORAM	Ontario risk-assessment model
UBCIC	Union of British Columbia Indian Chiefs
VRB	Vancouver Resource Board

Introduction:
People, Politics, and Child Welfare
Brian Wharf

The story of the evolution of services for abused and neglected children in British Columbia has been told only in a scattered and incomplete fashion: in scholarly articles (see, among others, Armitage, 1998; Sullivan, 1998), judicial inquiries and reviews (Gove, 1995; Hughes, 2006; Royal Commission on Family and Children's Law, 1975), reports from government (*Making Changes* [Community Panel, 1992] and *Liberating Our Children, Liberating Our Nations* [Aboriginal Committee of the Community Panel 1992]), and chapters in books (Callahan, 1987; Cruickshank, 1987). Each of these reviews has chronicled a particular time or event in the history of child welfare services. This book marks the first attempt to tell the story from its beginnings to mid-2006.

The first objective of the book is to provide a historical description of the development of services, but it is not the only objective. Other aims, described in more detail below, are to explore the philosophies and ideologies that have guided the development of policy and practice in child welfare; consider whether large bureaucratic organizations, such as provincial ministries of child welfare, can accept and implement innovations; and inquire into the impact of the many organizational changes that have occurred in the ministry responsible for child welfare in British Columbia.

Philosophies and Ideologies in Child Welfare
As mentioned, the second objective of the book is to look at the number of conflicting philosophical positions and ideologies that have swirled around policy and practice in child welfare. The first such conflict is articulated by the concept of public issues and private troubles (Mills, 1959). Public issues are those such as poverty, an inadequate supply of low-cost housing, and high levels of unemployment. Individuals experience these public issues in a very direct way but are largely powerless to change them. To be sure, some individuals, by dint of hard work, perseverance, and resiliency, are able to cope with and overcome public issues. Nevertheless, these issues remain as

a continuing feature of Canadian society, and their eradication requires intervention by the state.

Private troubles refer to personal matters such as marital breakdown or emotional and mental health problems. Although they may be affected by public issues, private troubles are, to some extent, amenable to resolution by individual effort. The welfare of children is an example of an area influenced by the combined effect of public issues and the private troubles of parents. Yet even though public issues can have an impact on families, they have remained in the background, and the attention of policy-makers has been focused primarily on private troubles. Thus, despite the significant growth of programs and services and the many changes that have been made, the child welfare enterprise remains anchored in the position that the welfare of children is the responsibility of parents and that the appropriate role of the state is to intervene only when parents neglect and abuse their children. The philosophy holds, further, that state intervention should occur as a last resort when the resources of parents, relatives, friends, and voluntary organizations have been exhausted. In the social welfare literature, this philosophical position focused on private troubles is known as "residualism." The essence of this position has been captured in the words of a historian: "The prejudices of the dominant belief system have regularly encouraged many Canadian child savers, whether private philanthropists, professional social workers or reform-minded citizens, to be blind to collective injuries whether they be of gender, race or class. Not surprisingly, such myopia favours techniques such as casework, but also psychologizing of all sorts that pathologize the individual. In contrast, community development approaches that require a panoramic perspective on children in distress, struggle against a normative vision of the world that resists institutional change" (Strong-Boag, 2002, p. 35).

A second conflict has arisen between policy-makers who favour providing support to families versus those who hold that the priority in child welfare is to protect children. Viewed from an objective perspective, it seems foolish to set these positions in opposition to each other. Rather, as many scholars and practitioners have argued (see, for example, Cameron, 2003; Peters, Peters, Laurendeau, Chamberland, and Peirson, 2001; and Chapters 3, 6, and 9 in this book), both are necessary and support each other. However, proponents of the two positions have had difficulty reconciling their views because of a significant difference in the assumptions that lie behind the positions. Proponents of the support position have argued that all families, not just those who neglect or abuse their children, require programs such as daycare and other support services (Cameron and Vanderwoerd, 1997; Wharf, 2002). They view such services as social utilities (Kahn and Kamerman, 1975) that are as necessary in today's society as public health and education and, therefore, should be available on a universal basis.

The advocates of the protection argument hold that most families manage well and that resources should be targeted to those experiencing difficulties in raising children. The differences are further heightened by the availability of resources. Obviously, developing universal programs for all children is an expensive proposition, an expense not incurred when only the vulnerable few are targeted. In rebuttal, advocates of universality argue that targeting inevitably stigmatizes users, and in doing so it adds to their feelings of inadequacy and powerlessness.

It is important to note at the outset that the contributors to this book hold the view that despite the many changes that have occurred in policies and practices, the enterprise of child welfare remains anchored in a paradigm of saving the child from abusive and neglectful parents. The child-saving paradigm is philosophically consistent with residualism and with a Western/white view of families and children. Numerous research studies have documented that neglect and abuse occur in large part because parents do not have sufficient resources to care for their children (Kitchen et al., 1991; Pelton, 1994; Peters et al., 2001; Ross and Roberts, 1999). Contributors to this book hold that universality and a commitment to cultural values are appropriate and helpful philosophies.

Nowhere has the child-saving paradigm been practised with more pernicious effects than in Aboriginal communities, where First Nations children were "saved" from environments that Western, middle-class social workers and judges saw as inappropriate for the care and proper upbringing of children. The disastrous consequences of child welfare's wholly mistaken efforts to protect First Nations children have long been known to First Nations families, but they received national attention with the publication of *Native Children and the Child Welfare System* (Johnston, 1983). Johnston characterized the era in which literally thousands of First Nations children were taken from their parents as the "Sixties Scoop." Subsequent chapters tell of the struggles of First Nations communities to cope with the effects of this scoop and, more recently, to gain control of child welfare services and provide them in culturally appropriate ways.

Innovations in Child Welfare

Despite the dominance of the Western/white view of the world and of the philosophy of residualism, there have been attempts to develop programs to prevent problems from arising. Such preventive thrusts have typically taken the form of programs to support families and develop the capacity of communities. One significant change occurred during the 1970s with the establishment of community resource boards (CRB) based on the principles of citizen participation, integration, and decentralization of services (Clague, Dill, Seebaran, and Wharf, 1984). The CRB experience is examined in some detail in Chapter 3, and the Ministry of Children and Family Development's attempt to implement a community development program is described in Chapter 6. Other more recent examples include the development of First Nations community control of child welfare. Despite innumerable jurisdictional difficulties, excellent examples of a holistic and community-wide approach have emerged in some First Nations communities (see, for example, Brown, Haddock, and Kovach, 2002; McKenzie, 2002).

The third objective of the book is to identify these efforts and inquire into their outcomes. Since innovations interrupt the established ways of doing things, can they be implemented and continued in a large bureaucracy like the Ministry of Children and Family Development, which is, by definition, bound by rules and regulations? What does it take for innovations to stick and to continue not merely as cosmetic additions to an array of individually oriented services but as genuine efforts to address the lack of resources that face parents?

The fourth objective is to examine the many organizational changes that have occurred. For example, the ministry changed its name on numerous occasions, reorganized the boundaries of its regional and local offices, relinquished responsibility for income assistance, added programs in the area of juvenile justice and mental health, and introduced new service protocols such as risk assessment. All changes were made with the stated intent of improving the effectiveness and efficiency of services. A number of chapters examine whether these organizational reforms have yielded any lasting benefits.

It will be readily apparent that this list of objectives is daunting. Certainly not all are applicable to all chapters, but some will be extremely pertinent to a number of chapters. For example, Chapter 4 describes the residual philosophy that held sway in the 1980s, and spirited arguments for community approaches to child welfare are featured in a number of chapters. When these objectives are considered together, they constitute a detailed inquiry into the troubled and dispute-ridden nature of child welfare.

Adding to the troubles of the child welfare system is the opportunity that mistreatment of children gives the media to bring examples to the attention of the general public. Indeed, the public has a right to know, but the problem occurs when the media tell the stories in lurid prose, criticizing parents and social workers in no uncertain terms. An example is provided by the *Vancouver Sun*'s coverage of the 1994-95 Gove Inquiry:

> After examining literally thousands of pages of transcripts and hundreds of articles we have come to a simple conclusion. The very first article written about the case ... set the tone for all that followed. The story told in the press is one of an evil mother who cared more for herself, her boyfriends and her seedy life-style than for her child. According to this account, many social workers knew about the mother's wholly inadequate care but did

nothing about it. The press stories maintain that social workers behaved in this fashion because they are simple minded and easily duped by a deceitful mother. (Callahan and Callahan, 1997, pp. 42-43)

This kind of coverage is not unexpected when tragedies occur in child welfare. Blaming individuals, be they parents or social workers or foster parents, makes for dramatic reading and grabs the attention of the general public. Like policy-makers, reporters and editors find it easy to focus on private troubles and ignore public issues. By doing so, the media make a huge contribution to maintaining and reinforcing the residual approach.

It should be noted that the day-to-day work of child welfare staff and the many instances of effective assistance to families go unnoticed and unrecorded in the media. However, not all reporters are blind to societal factors. British journalist Melanie Phillips admitted as much when she wrote: "But in crucifying them [social workers] we deflect attention from the real villains. A society which systematically beats up, tortures, buggers and murders children is a deeply sick society. A society which does all of these things and then sets up social workers to take the blame, turning the notion of doing good into the deepest insult, is even more vile, we leave social workers struggling to make a better society than we deserve" (1995, p. 17).

Sources of Information

Information for this book has been collected in a variety of ways. As noted earlier, there are a number of books, articles, and monographs that chronicle a particular era or a unique experience, and these have provided useful information. Annual reports and other documents from the Ministry of Children and Family Development and its predecessor organizations have provided data on changes in personnel and in the structure of the ministry and on the number of children in care. Chapter 2 relies heavily on these sources. In addition, contributors have conducted interviews with individuals who have made a distinct contribution to the evolution of services. The names of these individuals, along with their positions, are noted at the end of each chapter.

At the outset, the editors and contributors agreed that it would not be appropriate to use a detailed interview guide for all interviews. Rather, they decided that contributors would seek information on the following matters:

- the influence of philosophical positions (public issues/private troubles, universal/residual, and support/protection) during the era under review
- changes in legislation and policy, in the structure and organization of the ministry, and in the number of children in care
- changes in the day-to-day practice of child welfare workers
- relationships and changes vis-à-vis the voluntary sector.

Authors were also encouraged to elicit information about, and comment on, unique and important events that occurred in the era under review.

It should be noted that contributors did not disclose their philosophical positions during interviews unless specifically requested to do so. (They did reveal them at the end of the interview.) The intent was not to engage in a debate about philosophies, but to identify the philosophy of those being interviewed and to determine the extent to which their views shaped their work.

We recognize that philosophical positions are difficult to change. They are rooted in values, and, as Nicholas Lemann has pointed out, "it is not what we know, but what we believe in that matters" (2002, p. 99). Values and beliefs are formed in childhood and reinforced by experiences and relationships in adulthood. They represent deeply held convictions about the division of responsibility between individuals, families, and the state, and although some individuals are able to alter their philosophies in response to experience and new information, many cling to early established positions throughout their lives.

People in the Book
We have chosen to tell the story by identifying particular eras in child welfare. All these eras contain a notable event or development, and in each a particular individual or group assumed a leadership role. By tying the story to some dynamic and charismatic figures, the book personalizes and dramatizes the evolution of child welfare services. Thus, chapters profile politicians, senior civil servants, leaders in First Nations' communities, and practitioners.

With two notable exceptions, the chapters do not conspicuously feature the voices of practitioners and, particularly, parents and children who use child welfare services. The exceptions are Chapters 5 and 8. Chapter 5 describes the often-disastrous experiences of First Nations families and children with the Eurocentric child welfare system. Chapter 8 captures the views of both parents and practitioners regarding the use of risk-assessment instruments.

However, some recent literature in child welfare has recorded the opinions of both practitioners and service users, and we rely on this literature to represent their views (see Callahan, Hooper, and Wharf, 1998; Callahan and Lumb, 1995; de Montigny, 1995; Diorio, 1992; Grant, 1998; Mayer and Timms, 1970; Swift, 1995; Weller and Wharf, 2002). When asked, service users present a devastating critique of the child welfare enterprise. They report that all too often the programs and services offered are inappropriate and inadequate. Not only are the public issues of poverty, substandard housing, and unsafe neighbourhoods almost entirely ignored, but the programs aimed at private issues are also inappropriate.

Child welfare staff are typically so harried and preoccupied with investigations and paperwork that they have little time to provide support and counselling. Their response is to refer clients to voluntary agencies that provide short-term programs such as parent education, anger management, and budget preparation. Although they are well-intentioned, such referrals mean that clients are spun like tops between the staff of a number of agencies when what they need is a constant, reassuring, friendly, and practical person in their lives. It is also typical that clients are referred to such programs because they exist and have to be used, not because they are always, or even usually, configured to meet the needs of clients. The remark of a client in one research project summed up the frustration of many: "What I need is a bus pass, what I get is a referral to a parenting program that I do not need and can't get to anyway" (Callahan et al., 1998, p. 13).

As noted earlier in this introduction, many contributors find it difficult to escape the dismal view that little of substance has changed in the efforts to protect children from abuse and neglect. To be sure, the state has greatly expanded the number and range of services it offers to children and families; it has introduced such measures as risk assessment, which are designed to bring certainty to the job of investigation; and it has initiated a dizzying array of organizational and managerial changes. But despite these efforts, the pessimism remains.

We hope that this volume will provide a historical perspective on and analysis of efforts to make change and the results when the public issues of racism, poverty, housing, and employment in these reforms are ignored. Without heeding these lessons, are we doomed to focus our efforts on developing more and more different and ultimately ineffective ways of dealing with personal troubles?

References

Aboriginal Committee of the Community Panel on Family and Children's Services Legislation Review. (1992). *Liberating our children: Liberating our nations*. Victoria: Ministry of Social Services.

Angus, M. (1991). *And the first shall be last*. Toronto: NC Press Limited.

Armitage, A. (1998, Summer). Lost vision: Children and the Ministry for Children and Families. *BC Studies, 118*, 93-122.

Brown, L., Haddock, L., and Kovach, M. (2002). Watching over our families and children: Lalum'utul' Smuneem child and family services. In B. Wharf (Ed.), *Community work approaches to child welfare* (pp. 131-52). Peterborough, ON: Broadview Press.

Callahan, M. (1987). Public apathy and government parsimony. In K.L. Levitt and B. Wharf (Eds.), *The challenge of child welfare* (2nd ed., pp. 1-28). Vancouver: UBC Press.

Callahan, M., and Callahan, K. (1997). Victims and villains: Scandals, the press and policy making in child welfare. In J. Pulkingham and G. Ternowetsky (Eds.), *Child and family policies: Struggles, strategies and options* (pp. 40-58). Halifax: Fernwood Press.

Callahan, M., Hooper, L., and Wharf, B. (1998). *Protecting children by empowering women*. Victoria: University of Victoria, School of Social Work.

Callahan, M., and Lumb, C. (1995). My cheque or my children. *Child Welfare, 74*(4), 796-820.

Cameron, G. (2003). Promoting positive child and family wellness. In K. Kufeldt and B. McKenzie (Eds.), *Child welfare: Connecting research, policy, and practice* (pp. 79-101). Waterloo, ON: Wilfrid Laurier University Press.

Cameron, G., and Vanderwoerd, J. (1997). *Protecting children and supporting families.* New York: Aldine de Gruyter.

Clague, M., Dill, R., Seebaran, R., and Wharf, B. (1984). *Reforming human services: The experience of the community resource boards in B.C.* Vancouver: UBC Press.

Community Panel on Family and Children's Services Legislation Review. (1992). *Making changes: A place to start.* Victoria: Ministry of Social Services.

Cruickshank, D.A. (1987). The Berger Commission report on the protection of children: The impact on prevention of child abuse and neglect. In K.L. Levitt and B. Wharf (Eds.), *The challenge of child welfare* (2nd ed., pp. 182-200). Vancouver: UBC Press.

de Montigny, G.A.J. (1995). *Social working: An ethnography of front line practice.* Toronto: University of Toronto Press.

Diorio, W. (1992). Parental perceptions of the authority of child welfare caseworkers. *Families in society: The journal of contemporary human services, 73*(4), 222-35.

Gove, T. (1995). *Report of the Gove Inquiry into Child Protection in BC* (2 vols.). Victoria: Ministry of the Attorney General.

Grant, L. (1998). *Moving from punishment and treatment to empowerment in child welfare practice: Is it possible?* Unpublished paper, York University, School of Social Work.

Hughes, E.N. (2006). *BC children and youth review: An independent review of BC's child protection system.* Victoria: Ministry of Children and Family Development.

Johnston, P. (1983). *Native children and the child welfare system.* Toronto: Canadian Council on Social Development in association with James Lorimer.

Kahn, A., and Kamerman, S. (1975). *Not for the poor alone.* Philadelphia: Temple University Press.

Kitchen, B., Mitchell, A., Clutterbuck, P., and Novick, M. (1991). *The state of child and family poverty in Canada: Unequal futures.* Toronto: Child Poverty Action Group and Social Planning Council of Toronto.

Lemann, N. (2002, 4 November). Paper tiger: Daniel Ellsberg's war. *The New Yorker, 78*(33), 96-99.

Mayer, J.E., and Timms, N. (1970). *The client speaks.* London: Routledge and Kegan Paul.

McKenzie, B. (2002). Building community in West Region Child and Family Services. In B. Wharf (Ed.), *Community work approaches to child welfare* (pp. 152-63). Peterborough, ON: Broadview Press.

Mills, C.W. (1959). *The sociological imagination.* New York: Oxford University Press.

Moran, B. (2001). *A little rebellion.* Vancouver: Arsenal Pulp Press.

Pelton, L. (1994). Is poverty a key contributor to child maltreatment? Yes! In E. Gambrill and T. Stein (Eds.), *Controversial issues in child welfare* (pp. 16-22). Boston: Allyn and Bacon.

Peters, R. DeV., Peters, J.E., Laurendeau, M.-C., Chamberland, C., and Peirson, L. (2001). Social policies for promoting the well-being of Canadian children and families. In I. Prilletensky, G. Nelson, and L. Peirson (Eds.), *Promoting family wellness and preventing child maltreatment* (pp. 177-219). Toronto: University of Toronto Press.

Phillips, M. (1995). A case for bad blood for social work. *Perspectives* (BC Association of Social Workers newsletter), *17*(2), 17 (reprinted from the *Manchester Guardian*).

Ross, D., and Roberts, P. (1999). *Income and child well being.* Ottawa: Canadian Council on Social Development.

Royal Commission on Family and Children's Law. (1975). *Report of the Royal Commission on Family and Children's Law.* Victoria: Queen's Printer.

Strong-Boag, V. (2002). Getting to now: Children in distress in Canada's past. In B. Wharf (Ed.), *Community work approaches to child welfare* (pp. 29-46). Peterborough, ON: Broadview Press.

Sullivan, R. (1998). Implementing the B.C. risk assessment model. *Perspectives* (BC Association of Social Workers newsletter), *20*(3), 1, 21.

Swift, K. (1995). *Manufacturing bad mothers.* Toronto: University of Toronto Press.

Weller, F., and Wharf, B. (2002). Contradictions in child welfare. In M.V. Hayes and L.T. Foster (Eds.), *Too small to see, too big to ignore: Child health and well-being in British Columbia* (pp. 141-58). Canadian Western Geographical Series, Vol. 35. Victoria: Western Geographical Press.

Wharf, B. (Ed.). (2002). *Community work approaches to child welfare*. Peterborough, ON: Broadview Press.

1
Rethinking Child Welfare Reform in British Columbia, 1900-60

Marilyn Callahan and Christopher Walmsley

The history of child welfare in Canada and elsewhere has often been re-counted as a largely unsuccessful endeavour undertaken by well-meaning middle- and upper-class women intent on teaching the poor the values of "proper white society" and integrating them into the mainstream (Noble, 1980; Struthers, 1987a, 1987b). According to this account, social workers were the paid agents of the state, using the principal strategy of removing children from their homes and placing them in contexts that would social-ize them to the dominant middle-class values of Euro-Canadian society. Although we do not dismantle this account, in this chapter we reflect upon the thinking and actions of early social workers who actually raised a number of questions about the "middle-class values" they were supposed to support. While they challenged orthodoxy about women's economic dependence, championed a broad vision of child welfare beyond removing children from their homes, and created for themselves a new profession with more freedoms than other women's professions, they did not confront some of the most egregious policies concerning children that took hold during this period: the development of residential schools and, later, the placement of Aboriginal children in foster care. We explore some of the reasons for this. Our exam-ination focuses on British Columbia, but a similar story might be told of other Canadian provinces and settler societies.

The Legacy of Early Child Welfare Reforms

When construction of the Canadian Pacific Railway began in the early 1880s, British Columbia was home to 49,459 people and had a population mix of 52 percent Aboriginal, 35 percent European, and 9 percent Asian. After the railway's completion in 1886, a population explosion brought settlers from Ontario, the Maritimes, and Great Britain, and by 1901, BC's population had increased to 178,657, of which 72 percent were European, 11 percent Asian, and only 16 percent Aboriginal. By 1911, the Aboriginal population had declined to 5 percent of the total (20,174) and remained under 5 percent for most of the twentieth century (Barman, 1991). The reduction in the Aboriginal proportion of the population was the result of death from disease and social upheaval brought by white settlers and the explosion in the numbers of immigrants overall. In the 1890s, Vancouver began to dominate Victoria as the centre of British Columbia's economic life, and by 1901 its population was greater than Victoria's for the first time (ibid.).

A range of charitable organizations emerged in British Columbia in the late nineteenth century, the result of prodigious community organizing that was largely carried out by women. Child welfare activities in the province began in earnest in 1892, when several women raised funds for the development of the Alexandra Orphanage in Vancouver (see Appendix 1):

> The Alexandra Orphanage can justly claim to be Vancouver's earliest institution devoted exclusively to children ... Before that time, whenever a child was found orphaned and friendless, such women as the late Mrs. Haskett, Mrs. T.H. Morrison, Mrs. Foxley, and Mrs. J.J. Southcott, would come forward and find a home for it, even if it had to be paid for out of their own pockets ... Realizing that in a fast-growing community such contingencies were likely to re-occur, these women with Mrs. James Macaulay, Mrs. F.T. Schooley, Mrs. H. Mutrie and others decided to establish a home for the purpose. They rented a house on the corner of Homer and Dunsmuir Streets, which was formally opened on Thanksgiving Day of that year, with Miss Bowes as matron ... Within a year the number of children had increased to nineteen necessitating larger premises which were found on Hornby Street. (Nelson, 1934, p. 14)

Given the inadequacy of such voluntary efforts, women continued to organize. On 20 March 1901, the local Council of Women of Vancouver successfully petitioned the Legislative Assembly of British Columbia to pass a child welfare act because "all the efforts to care for neglected, orphaned or abandoned children are greatly hindered and in many cases wholly prevented owing to the absence of any law in this Province regulating such work. This want has been very much felt, not only by the various Philanthropic and Charitable Societies, but by the Police Officials as well" (Annual Report, Vancouver Children's Aid Society, 1902). Soon afterwards, the government passed the *Children's Protection Act*, which provided for state guardianship of orphaned or neglected children and for the incorporation of children's aid societies to care for these children.

The Vancouver Children's Aid Society, with its motto "We Protect the Little Ones," was incorporated in the same year. Although the first board of directors was composed solely of men, an active women's committee carried out the day-to-day work of the society and soon after took over its leadership. The first annual report, in 1901, stated that the work of the society far surpassed expectations; twenty-nine children were committed to care "by force of the evil conditions existing in the City." In the 1902 annual report, Mrs. T.E. Atkins, an early director, described the purpose of the society: "The Children's Aid Society stands first and last for the rights of children. It is authorized to investigate all cases of neglect, destitution and cruelty to ameliorate and better home surroundings when practicable, and when hopeless to remove the children from an environment of uncleanliness and vice; only when every effort in the home fails is the matter brought to the courts for adjudication."

The Council of Women stimulated the development of another charity movement, the Friendly Aid Society, "to assist families in distress." It began in Victoria in 1895 and Vancouver in 1896. Friendly visitors, women from the council, "investigated each family case, reporting to the Health Department the conditions and need they found" (Nelson, 1934, p. 16). This friendly visitor tradition was picked up later by family service and child welfare agencies.

Another significant child welfare plank in British Columbia, emanating from the actions of pioneer women, was the mothers' pension. Such women's groups as the National Council of Women (the national organization of the local Councils of Women), the Women's Christian Temperance Union, the Women's Institutes, the Canadian Club, the Daughters of the Empire, the University Women's Club, and the Equal Franchise Association, among others, petitioned the Legislative Assembly in 1918 for a mothers' allowance. The premier of the time, John Oliver, "in eulogizing the delegation, said it was the most businesslike and representative delegation that had ever appeared before the government" (*First Annual Reports of the Superintendent of Neglected Children and Mothers' Pensions*, 1920, p. 8). The *Mothers' Pension Act* was passed on 17 April 1920 and proclaimed on 1 July, following similar legislation in Manitoba (1916), Saskatchewan (1917), and Alberta (1919). According to the 1920 report of the Superintendent of Neglected Children and Mothers' Pensions, "it was a great boon to many of the mothers to receive the pension ... They were enabled in many cases to take their children out of the orphanages, rent little homes or rooms, purchase furniture, and provide for the winter clothing and fuel" (p. 9).

Initially, six temporary investigators were appointed to determine the need of each case under the *Mothers' Pension Act*, which was administered by the Superintendent of Neglected Children. These investigators were all women and came to be known as the "mothers' pensions visitors," "friendly home visitors," "welfare visitors," or merely "the visitors."

Early child welfare efforts included some attention to juvenile justice, although the distinction between those who entered children's aid services and those sent to reformatories seemed largely related to age and race. A juvenile reformatory opened in British Columbia in 1890. With the construction of a new facility at Point Grey in 1905, it became known as the Boys' Industrial School, serving boys nine to nineteen years. The first superintendent, David Donaldson, a Vancouver men's clothier, was also a member of the board of directors of the Vancouver Children's Aid Society. Under his leadership, the school aimed to be self-supporting, with the boys producing most of their own food, uniforms, shoes, furniture, and firewood. The most common reason for committal was "incorrigibility," which meant the child was beyond the control of parents or guardians, although neglected children and the rare child convicted of murder were also committed. From 1916 onwards, the school was plagued with unsanitary conditions, deteriorating facilities, and unfilled staff positions. By 1919, interest in juvenile justice shifted to the establishment of juvenile courts, which were viewed as capable of giving more individual attention to the needs of boys (Matters, 1980).

The Provincial Industrial Home for Girls opened in Vancouver on Cassiar Street in 1914 "to provide custody and detention with a view to the education, industrial training and moral reclamation of females under the age of sixteen" (Matters, 1984, p. 268). Between 1914 and 1937 there were 600 admissions for reasons primarily related to incorrigibility and morals offenses (88 percent), with only a few related to actual crimes. The home's matron advocated strenuously for a proper trade school for the girls in her care, but for the most part it prepared the girls only for domestic service. As Matters (1984) notes, committal to the home provided girls with a "way out" of their existing life by providing them with medical and physical care, some education, and work placement. At the same time, it robbed families of a teenage daughter's wages, as well as her home management and childcare contributions. In many cases it moved girls from one form of exploitation to another.

There are important legacies from these early developments that influenced subsequent child welfare policy and practice. While the development of orphanages and correctional facilities was featured during this early period, it is clear that proponents of these services recognized that child welfare was defined more broadly than institutional care. They worked earnestly to advance the case for preventive and family-based services, recognizing that most of the children in their care were not actually orphans but children from working-class families who required short-term substitute care to help them hold their families together in the long term (Purvey, 1991). For instance, most children at the Alexandra Orphanage were placed there during a critical stage of the family life cycle, such as death, illness, unemployment, or desertion, with most children staying a year or two before being reunited with their parents.

Orphanages were complemented by foster care. The Protestant Orphans Home was originally created in 1873 by Methodist, Anglican, and Presbyterian church leaders in Victoria "to give care, secular education and practical training and Christian education to the children" in its charge (Storey, Worobetz, and Kennedy, 1999, p. 52). However, by the early twentieth century, about half of the sixty children in its care were placed in foster homes.

Unfortunately, early government and municipal funding for child welfare was earmarked only for the institutional care of children (Angus, 1951). Government funding policies were influential in shaping the direction of child welfare services from the beginning of their formal development.

From the outset, the services developed along segregated lines according to class, race, religion, and "characteristics of children." For instance, the Protestant Orphans Home in Victoria initially admitted only Protestant children aged two to ten who were homeless. It excluded "delinquents," "defectives," and those "with serious social problems" (Storey et al., 1999, p. 51). Although it broadened its admission criteria in the 1920s, it refused children of Asian origin or Roman Catholics (Storey et al., 1999). There is sparse evidence of other minority cultures' participation in child welfare services. A sample of 303 children in the care of the Vancouver Children's Aid Society between 1901 and 1930 revealed only four children of Asian or African heritage (Adamoski, 2002). Of the 154 families in the sample, only ten were families of Aboriginal heritage, and most were interracial families, with a Caucasian father and a Native mother. Adamoski (1988) argues that during this period the Vancouver CAS "sought in practice if not in policy to avoid involvement with Native families" (p. 317). Aboriginal youth appear to have been sent to the Boys' Industrial School (Matters, 1980). We take up the subject of Aboriginal youth in later sections of this chapter.

Child welfare was a new field in which women's social and political action provided the leadership for change. Working outside the home, with little formal political influence and modest experience in public affairs and without the right to vote, women moved from the position of caring for indigent children on a voluntary basis to caring for children in orphanages funded by donations and then to pressing for legislation that provided government funding for the care of children and a pension for their mothers. At the same time, these women created paid employment for themselves. These were considerable achievements that required insights into the relationships between income and child welfare and that challenged some of the moral considerations and patriarchal values that were highly influential at the time.

A Crossroad: The BC Child Welfare Survey

From its inception, the Vancouver Children's Aid Society (CAS) was beset by overcrowded conditions, underfunding, the risk of fire, and public criticism of its work. In 1927, amid "charges of graft, perjury, falsifying of accounts and general scandalous conditions" against the Vancouver CAS, the BC Child Welfare Survey was initiated (Adamoski, 1988, p. 30). Conducted by Charlotte Whitton (of the Canadian Council on Child Welfare), the survey analyzed the services of fourteen BC child welfare agencies and was funded by four Vancouver service clubs (Adamoski, 1988; Whitton, 1927).

The survey, similar to those conducted later in other provinces, consisted of measuring public opinion for change, scrutinizing carefully the credentials and practice of the social workers of the day, and giving wide publicity to the results. Through the process, Whitton focused on endorsing preventive work with families and replacing "the casual appointee indiscriminately chosen from any trade or calling" with a skilled expert who possessed the "analytical attitude of a trained mind" (Rooke and Schnell, 1981, p. 495).

Barbara Finlayson, later a staff member of the Family Services Society in Vancouver describes the events leading up to and following the survey:

> You have heard of the three wise women from the east. Again we come to Charlotte Whitton and the unestimatable contribution that she made to Canada and social work development in the surveys for which the Canadian Council was responsible throughout this period, the 1920s and the 1930s. To mention one of them only, a survey of child welfare in B.C. Four able people from Toronto came here and were really digging. They came because of the wisdom of one of the board members of the Children's Aid Society in Vancouver who at a time when they had collected money and were planning for a bigger and better institution for the children, the increasing number of children that needed protection. They had the money, they had the architect's plan, were purring in anticipation when this board member said, "I think we shouldn't spend a cent until we have the opinion of the Canadian Welfare Council," and so Charlotte arranged for these four workers from Toronto to come
>
> Mr. R.E. Mills, Director of the C.A.S. of Toronto, was in charge. Margaret Main from the Neighbourhood Workers Association, she was the secretary throughout. Miss Leila O'Gorman came from the Roman Catholic Family Agency and Miss Vera Moberly from the Infant's Home in Toronto, she had a family understanding ... The able report that came back to the board of the C.A.S. in Vancouver stunned them. But as a result, fortunately, the institution didn't get built and the three wise women came from the East. Two of them, Miss Laura Holland and Miss Zella Collins, to bring about a change in the plan of care for children, a change from institutions to foster homes living with real families. The third member, Miss Mary MacPhedran came a year later ... to start a family service agency, as the report indicated, that was needed hopefully to give services to families before the child was neglected and so those three became known as the "three wise women from the East" and they were all extremely able. (Hill, 1990, pp. 21-22)

Although the survey was widely praised, it was not without its critics. Mary MacPhedran, Zella Collins, and Laura Holland, who were appointed by Charlotte Whitton to lead the reform and professionalize BC child welfare services, all came from Ontario. Mrs. T. Morward-Clark derided these young women who had never set foot on BC soil before, but who had the audacity to criticize the "wild and woolly west" (Rooke and Schnell, 1981, p. 496).

A future staff member of the Vancouver Children's Aid Society was twenty-seven-year-old Katherine Whitman, who was working in downtown Toronto as a family services worker when she accepted an invitation to join Laura Holland and Zella Collins in Vancouver. Many years later, she recalled her first winter on the coast:

> Miss Holland and Miss Collins were wonderful people to work for. We were sort of in it together. I don't know how Miss Holland managed it. Miss Collins was laid up with bronchitis that first winter, it was a very bad winter anyway, rained continually and the doctor told her she'd have to give it up all together unless she kept right indoors, which confined her to office work. She went over all these old dusty records, opening them up, they were long legal forms and folded over the way lawyers forms are ... and you couldn't pull out a folder and open it, you had to pick out one of these things tied with tape and undo it, and mice had been in them and dusty and dirty, some had been there for years. This was only 1927 but after all the Society had been operating since, well, before 1900.
>
> The plan was that children were to be placed in foster homes. They were all in a big institution out on Wall Street and there were close on two hundred children in the big building. I think another smaller building that had the babies in it. And I think the large building had already been condemned as not safe from the fire standpoint and the idea was to get them placed in foster homes as soon as possible ... The first thing to do really was not to look for foster homes, not right away, but to look up lost wards ... I don't know how many children [were] legally under care of the Children's Aid Society, well you know five or six hundred anyway ... and a good many had been placed in private homes and were still under sixteen years of age which was the legal age and the Society was legally responsible for those children. (Hill, 1990, pp. 7-15)

The survey was crucially important to the development of child welfare in British Columbia for a number of reasons. It provided the impetus for the reform of child welfare services in the province, but its influence was restricted to the fourteen childcare institutions that were the focus of the survey, all orphanages supported by religious, secular, or women's organizations. It did not consider correctional facilities for children, institutions for the mentally challenged or disabled, or the Indian residential schools. It had the effect of solidifying the field of child welfare in British Columbia as one focused on individual children and their parents. It also enshrined the focus on parents as the source of child maltreatment and established the two often-conflicting purposes of child welfare: supporting parents to care for their children and removing children from families where the parents failed to measure up. Funding policies were set up, and the children's aid societies, now funded by the provincial government, were charged primarily with investigating complaints and caring for children. The new Vancouver Family Services, with a focus on strengthening families, was funded by voluntary monies. The survey took a Eurocentric and urban-centred view of child welfare, and its effect was to confirm separate and unequal child welfare services in British Columbia. At the same time, however, the survey advanced the development of social work as a profession and solidified professional roles for women for services previously provided on a volunteer basis. The survey, the first of its kind in Canada, provided the impetus for surveys in eight other provinces between 1927 and 1949 (Adamoski, 1988) and thus had far-reaching effects beyond British Columbia.

Residential Schools and Institutional Care for Aboriginal Children

Charlotte Whitton and others involved in the survey paid little attention to Aboriginal children and families, in part because Canada was a nation divided along racial and class lines. The Depression, following shortly after the survey, placed many Canadians in dire poverty. Writing of that time, the historian Desmond Morton (2005) states that "our ancestors took poverty for granted and accepted the selfish cruelty that usually accompanies deprivation. In the struggle to live, most Canadians could only be looked after by 'their own kind.' Outsiders, be they immigrants or people of a different faith or ethnicity, seldom met generosity; exclusion, contempt and fear were the rule. We should not be astonished to find these qualities in so-called 'Third-World countries.' Before 1945, that was our state too" (p. 46).

Another reason Aboriginal peoples were left out of the survey was because they were defined as a federal responsibility under the *British North America Act*. All services to Status Indians were provided under the *Indian Act*, a set of laws that embodied separate and unequal social relations between Aboriginal peoples and the European population in Canada. This legislation provided for the construction and operation of residential schools, funded by the federal government but operated by the Anglican, Roman Catholic, and Methodist Churches. Residential school construction in British Columbia began a decade after the introduction of residential schools in other provinces, and about a decade and a half after the *Indian Act* was passed, but it occurred concurrently with the Canadian government's consolidation of reserves throughout the province. It also paralleled the great influx of white settlers to the province, which took place following the construction of the Canadian Pacific Railway in 1886.

In British Columbia, St. Mary's Mission was the first to operate a residential school, which opened in 1863 with forty-two boys from the Sto:lo people in the lower Fraser Valley. The Sisters of St. Ann were recruited in 1868 to run a girls' residential school, and about thirty girls were enrolled. In the 1880s, the boarding school received only minimal government funds, but when the Canadian government initiated its residential school program in British Columbia in the 1890s, St. Mary's was quick to respond to the offer of government assistance (Gresko, 1986). When the Canadian government offered funding to the churches, eight schools were built between 1888 and 1893, and a further six between 1900 and 1910. Altogether, at least twenty-two schools operated in BC; the last, St. Mary's, closed in 1984 (see Table 1.1 and www.turtleisland.org).

The aim of the residential school policy was to erase Aboriginal identity by separating generations of children from their families, suppressing their Aboriginal languages, and re-socializing them according to the norms of non-Aboriginal society (Royal Commission on Aboriginal Peoples, 1996a, chap. 10). The deputy superintendent general of Indian Affairs, Duncan Campbell Scott, told the House of Commons in 1920 that the department's object was "to continue until there is not a single Indian in Canada that has not been absorbed into the body politic and there is no Indian question, and no Indian department, that is the whole object of this Bill" (Haig-Brown, 1988, p. 27).

For most of the twentieth century, until the late 1980s, the residential schools operated outside the consciousness of the Euro-Canadian public. There was only one public inquiry that considered conditions in a residential school in British Columbia. That was a coroner's inquest into the death of eight-year-old Duncan Sticks, who had run away from the Williams Lake

Table 1.1

Indian residential schools in British Columbia

School	Years of operation	School	Years of operation
St. Mary's	1863-1984	Kitimat	1893-1941
Coqualeetza	1888-1941	Christie	1900-83
Kamloops	1890-1978	St. George's	1901-78
Kootenay	1890-1970	Squamish	1902-60
Kuper Island	1890-1975	Ahousaht	1904-39
Port Simpson	1890-1948	Sechelt	1905-78
Alberni	1891-1973	Lejac	1910-76
Cariboo	1891-1981	Alert Bay	1929-74

Source: York, G. (1998), *The dispossessed: Life and death in Native Canada* (Toronto: Little, Brown).

Residential School in 1902 and had been found dead the next day (Furniss, 1995). The schools were all located in rural British Columbia, miles away from centres of government, media, higher education, and social reform.

In the 1950s, the schools began to be phased out as Aboriginal children were integrated into provincial schools, but many schools continued to function as a child welfare resource or as a residence for children who lived in remote communities and attended provincial schools in larger centres. In these cases, the schools operated until the 1970s or 1980s.

Thus, while institutionalization was being derided for Euro-Canadian children by the social reformers involved in the 1927 BC Child Welfare Survey, it was being entrenched for Aboriginal children. Child welfare in British Columbia has been greatly shaped by the legacy of the residential schools. They had a genocidal effect on Aboriginal peoples as they eliminated language, religion, history, family ties, and knowledge of community traditions across the many distinct languages and nations found in British Columbia (Fournier and Crey, 1997; Furniss, 1995; Haig-Brown, 1988; MacDonald, 1993; Miller, 1996; York, 1990). In testimony to the Royal Commission on Aboriginal Peoples, Chief Cinderina Williams of the Spallumcheen Band summarized the effects of the residential school in her community:

> Later when these children returned home, they were aliens. They did not speak their own language, so they could not communicate with anyone other than their own counterparts. Some looked down on their families because of their lack of English, their lifestyle, and some were just plain hostile. They had formed no bonds with their families, and some couldn't survive without the regimentation they had become so accustomed to ... Perhaps the greatest tragedy of this background was the unemotional upbringing they had. Not being brought up in a loving, caring, sharing, nurturing environment, they did not have these skills as they are not inbred but learned through observation, participation, and interaction. Consequently, when these children became parents, and most did at an early age, they had no parenting skills. (1996b, chap. 2, p. 35)

The residential schools played a significant role in constructing the "Indian" stereotype held by the Euro-Canadian population as they eliminated differences between various Aboriginal cultures and collapsed this diversity to one homogenous "other." Most of the European population in British Columbia had little day-to-day contact with Aboriginal people, but all felt they knew enough to employ stereotypes in daily discourse within their community.

In addition to residential schools, the colonizing policies and practices of the Canadian government (the *Indian Act,* the creation of reserves, and the lack of political, legal, and economic rights for Aboriginal people) contributed to the decimation of British Columbia's Aboriginal people. At the same time, the rapid liberalization of provincial liquor laws in the 1950s and the repeal of century-old liquor laws that discriminated against Aboriginal people created rapid change for Aboriginal communities. Thus, when the provincial government began to take responsibility for Aboriginal child welfare after changes to the federal *Indian Act* in 1951, Aboriginal communities were greatly weakened; the values they held related to family, community, and children were virtually unrecognized; and child welfare policy and practices based on British Canadian values were well entrenched. The removal of Aboriginal children that occurred over the next decade and continues today was the result of this history.

Child Welfare Policy and Practice, 1930-60

The 1930s were a time of significant social policy change in British Columbia. The 1933 election of T.D. Pattullo's Liberal government on a "New Deal" platform began a transformation of health and welfare services. The province appointed its first Director of Social Welfare, Harry Cassidy, in 1934, and in 1935, "a welfare field service was set up to bring together within one division all of the department's skilled social workers, whose services could then be used over a larger geographic territory or by more than one division of the health and welfare branch" (Irving, 1987). This development led to a schism between those who sought the adventures of rural British Columbia and those who remained in urban areas, one that remains today. As Isobel Harvey, the Superintendent of Neglected Children, described it, "in the City of Vancouver, where there are numbers of social workers, practically all doing specialized jobs, I doubt whether nine people out of ten could enlighten you as to the difference between a family agency and a children's agency, and which you should consult in a given instance ... In the district, however, the welfare visitor is social work, and social work is what the welfare visitor does" (1937, p. 40).

University of BC School of Social Work graduates and others began to find employment in this expanded provincial service and in the children's aid societies and family service agencies in the larger urban areas. This raises the question: How did these new social workers take up the issues of inequalities built into the child welfare system from its early history?

Accounts of the provincial social workers in rural areas of British Columbia provide rare and interesting insights into the aims of these workers during this period. Without doubt, they found their work adventuresome and unpredictable. This was particularly the case for young, middle-class women, who would be a rare sight in many provincial outposts, logging camps, institutions, and urban slums. The sense of being an unusual, courageous woman who escaped the more predictable life of wife and mother is suggested in their accounts. Anne Angus describes mothers' pension visitors as "well motivated, hard working, but young and strong willed. As I've grown older I have often thought we were like a team of wild young horses" (1965, p. 227). Isobel Harvey recalls one such adventure:

> I wonder how many of us would come back cheerfully at the end of the day after having driven one hundred miles over a bad road, walked ten miles, three of them down a railway track and the rest in the bush – walked a boom of logs and crossed the Fraser River twice in a dugout canoe with half a foot of water in it. Our youngest visitor did just that on her second week in the field. The only reason I heard about it was because she was apologizing for having a hotel bill instead of returning to headquarters. She was quite tired and felt she could not start back after dark over thirty miles of bad road. (1937, p. 32)

Barbara Finlayson, a worker at the Family Services Association of Vancouver, describes a different sense of adventure and creativity in social work practice at the time: innovations such as homemakers for families where the mother was absent, the placement of family service workers in the Settlement Houses to bring some family counselling, and the introduction of group work,

> sometimes with a parent and child together, or a group of two parents and children, or groups not for a particular family but for groups made up of maybe mothers of several families that are meeting the same kind of problems or a group of people that have just been divorced, or a pre-marital group of young people ... and so on ... there was a person put in charge of that work, Mary Rupp, who had been on the staff of the School of Social Work and was a member of the Family Services staff at that time, took over and she gathered a staff of social workers who mostly had been in the agency on the staff but had resigned because of having children. Their children were older and they gave part-time to this group work. (Hill, 1990, p. 17)

The work was enormously varied in both urban and rural practice. Women spoke about the wide diversity of cases and programs in their charge, the expectation that they would and could create needed resources, the varied work settings, and the fascinating travel. Bessie Snider, who began her career in social work in northern BC, recalls the diverse nature of the work:

> We were providing a generalized service which we pioneered in B.C. and of which I am still very proud. ... [A]bout a third of our caseload would be mothers on Mother's allowance [$35 for a mother and child] and then

about 10% of our load ... would be single people on relief. They got nine dollars a month and the next classification were those that were unemployable ... the Destitute, Poor and Sick [$20 per adult person] and ... then we did all the families where the breadwinner or main person in the family had T.B. T.B. was still rampant then and we, though we were not nurses, had to go at certain intervals and pick up the sputum cups and get them back to head office here ... To be on Mother's Allowance, you had to have three years residence in the province. You had to be a British citizen. You had to produce your marriage certificate and your divorce papers, if you were divorced. A single mother, an unmarried single mother, that is, would not be eligible for Mother's Allowance, but she probably would be eligible, if she was unable to work, for Destitute, Poor and Sick Allowance ... And then we did all the social work histories for the provincial mental hospital and we would have to go and interview the family of the patient and get the social history. And we had a good number of unmarried parents and we visited them and helped them make the decision about whether or not they would keep their baby, or ... have it placed for adoption, and then in Salmon Arm, I had a good number of children in foster homes. Then we had also another category, juvenile delinquents, because we would have to make the arrangements if the boys or girls (principally they were boys) who'd be coming down to the Boys' Industrial School in Vancouver ... (ibid., pp. 8-10)

Theresa Kofman, who worked at the Vancouver Children's Aid Society, recalled that,

right from the beginning [I worked in] ... child protection but the Child Protection Division included many things ... we did some adoptions although we weren't the adoption department but it would occur. Work with unmarried mothers, a fair amount of that ... But those areas would be definitely part of your daily work. I was an apprehending officer which meant I would have to go out at all hours of the day or night to pick up children which we often did ... I worked very closely with the court worker and we had a great many court cases that we shared ... Child abuse has been highlighted so much today it rather amazes me in one way ... We had it less often ... this wasn't our major emphasis in those days, our major emphasis was general neglect. (ibid., pp. 29-30)

The women felt hugely independent in making decisions. There were few regulations, and they had the confidence to challenge and change those that did not serve them or their clients. The major programs that these women administered – child welfare, mothers' pension, and social assistance –

provided a great deal of discretion for the individual social worker. Little (1993) has identified the difference between the male and female welfare systems during this period. Welfare systems mainly used by men were those associated with the workplace, such as worker's compensation and pension plans. They were mostly contributory programs with little stigma and with firm rules governing entitlements. In contrast, welfare systems directed at women, such as mothers' pensions, child welfare, and, later, social assistance programs, were highly discretionary and gave the largely female staff administering them a great deal of room for decision making.

Above all, the few accounts of practice during this time emphasize the optimism that social workers felt about their endeavours and the potential of these services to create major social changes. Like Charlotte Whitton, these women believed that sufficient numbers of well-trained social workers could lead to vast improvements for clients and communities. Bessie Snider states that "[I] went out feeling that ... I was going to cure the ills of the community. There would not be any more social problems" (Hill, 1990, p. 11). Each individual social worker was a vehicle for change and devoted all her energies and resources to the task.

The notion that each individual had a remarkable capacity to create change appears ingenuous, even arrogant, in retrospect, particularly since the enormous task of changing structural inequalities is the focus of much social work education today. However, what is often forgotten is that at this time many social reformers were optimistic about the prospects of social change and the promises of the emerging welfare state to bring about such changes. This optimism was supported by the numerous accomplishments of these years. A tribute to Laura Holland on the occasion of her retirement captures some of these remarkable changes:

> In four years, the agency was changed over completely from institution to foster home care. The old buildings were replaced with a small receiving home in a new building which housed many of the private agencies also ... In the new position [deputy superintendent of child welfare, 1931] ... the list of things she accomplished includes cleaning up of the "adoption rackets," the commercial baby homes and maternity homes; the growth of preventive work everywhere in the province; increased help for unmarried mothers. She administered the acts as their own provisions required, with fear or favour for none ... Miss Holland concludes: "Nothing comes from one person. It's the combined effort of many that works miracles." (*Victoria Times*, 21 January 1946, p. 7)

These women also stood up for their beliefs. At the time of Amy Leigh's retirement from the provincial government, Martha Moscrop writes that

Miss Leigh was a strong advocate for the indigent when she worked as a welfare worker in Vancouver's City Relief Department during the early years of the Depression and left because of her treatment:

> Her male colleagues of those days, among them elected personages, could say in 1958 that their contempt for her advocacy of the luckless little people had changed slowly to respect, even though they were not prepared to acknowledge it then. Her administrators of those times were deaf to her arguments, blinded by the numbers who needed bread, adamant in their belief that hard, even punishing, treatment would soon clean up the economic mess ... Some say, thinking to find fault with her, that she is aggressive, that her weakness is her strength. To this her staff reply, "Had she not been strong, had she not been aggressive on our behalf, we would not be what we are today." (1958, p. 122)

Rural social workers were in a position to observe the conditions experienced by many Aboriginal families. Child welfare was not their responsibility, but they did have charge of other programs that could be useful to Aboriginal families. Bessie Snider recounts one effort to extend financial support:

> [While working in Prince Rupert as a child welfare worker,] I did an interesting little piece of research of my own. I was able to get an Indian family on one of the islands down the Skeena River on Mother's Allowance and I had to fight very hard with our supervisors who received our reports at head office to make this happen ... You see, you got more on Mother's Allowance for awhile. And I was so pleased ... Her husband had been a fisherman and had drowned ... When I would visit her, and I would have to go with the Indian agent on his boat to visit this family, I had said to the mother, you know, we do have some of our Mother's Allowances recipients ... keep a record of what it costs for them to buy certain items. And I had to explain to mothers when I was asking them [to do] this ... how it would be helpful if I had this information so that I could get it back to our office to get the allowance revised.
>
>   So I said to this mother in the presence of her teenage boy, who would be about twelve, no more, "We have a column for miscellaneous. If you can't remember everything and anything that you do have to spend money on, you put it in the miscellaneous." So the little boy said to me "How do you spell miscellaneous," and I spelled it out for him. Well, when I came back the next time, they had this beautifully outlined in a scribbler and the boy had done this and he was so pleased about this. Of course, I heard in the course of time about my McLeod family down the Skeena River, how she was occasionally in the beer parlour you know, and I thought, "So what, so

what!" that was one of the things I didn't record in my report down to head office as they would have felt that she was spending her money foolishly ... but they never saw these books that the mothers were keeping, though I would send down reports telling them how inadequate the allowance was.

[After leaving direct practice, Ms. Snider became the research director in senior administration in Victoria.] One thing was interesting [during this time]. I was a member of the federal-provincial committee on Indians and I was the chief representative of our department, and Shirley Arnold who was the head social worker for the federal department of Indian Affairs and the co-chairman and we had one of our district supervisors on the committee. We had a couple of Indian agents on that committee ...

We met once a month, and it took us ten years to get a similar amount of social assistance to Indian peoples as to non-Indians. We went all over the province, we talked to municipal people and so on and so on. We talked to our regional administrator and finally we convinced them that these people were people, Indian children were like our children and they could not subsist on the amount of Indian relief. And for sure, Shirley Arnold, who's still living and a very great friend of mine, would concede that was the one thing that we did, probably the only thing we did, after ten years of meeting. (Hill, 1990, pp. 9-29)

This era ended with the resignation of several prominent women in child welfare, in particular Ruby McKay, who resigned from the position of Superintendent of Child Welfare in 1960. Her reason for resigning might ring true today:

I reached my decision for one reason and one reason alone. It was no longer possible in the face of the government's restrictive policies to fulfill the responsibilities of Superintendent of Child Welfare. The job simply couldn't be done without more staff and money ... Despite many personal pleas for help, the government did nothing ... A few dedicated workers carrying on the program of child welfare have been so overloaded that necessary child care and adoptions could not be kept up. A staff twice the size would not be enough.

No recognition was being given to the extra heavy workloads resulting from the growing unemployment situation ... In addition, resources needed for the care of children were not forthcoming. Seriously disturbed children, urgently needing treatment in a properly controlled setting, presented heartbreaking problems to staff who could offer only foster home care ... Families applying to adopt a child had to wait months and in some instances years before a worker could even acknowledge their applications. And yet daily, children who desperately needed the security of adoption were having to be placed in paid temporary foster homes.

Overtime had become the rule for staff because of the workers' dedication to their jobs and their earnest desire as far as humanly possible to meet the needs of children ... [C]hild welfare services can only be as good as communities want them to be and my purpose in making this statement is to say to the people of B.C. that they must communicate their wishes to the government and through their local representative in the legislature so that the standard of service they desire for children is maintained. (*Victoria Times*, 6 January 1961, p. 1)

Concerns about resources for child welfare had been expressed a year earlier by Dave Barrett, a member of the Legislative Assembly and later premier of British Columbia, who decried the diminishing number of trained social workers employed by government and the rapidly increasing caseloads.

Contributions and Contradictions

The practice of social workers during this era is marked by a number of features, but none is more pervasive than their deep commitment to reform as they brought professional services to families and children and attempted to get to the root of problems rather than bandaging them up. They understood "getting to the root of the problem" in child welfare as replacing voluntary efforts with social programs such as child welfare, juvenile justice, and counselling to people living anywhere in British Columbia.

In this period, community work did not focus on developing community strengths to respond effectively to family and children's needs. Instead, social workers viewed community work as gaining commitment from government to extend programs to communities and convincing community elites and professionals of the value of the social programs and services on offer. They also thought that community work involved removing "problematic" people, such as delinquents, those with mental and physical disabilities, and the infirm, from communities to centralized resources in the Greater Vancouver area. Today, this view of "helping" can be criticized, but the idea that material resources and social programs could help families who were struggling is still valid.

As social workers espoused the power of government programs to create change, Aboriginal peoples were experiencing the devastation caused by government programs. Wholesale destruction of their communities and their culture was occurring as a stated objective of government. When provinces took over responsibility for Aboriginal child welfare in the late 1950s and early 1960s, social workers assumed the tasks of working with Aboriginal peoples without any understanding of their cultural traditions to build upon. They also took on these responsibilities at a time when resources for child welfare were diminishing and government programs were dedicated to individuals and their families but not to community development. By this time, Aboriginal traditions of community members caring for children within the context of communal life had been severely damaged by both the residential schools and child welfare removals.

Social workers lobbied for changes to the *Indian Act* in their 1947 submission to a Senate and House of Commons committee charged with reviewing the act. In their joint brief, submitted with the Canadian Welfare Council, they argued that Aboriginal peoples were unfairly treated because they were not offered child welfare services comparable to those available to other Canadians. The brief also condemned the practice of putting neglected children in residential schools, and

> concluded that the best way to improve this situation was to extend the services of provincial departments of health, welfare and education to the residents of reserves. It recommended against the development of a federally operated service system parallel to those of the provinces ... The extension of provincial child welfare and other social service programs seemed to be a logical way to overcome some of the problems facing the residents of reserves. The recommendation was obviously made with the best of intentions but little attention was paid to the effect that extending provincial services would have on Indian families and communities. Nor did there appear to be any concern that provincial services might not be compatible with the needs of Indian communities. (Johnston, 1983, p. 3)

When the changes that social workers championed became law, the results were damaging. From the mid-1950s until the early 1970s, large numbers of Aboriginal children entered the child welfare system for the first time. In 1955, only 29 Indian children were in the care of the BC Superintendent of Child Welfare. By 1960, this number had risen to 849, and in 1964 to 1,446. In a period of ten years, Aboriginal children went from making up less than 1 percent of the total number of children in care in British Columbia to comprising about 32 percent (Stanbury, 1975). This period was later described as the "Sixties Scoop" (Johnston, 1983), and it set a trend that continues today.

Resistance

Although statistics show the increasing numbers of Aboriginal children in care during this period, there is little systematic analysis of the thinking and practice of social workers, nor of the views of Aboriginal leaders, elders, and parents. However, a small but powerful literature on this period is emerging (Furniss, 1995; Herbert, 1994). Robina Thomas tells the stories of Aboriginal peoples, their reflections on the residential school at Kuper Island, and the devastating impact of separation on children and their families (Thomas, 1998). Bridget Moran's book *A Little Rebellion* (1992) documents her torments as a social worker in Prince George during the 1950s and 1960s, working mostly with Aboriginal families, but without the resources to help them rebuild. From these accounts and our own memories, stories of resistance emerge.

Social workers generally met with deep suspicion and hostility in Aboriginal communities. As a young social worker in Prince George during the 1960s, one author of this chapter remembers well her own discomfort on entering the nearby reserves and the pervasive feeling that people were doing what they could to avoid co-operation. Often their efforts paid off, and she left without seeing the family in question or learning anything about their whereabouts. She also remembers her job in the summer of 1966 at the Catholic Children's Aid Society in Vancouver, where she was to locate parents of children in care and assess the possibility of returning children home. Many of the parents she tried to find were Aboriginal, and her supervisor argued valiantly for their reconciliation with their children. One mother wept uncontrollably when she learned that her children, apprehended at birth, were living only a few miles away from her Capilano Reserve. The children were returned to her later that year.

An Aboriginal woman, now a child protection social worker, describes her father protecting her from state intervention:

> My parents ended up separating so my dad raised me on his own. Being a single parent, I guess the Ministry decided that it wouldn't be a good thing for a single man to raise a daughter so, um, my dad told me this one story actually where a social worker came up to check on the situation, decided that a single parent man couldn't raise a daughter, and said "Well, we have to take her out of the home." My dad, I guess, became somewhat threatening and I was sure [he was] somewhat verbally reprimanding – whatever word you want to use and said you're not taking her and she said "Well, I'll be back up with the RCMP, Mr. –," and he said "Well you go right ahead. My shotgun will be waiting for you." And I guess the social worker never came back. (Walmsley, 2001, p. 141)

This story, both a description of a defensive strategy and an account of success, demonstrates the strength and power of a father determined to raise his daughter autonomously without state regulation or control. The social worker describes a childhood experience, but one wonders what significance this story might have to an Aboriginal community's understanding of the practice of state child protection.

Rethinking Reform and Reformers

Child welfare for Aboriginal and non-Aboriginal children developed in two separate worlds informed by widely different values. For Euro-Canadians, prominent members of the community promoted the early development of family support, income maintenance, and family care (foster) services rather than institutionalized services. Services grew unevenly, but there was steady progress toward more humane and family-based services. For Aboriginal children throughout the province, there was an early commitment to institutionalized care, and there were no champions to challenge this policy outside the Aboriginal community. Later, when the provincial government took over child welfare services, this removal of children from families continued.

In this chapter we have argued that social work pioneers were impressive women. Although predominately Euro-Canadian women, they were in but not always "of" their times. They thought creatively and independently. They challenged some entrenched views prevalent at the time and argued for public funds to support individuals in need. They also lobbied for people who were largely excluded in a classist and racist society, and challenged views about gender and mothers' roles. They insisted that women required their own source of funds to support their families. Their own careers did not fit the script set for middle-class women, as they were educated, independent, and dedicated to a career that often eschewed marriage and children. They created a new profession for women that was less restrictive, more independent, and more flexible than the professions of nursing and teaching, the only others available to them at the time.

How was it that these women did not take up the cause of Aboriginal children from the beginning? We have proposed several interlocking reasons. First, the development of Aboriginal and non-Aboriginal child welfare services was complicated by the original division of powers between the federal and provincial government. Early women championing the development of child welfare were intent on achieving provincial government responsibility for services previously offered by volunteers and ensuring that these services were evenly available throughout the province. Tackling the federal government policies, had they thought about them, would have diverted from this task. But they didn't give the federal policies much thought. When formal child welfare services were first established at the beginning of the twentieth century, most Aboriginal peoples lived in remote areas of the province and had been severely diminished in numbers. The impetus for child welfare reform came mainly from women in the urban centres of Vancouver and Victoria. At that time a largely British population, which was either intolerant of or indifferent to the different cultural groups that shared the province, dominated British Columbia. This society lived in a separate world from the Aboriginal communities of the province, and its gaze barely extended beyond "people like us."

Another reason was the importance of funding formulas in shaping child welfare policy and practice that existed from the beginnings of child welfare and continues today. Initially, government funding was only available for institutional services. A quarter century passed before it was available for non-Aboriginal children in foster care. Statutory funding for group and community work was then, and is now, almost non-existent for both Aboriginal and non-Aboriginal child welfare. Yet our history underscores the vital importance of these approaches. It was from community work that the early pioneers gained the support to develop formal services. Later, social workers counted on the support of community members to gain general acceptance for their services. Group work encourages self-help and non-blaming practices. It is tempting to speculate what might have happened if, when the province took over Aboriginal child welfare from the federal government, it focused upon rebuilding groups and communities rather than removing children.

However, the transfer of responsibility for Aboriginal child welfare to the provinces took place without preparation. A great off-loading occurred. Child welfare workers were not recruited from Aboriginal communities, members of these communities were not consulted about what should replace residential schools, and the province and its social workers were expected to pick up the pieces with no extra resources to do so. By this time, a model of child welfare entrenched in individual pathology and individual approaches, evident as a thread throughout our history, had thoroughly taken hold.

Yet it was social workers' own understanding of equality that contributed significantly to their inability to champion the cause of Aboriginal children and families. Social workers argued for the provincial takeover of Aboriginal child welfare, believing strongly that social justice would occur if everyone received the same kind and quality of service. This view did not quickly disappear as a result of the Aboriginal experience with child welfare services; in fact, it remains today. Yet equal does not have to mean identical or "the same"; it could mean equal recognition of differing cultural values and traditions with respect to the welfare of children, appreciating rather than denying diversity. The ongoing challenge for child welfare, then as now, is to recognize difference while achieving equality. Requiring Aboriginal peoples to develop services that mirror our own, a current policy in child welfare, is one example of the injustice of "sameness" repeating itself.

This chapter opened with the remark that the history of child welfare often describes it as an endeavour that oppressed those it was supposed to assist. There is some truth to this account, but it is incomplete. It ignores how early social workers challenged some of the prevalent assumptions about class, gender, and parenting, and how they transformed the volunteer work of women into fully paid professional employment. This chapter highlights the importance of not discarding our past but, rather, understanding the actions of social work pioneers within the context of their times and gaining appreciation for their accomplishments. Such analysis can also help social workers face their guilt and anger about the Euro-Canadian past of their profession and some of the injustices it perpetrated. It can ensure that we do not continue to repeat the mistakes of our history. The philosopher Conor Cruise O'Brien offers sage advice:

> We need to dig up that buried guilt of ours and ascertain its extent and its limits. We need to find how much there is that we can do something about, and how much that we can do nothing to remove. Then we need to get on with doing what we can do and get on also with living with conscious acceptance of that degree of guilt which is inseparable from our condition as the kind of people we are, in the kind of world we happen to live in. (1994, p. 145)

References

Adamoski, R. (1988). *The profession of casework: The organizational expediency of the British Columbia Child Welfare Survey.* Unpublished master's thesis, University of Toronto, Toronto.

–. (2002). The child – the citizen – the nation: The rhetoric and experience of wardship in early 20th century British Columbia. In R. Adamoski, D. Chunn, and R. Menzies (Eds.), *Contesting Canadian citizenship: Historical readings* (pp. 315-36). Peterborough, ON: Broadview Press.

Andrews, J. (1990, Summer). Female social workers in the second generation. *Affilia: Journal of Women and Social Work, 5,* 46-59.

Angus, A. (1965). Profiles 3: Winona Armitage. *Canadian Welfare, 41*(5), 226-31.

Angus, H.F. (1951, April). Vancouver Children's Aid Society, 1901-1951. *Canadian Welfare, 27*(1), 20-24.

Barman, J. (1991). *The west beyond the west: A history of British Columbia.* Toronto: University of Toronto Press.

Becker, D. (1964). Exit Lady Bountiful: The volunteers and the professional social worker. *Social Service Review, 38*(1), 57-72.

Chambers, C. (1986, March). Women in the creation of the profession of social work. *Social Service Review, 60,* 1-33.

Dixon, S. (1992). The enduring theme: Domineering dowagers and scheming concubines. In B. Garlick, S. Dixon, and P. Allen (Eds.), *Stereotypes of women in power: Historical perspectives and revisionist views* (pp. 209-25). New York: Greenwood Press.

Fournier, S., and Crey, E. (1997). *Stolen from our embrace: The abduction of First Nations children and the restoration of Aboriginal communities.* Vancouver: Douglas and McIntyre.

Furniss, E. (1995). *Victims of benevolence: The dark legacy of the Williams Lake residential school.* Vancouver: Arsenal Pulp Press.

Garlick, B., Dixon, S., and Allen, P. (1992). *Stereotypes of women in power: Historical perspectives and revisionist views.* New York: Greenwood Press.

Gresko, J. (1986). Creating little dominions within the Dominion: Early Catholic Indian schools in Saskatchewan and British Columbia. In J. Barman, Y. Hebert, and D. McCaskill (Eds.), *Indian education in Canada: Vol. 1. The legacy* (pp. 88-109). Vancouver: UBC Press.

Haig-Brown, C. (1988). *Resistance and renewal: Surviving the Indian residential school.* Vancouver: Tillacum Library/Arsenal Pulp Press.

Harvey, I. (1937). Public welfare with particular reference to British Columbia. *Proceedings of the Fifth Annual Conference: Canadian Conference on Social Work* (pp. 31-35). Ottawa: Canadian Council on Social Development.

Herbert, E.I. (1994). *Talking back: Six First Nations women's stories of recovery from childhood sexual abuse and addictions.* Unpublished thesis. University of British Columbia, School of Social Work, Vancouver.

Hill, K. (1990). *Final report: Pioneers in social progress; Oral history of social work in Canada.* Ottawa: Canadian Council on Social Development.

Irving, A. (1987). The development of a provincial welfare state: British Columbia, 1900-1939. In A. Moscovitch and J. Albert (Eds.), *The benevolent state: The growth of welfare in Canada* (pp. 155-74). Toronto: Garamond.

Johnston, P. (1983). *Native children and the child welfare system.* Toronto: Canadian Council on Social Development in association with James Lorimer.

Little, M.H. (1993, June). *"No car, no radio, no liquor permit": The moral reputation of single mothers in Ontario, 1920-1940.* Paper presented at the Canadian social welfare conference, St. John's, Newfoundland.

MacDonald, J. (1993). *Community study of the Spallumcheen Band child welfare program: Interim report.* Victoria: Royal Commission on Aboriginal Peoples.

Matters, D. (1980). The Boys' Industrial School: Education for juvenile offenders. In J.D. Wilson and D.C. Jones (Eds.), *Schooling and society in twentieth century British Columbia* (pp. 53-69). Calgary: Detselig.

Matters, I. (1984). Sinners or sinned against? Historical aspects of female juvenile delinquency in British Columbia. In B. Latham and R. Pazdro (Eds.), *Not just pin money: Selected essays on the history of women's work in British Columbia* (pp. 265-77). Victoria: Camosun College.

Miller, J. (1996). *Shingwauk's vision.* Toronto: University of Toronto Press.

Moran, B. (1992). *A little rebellion.* Vancouver: Arsenal Pulp Press.

Morton, D. (2005, 3 May). The VE-Day revolution: The end of the war triggered positive social change [Electronic version]. *Maclean's, 188*(29), 46.

Moscrop, M. (1958). The life and times of Amy Leigh. *Canadian Welfare, 34*(3), 120-25.

Nelson, L. (1934, February). Vancouver's early days and the development of her social services. *British Columbia's Welfare,* p. 14-17.

Noble, J. (1980). *Saving the poor and their children.* Unpublished master's thesis, University of Toronto, Toronto.

O'Brien, C.C. (1994). *On the eve of the millennium.* Concord, ON: House of Anansi Press.

Purvey, D. (2005). Alexandra Orphanage and families in crisis in Vancouver, 1892 to 1938. In D. Purvey and C. Walmsley (Eds.), *Child and family welfare in British Columbia: A history* (pp. 53-75). Calgary: Detselig.

Rooke, P., and Schnell, R.L. (1981). Child welfare in English Canada (1920-1948). *Social Service Review, 55*(3), 484-506.

Royal Commission on Aboriginal Peoples. (1996a). *Report of the Royal Commission on Aboriginal Peoples: Vol. 1. Looking forward, looking back.* Ottawa: Minister of Supply and Services.

–. (1996b). *Report of the Royal Commission on Aboriginal Peoples: Vol. 3. Gathering strength.* Ottawa: Minister of Supply and Services.

Sanders, M. (1957). Social work: A profession chasing its tail. *Harpers, 2,* 56-62.

Smith, M.J. (1948, November). Professional education for social work in British Columbia. *British Columbia's Welfare,* pp. 12-13.

Stanbury, W. (1975). *Success and failure: Indians in urban society.* Vancouver: UBC Press.

Storey, V., Worobetz, T., and Kennedy, H. (1999). *The home: Orphan's home to family centre, 1873 to 1998.* Victoria: Cridge Centre for the Family.

Struthers, J. (1987a). "Lord give us men": Women and social work in English Canada, 1918-1953. In A. Moscovitch and J. Albert (Eds.), *The benevolent state: The growth of welfare in Canada* (pp. 126-43). Toronto: Garamond Press.

–. (1987b). A profession in crisis: Charlotte Whitton and Canadian social work in the 1930s. In A. Moscovitch and J. Albert (Eds.), *The benevolent state: The growth of welfare in Canada* (pp. 111-25). Toronto: Garamond Press.

Thomas, R. (1998). *The legacy of the residential school at Kuper Island.* Unpublished thesis, University of Victoria, Faculty of Human and Social Development, Victoria.

Turtle Island Native Network. www.turtleisland.org.

Walmsley, C. (2001). *The social representations of child protection practice with Aboriginal children.* Unpublished doctoral dissertation, Laval University, Québec City.

Whitton, C. (1927). *Report of the British Columbia Child Welfare Survey.* Vancouver: BC Child Welfare Survey Committee.

York, G. (1990). *The dispossessed: Life and death in native Canada.* Toronto: Little, Brown.

2

Trends in Child Welfare: What Do the Data Show?

Leslie T. Foster

This chapter provides an overview of how some key events and individuals in child welfare influenced the trends affecting the numbers of children in the care of the state during the second half of the last century and the early years of the present one (see Appendix 1). Data from provincial government administrative files are used to examine the impact that particular policies and individuals had on the numbers of children taken into state care. The chapter describes the cyclical trend in both the numbers and rates of children in care and relates this to changing demographics, financial policies, and child welfare policies. In particular, it notes the impact of single events, such as a child death, on child-in-care rates. Sections of the chapter consider the different paths into care that are taken by Aboriginal children and children of the dominant culture, and the difference in rates of children in care by geographical location is described.

The data used provide a sense of the trends, but it is important not to lose sight of the fact that each "statistic" represents a child, one who has been separated from his or her biological family – and, in the case of Aboriginal children, their cultures – and placed in the home of a stranger.

The numbers of children in care and the rates per thousand children in the population are useful indicators for tracking the trends in the child welfare system. There are, of course, other indicators, such as spending or the reasons children came into care. Did they enter care through voluntary agreements with parents, did they enter through the court system because of severe physical, emotional, or sexual abuse, or were they admitted into care because of chronic neglect related to extreme poverty? Evidence suggests that since the 1994-95 Gove Inquiry into Child Protection, there has been an increasing tendency for children to come into care for reasons of protection rather than under voluntary care arrangements. Between March 1998 and March 2006, the number of children in care under voluntary arrangements fell from 1,379 to 664 (Table 2.1), mostly as a result of a lower number of non-Aboriginal children in these arrangements. It should be

Table 2.1

Reasons for being in care

	Voluntary care agreement	Special needs agreement	Protection need	Other	Total
1998	**1,379** *338 / 1,041*	**2,496** *345 / 2,151*	**11,609** *4,118 / 7,491*	**216** *72 / 144*	**15,700** *4,873 / 10,827*
1999	**1,293** *329 / 964*	**2,660** *381 / 2,279*	**12,925** *4,599 / 8,326*	**213** *63 / 150*	**17,091** *5,372 / 11,719*
2000	**923** *281 / 642*	**2,233** *347 / 1,886*	**13,597** *5,101 / 8,496*	**203** *61 / 142*	**16,956** *5,790 / 11,166*
2001	**897** *307 / 590*	**2,099** *393 / 1,706*	**14,699** *6,020 / 8,679*	**176** *50 / 126*	**17,871** *6,770 / 11,101*
2002	**831** *330 / 501*	**1,866** *395 / 1,471*	**14,293** *6,358 / 7,935*	**171** *65 / 106*	**17,161** *7,148 / 10,013*
2003	**749** *278 / 471*	**1,687** *379 / 1,308*	**13,863** *6,447 / 7,416*	**169** *69 / 100*	**16,468** *7,173 / 9,295*
2004	**712** *305 / 407*	**1,557** *355 / 1,202*	**13,198** *6,393 / 6,805*	**148** *58 / 90*	**15,615** *7,111 / 8,504*
2005	**728** *328 / 400*	**1,335** *345 / 990*	**13,328** *6,714 / 6,614*	**131** *58 / 73*	**15,522** *7,445 / 8,077*
2006	**664** *305 / 359*	**1,207** *313 / 894*	**13,664** *6,998 / 6,666*	**144** *59 / 85*	**15,679** *7,675 / 8,004*

Notes: Data are from March of each year. Top figures are totals; figures in italics are for Aboriginals; figures in roman are for non-Aboriginals. Figures taken from March active files and individual cases can have up to three different reasons for service. In March 2006, there were 9,157 total children-in-care (CIC) cases. Of these, 0.5 percent had no reasons for service, 46.1 percent had one reason, 34.1 percent had two, and 19.2 percent had three. Because of this, the numbers above will be higher than the CIC caseload.

Source: Ministry of Children and Family Development, Decision Support Branch.

noted, however, that sometimes children in care under a voluntary agreement were placed there for protection reasons.

The data raise an intriguing question: What is the right number of children to have in state care? Obviously, coming into state care should be seen as a last resort, as intended by the legislation of the day, because the results of children being in state care have not been promising. Research has shown that "adults who were in care as children had significantly higher depression scores, lower scores on marital happiness, less intimate parental relationships, and higher incidences of social isolation than adults who were never in care" (Foster and Wright, 2002, p. 103, based on Cook-Fong, 2000). There is also overwhelming evidence that many homeless people have been in the child welfare system and suffer disproportionately from the many social and health issues faced by this marginalized population (Downing-Orr, 1996; Leslie and Hare, 2003; Paliavin, 1993; Roman and Wolfe, 1997; Rutman, Hubberstey, Barlow, and Brown, 2005; Serge, Eberle, Goldberg, Sullivan, and Dudding, 2002; Tweedie, 2005; Zlotnick, Kronstadt, and Klee, 1998). Further, some, but certainly not all, children find themselves in state care because of an "intergenerational" component to child welfare. The children of parents who had been in the system have a much higher probability of being placed into state care because of their parents' social problems and poor parenting practices resulting in abuse and neglect. There are also many children in need of child welfare services or nurturing who do not get taken into care. One estimate has suggested that in 2001, as many as 8,700 children were being looked after by grandparents or other extended family because parents were not available or, if they were, could not provide for their own children (Callahan, Brown, MacKenzie, and Whittington, 2004, as quoted by BC Association of Social Workers, 2006). Despite these cautions, children-in-care data are readily available and so are used in this chapter as a key indicator with which to understand the impacts of certain policies and individuals on child welfare.

BC Trends from Post-Second World War to 2006

The numbers of children in care between 1950 and 2006 are shown in Figure 2.1. These statistics come from administrative files of the Ministry of Children and Family Development and its predecessor ministries and departments (see Appendix 2) and from ministry annual reports published after the Second World War. Data prior to 1950 are unreliable and inconsistent because children in care were looked after by several different children's aid societies (CAS), as well as by the province. It is only recently that there has been a consistent recording system to track the number of children in care.

During the mid-1980s, some pioneering work was undertaken to look at historical trends of children in care (Merner, 1983). Historically, however, the ministry reported data inconsistently, even within its own annual reports.

Figure 2.1

Children in care (CIC) since 1950

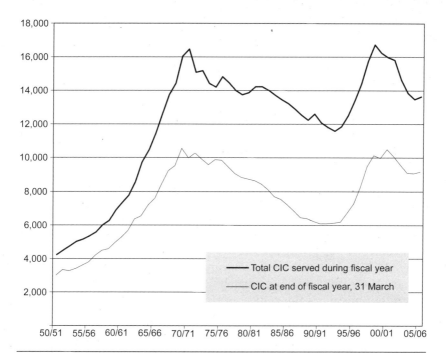

Source: Ministry of Children and Family Development, Decision Support Branch

In some instances, data were recorded for the calendar year; in others, for the fiscal year. Sometimes only the number of paid children in care was recorded. In addition, data would sometimes be provided only for children in the care of the ministry and would not include those in the care of CASs. These issues often resulted in reported undercounts of the total number of children in care and a relative over-calculation of the percentage of Aboriginal children in care because the large majority of Aboriginal children in care were looked after by the province and not by the CASs.

Further, by March 2006 there were twenty-four delegated Aboriginal authorities, of which seventeen currently look after Aboriginal children in care. Some of these children are financed entirely by the province; others are financed entirely by the federal government (see Appendix 3). For all these reasons, researchers examining historical documents must use extreme caution when obtaining and comparing numbers and rates of children in care. Nevertheless, the figures and tables that follow have, to the extent possible, avoided the pitfalls noted.

Merner (1983) was able to obtain counts going back to 1933, but only for children in paid care. In 1933 there were 533 children in state-paid care, rising to over 8,000 in 1970. Using the consistent data available from 1950 onwards, Figure 2.1 shows the number of children in care at each fiscal year-end (31 March) and also the total number of children in care during the fiscal year (April to March), including new removals or apprehensions and those discharged back home or aging out of the system during the year. It is worth noting that the total number of children in the care of the state throughout the year is approximately five to six thousand higher than fiscal year-end figures, the number normally contained in annual reports. This difference reflects the fact that the number of children in care represents a complex system of children entering care all the time while others leave to return home or age out. Still other children are in care for the whole year. Year-end figures tend to underestimate the total number of children in the system, as they only show the statistics at a moment in time.

Figure 2.1 shows an increase from 1950 onwards for two decades, peaking around 1970, after which there is a gradual decline until 1994. Following this, there is a rapid increase for five years or so, peaking in June 2001, when 10,775 children were in the care of the state. Since that time the numbers have fallen by approximately 15 percent, to 9,157, by March 2006.

Part, but not all, of this trend can be accounted for by the child demographics of the last half of the last century, characterized as the post-war baby boom, and a rapidly declining infant mortality rate. This was followed by a reduction in birth rate and then by an "echo" baby boom (Foot and Stoffman, 2001; Foster and Wright, 2002; Merner, 1983). The birth rate in the province went from a pre-war crude rate of less than 10 per thousand people to 25.2 per thousand in 1947, peaking at 26.1 per thousand in 1957, before beginning a gradual decline. Infant mortality rates have seen a consistent reduction from 29.7 deaths per thousand live births in 1950 to fewer than four per thousand in 2005.

The size of the child population is controlled for in Figure 2.2, which provides the rates of children in care. This shows a rather flat trend throughout much of the 1950s, even though three special groups of children came into care during that period: Jewish children starting in 1948, Hungarian children starting in 1956, and Doukhobor children starting in 1955. The first two groups came from abroad because of political issues, while the latter were removed and put in care because of their parents' failure to send them to public school. (This was not the first time that Doukhobor children had been placed in care in large numbers. In 1932, 364 children were placed in care after their parents had been imprisoned.) The rate of children in care started to increase late in that decade. The trends noted in Figure 2.1 are repeated, although the cyclical trends are somewhat "flattened." The fact

Figure 2.2

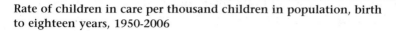

**Rate of children in care per thousand children in population, birth
to eighteen years, 1950-2006**

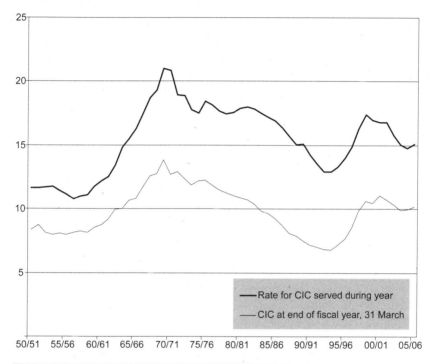

Source: Ministry of Children and Family Development, Decision Support Branch

that the cyclical trends continue to appear indicates that factors other than
the mere demographics of the "boom, bust, echo" phenomenon are also
important.

Non-Demographic Factors Related to the Increase in Children in Care between 1950 and 1970

During the second part of the twentieth century, changing financial relationships between the province, municipalities, and the federal government
undoubtedly had a major impact on child welfare practice and policy in the
province. Such relationships made the public costs of children in care more
affordable for municipalities and also for CASs, which received increasingly
more resources from the province to look after children in care. As well,
changes at the federal level also made it less expensive for the province to
cover the costs of child welfare services.

Of particular importance was the province's *Social Assistance Act* of 1945, which included the costs of foster and boarding care as social services and gave some financial relief to municipalities. Following the Royal Commission on Provincial-Municipal Relations in 1947, the province agreed to cover 80 percent of child welfare costs. This was later increased so that the province assumed 90 percent of the costs in September 1958. In 1966, the federal government introduced the Canada Assistance Plan, which resulted in provinces receiving 50 percent of their costs for welfare, including child welfare, from the federal government. In the early 1970s, funding for child welfare was provided entirely by the province, which took over complete control and oversight of the delivery of child welfare services from municipalities and CASs (see Chapter 3). Since the 1980s, however, as Aboriginal agencies started to assert control over the delivery of child welfare services to Aboriginal children, the federal government agreed to pay for some of the costs of First Nations children, especially those who were removed from their families while they or their guardians were living on reserves.

Another important factor was a change to the federal *Indian Act* that gave provinces responsibility for child welfare on reserves. This resulted in a rapid increase in the number of Aboriginal children in state care in the 1960s, which has been referred to as the "Sixties Scoop" (Johnston, 1983; see also Chapter 5). Based on various sources, more than half of the total increase in the number of children in care between 1950 and 1990 would have been Aboriginal children. Middle-class social workers were appalled at the poverty and living conditions of First Nations children on reserves. As residential schools were being closed down, the social workers saw little option but to have children put into care off-reserve, with minimal concern for or understanding of the cultural impact of doing so (see Chapter 1).

The 1960s saw the emergence of the "battered child syndrome" following the work of Kempe, Silverman, Steele, Droegemueller, and Silver (1962). This research resulted in an increasing realization that many childhood injuries resulted from physical abuse at the hands of the child's parents. There was an increasing push in the decade to introduce more preventive services for families, first through the *Families and Children's Court Act* in 1963 (Clague, Dill, Seebaran, and Wharf, 1984), and later through the introduction of the federal Canada Assistance Plan in 1966, which covered not only 50 percent of the costs of child welfare, as mentioned above, but also a similar proportion of the cost of family services.

In 1967, amendments made to the *Protection of Children Act* required people to report suspected maltreatment (Callahan and Wharf, 1982) and, as the 1968 Annual Report of the Department of Social Welfare indicated, provided for temporary care of a child "while the neglectful family is helped to overcome its problems" (p. 19) (throughout this chapter the term "annual report," unless otherwise specified, refers to the annual reports of the ministry or department responsible for child welfare; see Appendix 2 for appropriate department and ministry titles). Further amendments in 1968 allowed the Superintendent of Child Welfare to permit the adoption of permanent wards, as well as authorizing the closures of orphanages and industrial schools. In 1969, for the first time, the government created a full-time position of minister for social welfare, providing for more focus on child welfare. During this period, however, it is clear that the push to support families was overwhelmed by the development of more reasons for bringing children into care, as the numbers and rates of children in care continued to rise (Callahan and Wharf, 1982).

Twenty-Five Years of Reductions, 1970-94

The election of the New Democratic Party (NDP) government in 1972 solidified an emphasis on family and community supports (see Chapter 3), a trend that continued throughout the 1970s and beyond. Further, after 1975, a new Social Credit cabinet established an inter-ministry committee for children in an attempt to improve co-ordination of services. The committee, consisting of the deputy ministers of health, education, and human resources, along with the commissioner of corrections, was referred to as the "Children in Crisis" committee. Similar committees were established at the local level. In addition, the Social Credit government initiated a further review of children's legislation with the intent of integrating various statutes, as noted in the 1977 Annual Report of the Ministry of Human Resources. An earlier review, undertaken by Thomas Berger under the NDP government, came to naught with the change in government (see Chapter 3).

With the appointment of Grace McCarthy as minister in 1977, there was a further increase in emphasis on services to families and children, and 265 family support workers were added to the ministry field offices "to help keep families intact," as was noted in the ministry's annual report for 1977. In September 1978, the draft *Family and Child Service Act* was released for public review. The draft act emphasized the role of the family in caring for children and outlined the support services for families provided by the government. A toll-free help line for children was established the following year, and a policy handbook addressing the issues of child abuse and neglect was developed and distributed to various professions involved in child welfare to assist them in their work. As described in the 1979 Annual Report of the Ministry of Human Resources, the ministry introduced a tracking system to ensure regular review of formalized care plans for children in care (see Chapter 4).

Institutions such as Glendale, Tranquille, and Woodlands, which provided residential and other services to some children with developmental delays as well as to adults, started to close as residents were moved into the community. In addition, sex abuse was formally recognized as a problem in British Columbia several years before the 1984 publication of the Badgley Report shocked the country by identifying the nature and extent of child sexual abuse in Canada (Badgley, 1984). By the mid-1980s, ministry annual reports indicated that 5 to 6 percent of children in care were there because of sex abuse issues (see Chapter 4).

In 1983, following a provincial election that saw the Social Credit government re-elected, Premier Bill Bennett announced a major budget restraint initiative. The family support workers introduced in the late 1970s were eliminated despite a positive evaluation of their work (Ministry of Human Resources, 1979), and the number of other child welfare positions was reduced (Gove, 1995). Despite the elimination of family support workers, both the number and the rate of children in care continued to decline. When Bill Vander Zalm became leader of the Social Credit Party and premier in 1986, a major infusion of support resources was announced. Of the $20 million in new annual funding, the Ministry of Social Services and Housing received $16.4 million. Several new programs were introduced, based on community-identified needs, and, as stated in the 1989 Annual Report of the Ministry of Social Services and Housing, "299 contracts were signed with local not-for-profit agencies for a variety of services, including Family Advancement, Supports to Young Mothers, Parent Training Homemakers, and Supportive Living programs" for women in their final trimester of pregnancy. Known as "Initiatives to Strengthen the Family," the funding was an attempt to advance the anti-abortion stance of the premier. This investment undoubtedly assisted in continuing the decline in the rate of children in care, despite predictions by ministry staff that, based on demographics, the rate and numbers should start to increase in the mid-1980s (Merner, 1983) as a result of the "echo" baby boom (Foot and Stoffman, 2001).

At the end of the decade, the ministry undertook a major reorganization, particularly in terms of delivering services in urban areas. To this point the ministry had worked to provide integrated services, but it was argued that the services being delivered were now too complex for integration. Consequently, the ministry developed separate offices for its three major services: income assistance; family and children services; and services for people with mental handicaps (developmental delays). This was the start of increased specialization in the ministry, as well as the separation of child welfare from the income assistance program, despite the fact that the large majority of children in care came from families on income assistance (Foster and Wright, 2002; Weller and Wharf, 2002; see also Chapter 4). It is worth noting that the provincial ombudsman criticized this move in 1990, arguing that there was a need for more integration of services related to children, youth, and their families, not less (Welch, 2004).

The Rebound, 1994-2001

Events and changes in the 1990s and beyond would clearly eclipse events in previous decades. Child welfare became a major political maelstrom, rarely out of the media and public eye, and there was a return to increasing numbers of children taken into care. The decade also saw major reviews; new legislation; a continued quick turnover of ministers, deputy ministers, and superintendents (directors) of child welfare; and major concerns that successive ministry reorganizations were taking the focus away from child welfare services.

At the beginning of the 1990s, the NDP under Mike Harcourt swept into power after a decade and a half of uninterrupted Social Credit administration. Social Credit was all but wiped out, but in its place a revived provincial Liberal Party arose as the official opposition. Joan Smallwood became the new minister of social services and immediately established two Community Panels on Family and Children's Services Legislation Review, one of which was devoted specifically to Aboriginal child welfare, to examine the current child welfare system in the province (Aboriginal Committee of the Community Panel, 1992; Community Panel, 1992; see Chapters 5 and 6). These reviews led to a major overhaul of child welfare legislation that had started under the Social Credit administration. The *Child, Family and Community Service Act* became law in 1996, replacing the *Family and Child Service Act* of 1981. There were many new features; some key ones included an expanded definition of a child in need of protection – which included emotional abuse – and an emphasis on the preservation of Aboriginal culture (Armitage, 1998). Further, the safety and well-being of children were listed as paramount considerations, adding to the development of a risk-averse culture in the ministry (Foster and Wright, 2002; see Chapters 7 and 8).

There are several reasons for the rapid increases in both the numbers and rates of children in care in the 1990s (Foster and Wright, 2002). Although the previously noted community panel reports and new legislation were major events, they were overshadowed by changes underway in the welfare system that culminated in the emergence of the BC Benefits Program in 1996, and by the death of a child, Matthew Vaudreuil, who was "known to the ministry" but was not in its care. Controversy around both his death and the resulting internal government review led to the establishment of the Gove Commission in 1994. Almost immediately after the government announced that the commission had been set up, the number and rate of children coming into care started to increase.

The report by Thomas Gove, which contained 118 recommendations, called for nothing less than a complete overhaul of the child-serving system (see Chapter 7; Gove, 1995). Intense public and media scrutiny of the child welfare system created an even more risk-averse culture within the ministry. In addition, the public scrutiny brought issues related to child protection to the attention of the public and media. The result was an increase in the number of child protection concerns reported to the ministry, especially from professional groups such as the police, schools, and community professionals. Today, the police raise more child protection concerns with the ministry than any other group (Table 2.2).

Cynthia Morton was appointed transition commissioner to oversee how Gove's recommendations might be implemented, but government rushed to put a new face on child welfare before Morton had completed her work (Morton, 2002). A new child-serving organization, created in September 1996, was symbolically named a Ministry "for" rather than "of" Children and Families, contained over 100 programs from five different ministries (Allen, 1998; Morton, 1996; see Chapter 7). Significantly, the income assistance program, which supported many families whose children were in care, was also sent to a new ministry of human resources, divorcing the two long-connected program areas. A decentralized twenty-region administrative service model was developed for child welfare. New minister Penny Priddy vowed there would never be another Matthew Vaudreuil in the province, an almost unachievable goal in any child welfare system.

Government continued its overhaul of the income assistance programs, making it harder for families to receive welfare, reducing amounts to those on welfare, and tightening eligibility requirements for two programs that supported vulnerable children and teens, the Child in Home of Relative program and under age nineteen income assistance (Foster and Wright, 2002). These changes, combined with a reduction in budget for the first full year of operation (despite assurances by the premier, Glen Clark, that any "savings" found through consolidating children and family services would be reinvested in the system), meant the new ministry and its child protection workers were under major stress right from the start.

A new Children's Commission was established under the direction of Cynthia Morton, previously the transition commissioner, to oversee the work of the ministry. The creation of the committee and of the new Child, Youth and Family Advocate position, along with the minister's statement that there would never be another Matthew, increased scrutiny of the ministry. Also in 1996, nearly 350 new child welfare workers were hired to investigate the rapidly increasing number of child protection reports (which identified children who might be in need of protection) received by the ministry, and the number of children in care climbed to levels not seen since the early 1970s (Foster and Wright, 2002). This increase in the number of children in care was also fuelled by both the suspension of workers related to child welfare cases and the introduction of a risk-assessment model (see Chapter 8). Both factors encouraged workers to become more conservative in their practice, and the result was that workers were more likely to remove children from their homes rather than take the chance of supporting

Table 2.2

Percentage of protection reports by caller type, by fiscal year

	1997-98	1998-99	1999-2000	2000-1	2001-2	2002-3	2003-4	2004-5	2005-6
Police	8.8	9.3	11.4	12.5	13.2	14.2	15.0	16.0	18.3
Community professional	13.5	13.6	13.9	13.4	13.8	13.6	14.7	14.3	14.8
School	14.9	15.3	15.4	15.5	15.2	14.6	14.9	15.0	14.3
Parent	10.9	11.3	11.0	11.1	10.8	10.9	10.5	10.1	9.2
Relative	7.5	7.2	6.7	7.1	7.8	8.2	8.1	8.5	8.1
Concerned citizen	10.0	8.3	8.1	7.9	7.8	8.0	8.1	8.2	7.8
Friend/Neighbour	10.2	9.9	9.2	9.0	8.8	8.9	8.0	7.8	6.9
Health professional	5.5	5.1	5.1	5.1	5.5	5.7	5.5	5.8	6.2
Children and Family Development worker	5.2	6.5	6.1	5.6	5.2	5.2	5.3	5.0	5.4
Anonymous	3.4	3.2	3.1	3.4	3.0	3.1	2.7	2.8	2.5
Subject child	3.1	2.9	2.8	2.7	2.5	2.1	1.9	1.7	1.6
Probation officer	0.8	0.9	0.8	1.0	0.9	1.0	1.0	1.0	1.1
Ex-spouse	0.9	1.0	0.9	1.3	1.2	1.3	1.2	1.0	1.1
Financial assistance worker	2.5	2.8	2.8	2.2	2.0	1.4	1.4	0.9	0.8
Support service provider	1.0	1.0	0.9	0.7	0.8	0.6	0.5	0.5	0.8
Preschool/Daycare	0.9	0.9	0.9	0.8	0.7	0.7	0.7	0.8	0.7
Residential caregiver	0.8	0.6	0.6	0.7	0.7	0.5	0.4	0.3	0.4
Community living worker	0.2	0.2	0.1	0.1	0.2	0.1	0.1	0.1	0.1
Total number of reports	32,642	33,137	35,005	34,794	33,522	31,780	30,074	29,907	30,900

Notes: Figures are taken from March active files.
Source: Ministry of Children and Family Development, Decision Support Branch

the family so it could try to do better. Putting a child into care was much "safer" for the worker than leaving the child with the family, even if the child could be supported at home. If something went wrong with the latter scenario, workers were afraid of being disciplined or, worse, fired.

In the summer of 1999, a time of year when the number of children in care tended to fall, four boats carrying Chinese migrants from Fujian Province were intercepted off the coast of British Columbia. About 140 of these migrants claimed to be minors under the age of nineteen. These minors boosted the total number of children in care during that year. As the Ministry for Children and Families had little experience in dealing with large numbers of international children coming into care at one time (the last influx had come in the 1950s following the Hungarian Uprising), particularly those related to human trafficking, it was left scrambling to find appropriate, non-prison-based care, as well as education and health services for the children. (Over time the numbers declined as many of the children "disappeared." It is thought they were picked up by the "snakehead" handlers who organized the trafficking. Nevertheless, the ministry received an award from the United Nations for its sensitive handling of, and its protection of the rights of, these children.)

The Recent Reduction in the Number of Children in Care, 2000 to March 2006

The largest total number of children in care in a fiscal year was recorded at the end of the twentieth century (Figure 2.1). Subsequent reductions in numbers coincided with the introduction of budget restraints starting in the late 1990s; the push to increase adoptions, which rose from 117 in 1998 to well over 300 for each of the three fiscal years from April 2002 to March 2005; the introduction of a special Treasury Board-funded "utilization management" program, which, among other things, provided specific resources to examine whether it was possible to return children home safely; and changes to legislation that allowed social workers to monitor children under "supervision orders," which allowed the children to remain in their own home rather than being taken into, or kept in, care (Figure 2.3). The introduction of youth agreements in December 1999 gave financial support to teens while keeping them out of care (BC Statistics, 2002). For the fiscal year 2000-1, 300 youth received support through the Youth Agreement Program rather than being taken into state care; for the fiscal year 2004-5, a total of 789 youth received such support throughout the year.

In recent years, the federal government's increasing investments in early childhood development, flowed through provincial coffers, have provided more services for children from birth to age six and their parents. The aim of these resources was to improve both parenting skills and the development of young children. One hoped-for outcome was to reduce the number

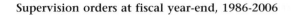

Figure 2.3

Supervision orders at fiscal year-end, 1986-2006

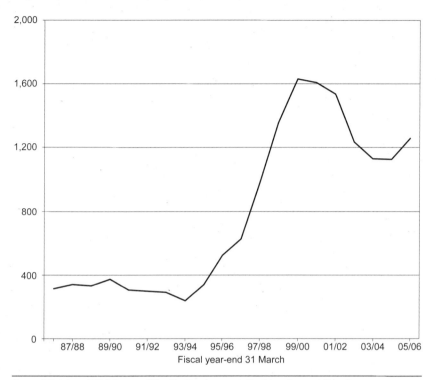

Fiscal year-end 31 March

Source: Ministry of Children and Family Development, Decision Support Branch

of very young children requiring state care. Figure 2.4, however, shows that the proportion of children aged 0-4 in care dropped only marginally since these program resources were introduced, and in recent years has actually increased. The relative reduction of caseloads in the fifteen-to-eighteen age group reflects the introduction of youth agreements and the increasing reluctance to take older youth into care.

In May 2001, the NDP lost an election to Gordon Campbell's Liberals, which created a new Ministry of Children and Family Development. The highest monthly number for children in care was recorded in June 2001; since then the numbers have dropped substantially. Reasons for this decrease include budget and staffing reductions, an increased emphasis on keeping children with their families – a philosophy promoted by Gordon Hogg, who was minister of children and family development from 2001 to 2004 – and increased investment in early childhood development programs. Minister Hogg also promoted the professionalism of child welfare workers so that they did not have to rely on the rigidity of the risk-assessment model

Figure 2.4

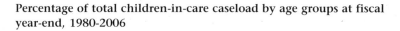

Percentage of total children-in-care caseload by age groups at fiscal year-end, 1980-2006

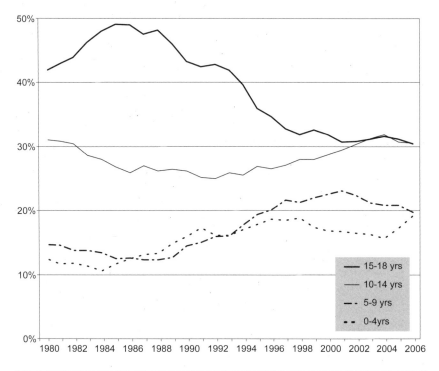

Source: Ministry of Children and Family Development, Decision Support Branch

introduced following the Gove Inquiry (see Chapter 9). Both funding restraints and the promotion of early childhood development were a continuation of measures introduced by the previous administration, and some of the measures for reducing the number of children in care were indeed paying off, especially for non-Aboriginal children. In addition, many children taken into care during and immediately after the Gove Inquiry were aging out of the system in large numbers during the early years of the twenty-first century, thus reducing the overall count.

Other factors of importance are related to the drop in number of concerns reported to the ministry about children from 1999/2000 to 2004/5 (Table 2.1). Furthermore, because of reduced staffing and more reliance on the judgment of child protection workers, the percentage of protection reports investigated also dropped substantially (Figure 2.5), although the rate for Aboriginal families remained higher.

Figure 2.5

Percentage of protection reports investigated, April 1998-March 2006

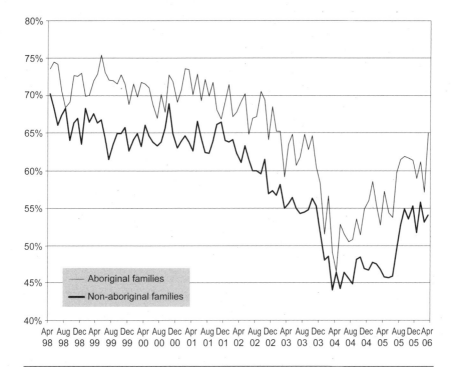

Apr Aug Dec Apr Aug Dec Apr Aug Dec Apr Aug Dec Apr Aug Dec Apr Aug Dec Apr Aug Dec Apr Aug DecApr
98 98 98 99 99 99 00 00 00 01 01 01 02 02 02 03 03 03 04 04 04 05 05 05 06

Source: Ministry of Children and Family Development, Decision Support Branch

Aboriginal Children in Care in British Columbia

Little mention has been made of Aboriginal child welfare issues so far in this chapter. This is not to belittle the drastic impact of successive federal and provincial governments' approaches to Aboriginal children. The devastating and intergenerational health and social effects on Aboriginal children, families, communities, and cultures rendered by colonization, forced assimilation and acculturation, and the residential school system are described elsewhere (see Chapters 1 and 5). At the outset, however, it should be noted that Aboriginal children coming into the care of the state suffered, and continue to suffer, from the double jeopardy of being separated not only from their biological and extended families, but also from their indigenous cultures and communities. This perpetuates the intergenerational social issues so common in Aboriginal communities that are related to the historical effects of the residential school system.

The trend of an increasing number and proportion of Aboriginal children in state care became apparent in the middle of the last century and continues in 2006. The Superintendent of Child Welfare, Ruby McKay, noted in her 1944 annual report that there were too many children of Aboriginal background who had numerous temporary placements, rather than one permanent foster home. In her 1952 annual report, Superintendent McKay opined that the 1951 changes in the *Indian Act* (noted earlier in this chapter) were responsible for bringing about changes in the traditional Aboriginal way of life. She noted that "there must continue to be social casualties during this period of adjustment unless more guidance and help is given the group than is presently available to them" (p. 55). She continued to express concern about legal impediments to Status Indian families taking Aboriginal children into foster care "despite there being a number of good adoptive and foster homes to be found through the Indian reservations of this Province" (ibid.).

The number of Aboriginal children in care increased disproportionately relative to the Aboriginal child population in the province as whole, and the Department of Social Welfare's annual report for 1961 noted that there was growing concern at that time about the great number of Aboriginal children coming into care in the north of the province and in the Kamloops area. Indeed, in 1992 the Aboriginal Committee of the Community Panel on Family and Children's Services Legislation Review noted that "the scope of the apprehensions and foster placement of our children in the 1950's and 1960's was so extensive it is now known as the '60's Scoop'. In 1955, 1% of the children in care of the Superintendent in British Columbia were Aboriginal children. By 1960, 40% of the children were Aboriginal. In some of our communities, every child was, at one point in his or her life, apprehended" (1992, p. 20; see also Johnston, 1983; Chapter 5). Some of this increase was likely motivated by the federal Treasury Board Minute Number 627879 in 1964, which gave even more power to the provinces for on-reserve social services (Montgomery, n.d.).

The Department of Social Welfare's 1967 annual report suggests that "this [increase] relates in part to the accelerated transition of Indian people to the urban centers and thus stress on Indian families" (p. 19). Remarkably, there was no mention of the impact of the residential school system nor of the dreadful housing, social, and economic conditions on reserves, which led to this urban migration.

A review of Aboriginal caseloads in 1969 noted that more than 5 percent of all Aboriginal children in the province were in the care of the state, compared to only 0.8 percent of non-Aboriginal children. In other words, an Aboriginal child was 6.25 times more likely to be in care. The report also warned that it would not be possible to care for Aboriginal children in Aboriginal foster homes given current resources. On the reserves, there was only one approved foster home for every four children in care; off-reserve there was only one approved Aboriginal foster home for every eleven Aboriginal children in care. Despite these poor ratios, this was apparently a substantial improvement over the availability of Aboriginal foster homes earlier in the decade (Rippon, 1969).

Norm Levi, the minister of human resources from 1972 to 1975, was the first to note, in the Department of Human Resources' 1972 annual report, that Aboriginal children, "once removed from their family and cultural roots, remain in care for longer periods and are frequently lost to their tribe" (p. 33). The same annual report also acknowledged the need to make contact with key Aboriginal organizations in order to solve the problem of the inordinate number of Aboriginal children in care. As noted in the Department of Human Resources' annual report for 1974, this led to government working with the Union of BC Indian Chiefs (UBCIC) and the BC Association of Non-Status Indians to help develop and find appropriate Aboriginal foster homes for Aboriginal children in care so that they could stay in their community. In contrast, a 1974 resolution by the Indian Homemakers Association of BC, which called on the federal government to recognize Aboriginal peoples' jurisdiction in child welfare fell on deaf ears (Walkem and Bruce, 2002).

Much of the information related to Aboriginal children in care that has been presented so far is gleaned from a variety of places, including ministry annual reports and other sources (e.g., Johnston, 1983; Walkem and Bruce, 2002). For example, ministry records indicate that in 1970, Aboriginal children in care comprised 40 percent of all *non-Vancouver* children in care, an often-quoted figure that, as noted previously, overestimated the relative proportion of Aboriginal children in care. Consistent data related to the numbers of Aboriginal children in care are available only from about 1980 onwards and are plotted in Figure 2.6. With three notable exceptions (1986, 1987, and 1992), the number of Aboriginal children in care fell until 1993, consistent with the trend for non-Aboriginal children in the care of the province. Since that time the numbers have increased for every fiscal year-end except 2003-4. By contrast, the number of non-Aboriginal children in care at fiscal year-end, which peaked in March 1999, has consistently fallen since then. One of the major reasons for an increasing proportion of Aboriginal children in care relative to the rest of the child population is the higher birth rate of Aboriginal peoples (Vital Statistics Agency, 2004). The other point to note is that since the late 1990s there has been increased vigilance in recording Aboriginal heritage. Nevertheless, analysis reported elsewhere has suggested that this latter point accounts for only a relatively small part of the Aboriginal increase (Foster and Wright, 2002). By March 2006, there were 4,542 Aboriginal children in care.

By the early 1980s, Aboriginal people were pressing more strongly for the right to look after their own children. This pressure only became stronger

Figure 2.6

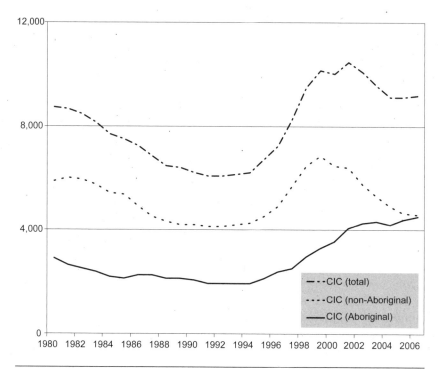

Children in care at fiscal year-end, 1980-2006

Source: Ministry of Children and Family Development, Decision Support Branch

over time. Members of the Spallumcheen Band, concerned about the high number of their children being removed into state care (eighty children were put into care during the 1970s, and by 1980, twenty-five children from this small band were still being cared for outside the community), passed their own "By-Law for the Care of Our Indian Children," which went into effect on 3 June 1980. The bylaw received "tacit, although far from enthusiastic support from the federal government" (MacDonald, 1985, p. 255). The band, along with hundreds of Aboriginal people from throughout the province, demonstrated in front of the home of Grace McCarthy, human resources minister, on Thanksgiving Day, 1980. The Indian Child Caravan, as it was known (Johnston, 1983), resulted in a handwritten agreement between the province and the band, with the province agreeing to respect the authority of the band council to take responsibility for its children (see Chapter 5).

By the mid-1980s, the ministry had entered into agreements with the Nuu-chah-nulth Tribal Council (in 1989, the Nuu-chah-nulth gained full delegated authority to look after children in care), the Carrier Sekani Tribal Council, and the McLeod Lake Band to give them a much greater say and a more active role in delivering child welfare services to their children on the reserve (Morgan, 1987). The number of bands with such agreements might have been higher had the federal government, which still bore the responsibility of covering the costs of First Nations children in care, not imposed a moratorium on further transfers of First Nations child and children services to bands in 1986. This moratorium was lifted only in 1991 when Federal Treasury Board Directive 20-1 was adopted following a complete policy review. The ministry, as it declared in its 1988 annual report, also committed to Aboriginal communities that if children taken into care were unable to return to their biological parents, the children's band would be consulted when permanent placement plans were being developed.

In 1989, the ministry initiated discussions with urban Aboriginal groups to consider what services were required for child welfare. This was a clear recognition of the effect of large numbers of families leaving reserves to live in urban areas. To give a sense of this trend, in 1986, 29 percent of Status Indians lived off-reserve. By 1996, 56 percent were living off-reserve (BC Statistics, 1998). In response, the government created the Native Family and Children Services Unit in Vancouver on 19 March 1990, the first such unit in the province. Two years later, in December 1992, a moratorium on adopting Aboriginal children into non-Aboriginal families was implemented. Gove (1995) has suggested that this resulted in more Aboriginal children staying in state care than otherwise might have been the case, although the evidence for this view is somewhat ambiguous. Certainly, between 1994-95 and 2000-1, only 173 Aboriginal children in care were adopted out of a total of 1,318 adoptions, or 13 percent. However, between 2002-3 and 2004-5, 394 Aboriginal children in care were adopted out of a total of 990, or 40 percent.

Even though authority for child welfare was transferred to selected Aboriginal agencies throughout the 1990s and early twenty-first century, Aboriginal children still constitute close to half of all children in care. While the relationship between child neglect and poverty is beyond dispute (Foster and Wright, 2002; Sullivan, 1998; Weller and Wharf, 2002), the challenges faced by Aboriginal communities – including unemployment, violence, and substance abuse (Bennett and Blackstock, 2002; Bennett, Blackstock, and De La Ronde, 2005; Blackstock, Clarke, Cullen, D'Hondt, and Forsma, 2004; Canadian Institute for Health Information, 2004; Kendall, 2002; Royal Commission on Aboriginal Peoples, 1996; Wade, 1996) – are also major factors leading to high counts of Aboriginal children in care. A 1997 report suggested that there were four other major reasons for the high

Figure 2.7

Number of Aboriginal children in the care of delegated agencies, April 1998-March 2006

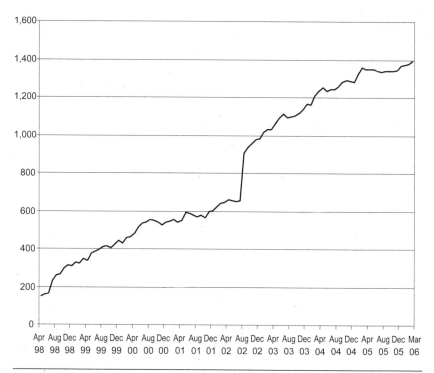

Source: Ministry of Children and Family Development, Decision Support Branch

number of Aboriginal children in care (Petch and Scarth, 1997). First, Aboriginal cultural values and parenting practices have been evaluated from the perspective of the dominant, white culture. Second, some non-Aboriginal social workers still wish to "save" Aboriginal children from traditional tribal ways. Third, there are few support services for Aboriginal families on or off reserve. And fourth, there has been a failure to consider the importance of the extended family in Aboriginal cultures (Foster and Wright, 2002).

Nevertheless, the ministry's approach has been, where possible, to move Aboriginal children in care to the jurisdiction of "delegated Aboriginal agencies." At the end of March 2006, seventeen of twenty-four delegated Aboriginal agencies (Appendix 3) were looking after 1,392 Aboriginal children in care, or approximately 30 percent of the total 4,542 Aboriginal children in care. (It should be noted, however, that the children were not necessarily in the care of Aboriginal families.) This compares with only 101 Aboriginal children in the care of delegated agencies in 1997 (Figure 2.7).

In 1999, the first modern-day treaty in British Columbia was signed by the provincial government and the Nisga'a people of northwestern BC. As part of this treaty, the Nisga'a Lisims government was given the right to make laws with respect to children and family services on Nisga'a lands. In the same year, the Ministry for Children and Families completed its strategic plan for Aboriginal peoples. The key principle of the plan reflected the desire to have Aboriginal peoples involved in the delivery of services for children and families, either through delegated service agreements contracted with the province or through consultations (Ministry for Children and Families, 1999).

An important event for Aboriginal child welfare in the province was the appointment of Grand Chief Ed John as the minister for children and families in the fall of 2000. John, who was a lawyer, had also attended residential school. Although not an elected member of the legislature, John took on the portfolio in order to bring a strong Aboriginal presence into cabinet, and also to try to ensure Aboriginal perspectives were taken into account in child and family issues. Under John's leadership, the government and Sto:lo bands reached an agreement on improved funding arrangements for child welfare, and in early 2001 he created an Aboriginal Advisory Committee consisting solely of Aboriginal members. This in turn led to the signing of a draft memorandum of understanding between the province and selected Aboriginal groups, including the United Native Nations, the Métis Provincial Council, and the First Nations Summit, on 22 March 2001 (Aboriginal Advisory Committee to the Minister for Children and Families, 2001). The draft memorandum of understanding established a dialogue on child welfare between the government and Aboriginal groups. As Ujjal Dosanjh, the premier at the time, noted when the agreement was signed: "This is a historic day in BC, with First Nations and government coming together to move aboriginal children back to their home communities safely" (Ministry for Children and Families, 2001).

Ironically, during John's tenure as minister, the number of Aboriginal children in care continued to increase rapidly. There are several possible explanations for this. First, workers paid more attention to recording Aboriginal ancestry than they had done previously. Second, several Aboriginal children died in John's own traditional territory, and these deaths could perhaps have been avoided had the children been in care. Third, the workers clearly became more risk-averse as a provincial election loomed. John was unsuccessful in gaining a seat in the legislature in the May 2001 election.

In June 2002, following a two-day meeting of key Aboriginal groups in Tsawwassen, the so-called Tsawwassen Accord, drafted by Chief Stewart Phillip of the UBCIC, was embraced by the major Aboriginal leaders in the province (UBCIC, 2002). This accord was a historic step in that all First Nations leaders, urban Aboriginal leaders, and Métis leaders agreed to put aside past difference for the sake of taking back their children. It led to the signing of a memorandum of understanding between numerous Aboriginal political and service groups and the provincial government in September 2002. This new memorandum of understanding set out how services to Aboriginal children and families would be transferred to Aboriginal authorities (Ministry of Children and Family Development, 2002). It was much more inclusive and comprehensive than the memorandum signed with the NDP government in 2001. The 2002 memorandum of understanding had its basis in that agreement, but it had more signatories, including the powerful UBCIC.

Major changes in the period from early 2004 to early 2006 have affected Aboriginal child welfare governance. First, the minister, Gordon Hogg, resigned in January 2004, and Christy Clark, who was also deputy premier, was appointed to the child welfare portfolio. Under Clark's stewardship, funding for governance planning for the Aboriginal authorities was reduced (it was eliminated entirely for non-Aboriginal governance planning), although the ministry service plan stated that Aboriginal governance of child welfare would still be in place by 2007 (Ministry of Children and Family Development, 2005, p. 29). Clark resigned in the fall of 2004, and Stan Hagen was appointed minister. In September 2004, a new assistant deputy minister position was created to oversee Aboriginal governance, and there was hope that a new focus on Aboriginal governance might emerge. Such optimism received a setback, however, following media revelations about the 2002 death of an Aboriginal child who was being looked after by a delegated agency in a "kith and kin" agreement (see Chapter 9). In early October 2005, the ministry established a new associate deputy minister position to oversee the move to regionalization of child welfare, although by February 2006 the individual in the new position became acting deputy minister after both the Director of Child Welfare and the deputy minister left the ministry. A new permanent deputy, Lesley du Toit, was appointed in April 2006, following the release of a review of the child welfare system that was undertaken as a result of the outcry over the child death in 2002. That review supported a move to Aboriginal governance, but only after Aboriginal communities had built up the appropriate capacity (Hughes, 2006; see Chapter 9).

The relative proportion of Aboriginal children in care has hovered between 30 and 40 percent of all children in care in the province since about 1960, but the percentage and total numbers have recently increased while the number of non-Aboriginal children in care has gone down. In March 2006, Aboriginal children constituted a little over 7 percent of all children in the province, but accounted for 49.6 percent of all children in care (4,542, out of a total of 9,157). Today, relative to non-Aboriginal children in care, Aboriginal children are three times more likely to have someone report a protection concern, double the rate from 1997. Reports about Aboriginal

Figure 2.8

Likelihood an Aboriginal child will be in care relative to a non-Aboriginal child, April 1998-March 2006

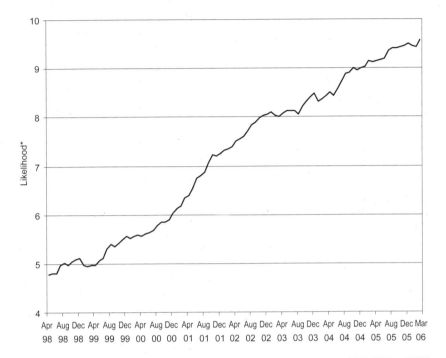

Source: Ministry of Children and Family Development, Decision Support Branch
* E.g., a likelihood of 9.5 means that if the CIC rate for non-Aboriginal children is 6/1,000, then the rate for Aboriginal children is 9.5 times this, i.e., 57/1,000.

families are more likely to be investigated (Figure 2.5), and Aboriginal children are twice as likely to be admitted into care following an investigation of a protection report (Wright, 2005). In early 2006, Aboriginal children in British Columbia were more than nine times more likely to be in care relative to a non-Aboriginal child (Figure 2.8). Sadly, these same inequitable statistics are reflected in other provinces and across the country in general (Blackstock, Prakash, Loxley, and Wien, 2005; Trocme et al., 2005; Trocme, Knoke, Shangreaux, Fallon, and MacLaurin, 2005).

Trends in the province over the last nine years (1998-2006) show some major differences between Aboriginal and non-Aboriginal children's experiences of being in care. Special needs agreements and voluntary care agreements have been much less common among Aboriginal families. The number of Aboriginal children in need of non-voluntary protection has always been relatively greater (Table 2.1). In March 1998, 84.5 percent of all Aboriginal children in care were there for protection reasons, compared to only 69.2 percent for non-Aboriginal children. By March 2006, the difference between the two groups had been reduced, with 83.3 percent of non-Aboriginal children in care for protection reasons, compared to 91.2 percent for Aboriginal children. These data show that, over time, the number of children in care because they need protection has increased substantially relative to the number of children in care for other reasons. The top two reasons for protection are the same for both Aboriginal and non-Aboriginal children – "parent unable/ unwilling to care" and "neglect by parent with physical harm" – but the third most frequent reason varies. It is "physical harm by parent" for Aboriginal children in care, but "emotional harm by parent" for non-Aboriginal children (Table 2.3).

Given current trends, by the time this volume is published there will be more Aboriginal children than non-Aboriginal children in care. The one bright spot, if it can be called that, is that over the past decade, the number of Aboriginal children in care being looked after by delegated Aboriginal agencies has increased to over 30.1 percent (Figure 2.7), but these children are not necessarily cared for by Aboriginal foster parents.

Geographic Patterns of Children in Care
Counts and rates of children in care vary substantially by region throughout the province (Foster, 2005; Foster and Wright, 2002; Kershaw et al., 2005). Figures 2.9 and 2.10, respectively, show the rate of Aboriginal and non-Aboriginal children in care per thousand children in each of the province's sixteen health service delivery areas (HSDA) for 2003. There are many revealing differences. The highest rate for Aboriginal children occurs in the Vancouver HSDA, where over 140 of every 1,000 Aboriginal children are in care. The other areas with very high rates are also in the Lower Mainland. Richmond and South Fraser show high rates, and they reveal a worsening of the situation when compared to information plotted for 1999 (Foster and Wright, 2002). The lowest rates occur in the Kootenay areas, a pattern similar to that recorded for 1999, and also in the Northeast, which has shown a marked improvement over the last five years.

The reasons for these variations are not entirely clear, but previous analysis has shown that the percentage of children in families receiving income assistance, the unemployment rate, and the percentage of the population between twenty-five and thirty-four years of age who did not graduate high school all display a statistically significant relationship to the rates of children in care regionally. It is also known that a high number of children in care come from lone-parent (mainly female) families (Foster and Wright, 2002). There is a statistically significant inverse relationship between the percentage of Aboriginal children in the total HSDA child population and

Table 2.3

Reasons for service – Protection need as percentage of total count

	1998	1999	2000	2001	2002	2003	2004	2005	2006
Parent unable/ unwilling to care	**40.0** *40.3 / 39.9*	**41.0** *41.0 / 41.0*	**40.6** *41.2 / 40.2*	**40.0** *39.9 / 40.1*	**40.5** *40.3 / 40.7*	**40.8** *40.7 / 40.9*	**40.6** *40.4 / 40.8*	**40.7** *40.0 / 41.4*	**40.1** *39.9 / 40.2*
Neglect by parent with physical harm	**20.9** *26.7 / 17.8*	**20.9** *26.5 / 17.8*	**20.8** *26.8 / 17.2*	**22.0** *27.4 / 18.2*	**23.1** *27.5 / 19.6*	**23.8** *27.5 / 20.6*	**24.5** *27.8 / 21.3*	**25.5** *28.6 / 22.4*	**26.7** *29.0 / 24.3*
Physical harm by parent	**10.1** *8.3 / 11.2*	**9.6** *7.9 / 10.5*	**10.1** *8.4 / 11.0*	**10.4** *8.9 / 11.4*	**9.8** *8.9 / 10.4*	**10.0** *9.2 / 10.8*	**10.2** *9.4 / 10.9*	**9.7** *9.1 / 10.3*	**10.1** *9.6 / 10.6*
Emotional harm by parent	**10.0** *6.9 / 11.7*	**10.6** *7.0 / 12.5*	**10.6** *6.9 / 12.8*	**10.8** *7.2 / 13.4*	**10.4** *7.6 / 12.7*	**10.0** *7.2 / 12.5*	**10.1** *7.8 / 12.3*	**10.1** *8.1 / 12.0*	**9.8** *7.9 / 11.7*
Parent not protecting from abuse	**4.2** *4.1 / 4.3*	**4.1** *4.2 / 4.0*	**4.4** *4.3 / 4.5*	**4.7** *4.7 / 4.7*	**4.9** *4.9 / 4.9*	**4.9** *4.8 / 5.0*	**4.7** *4.6 / 4.7*	**4.7** *4.9 / 4.5*	**4.5** *4.7 / 4.2*
Child abandoned: inadequate provision	**4.9** *5.4 / 4.6*	**4.4** *4.9 / 4.0*	**4.9** *4.6 / 5.1*	**4.3** *4.5 / 4.1*	**4.2** *4.2 / 4.2*	**3.9** *4.5 / 3.5*	**4.0** *4.3 / 3.7*	**3.8** *4.1 / 3.4*	**3.7** *4.1 / 3.3*
Sexual abuse/exploitation by parent	**2.8** *2.5 / 3.0*	**2.5** *2.5 / 2.6*	**2.5** *2.6 / 2.5*	**2.4** *2.4 / 2.3*	**2.2** *2.2 / 2.2*	**2.0** *2.0 / 2.0*	**1.7** *1.7 / 1.7*	**1.6** *1.5 / 1.6*	**1.4** *1.3 / 1.6*
End of agreement: parent unwilling to care	**1.7** *1.3 / 2.0*	**2.0** *1.8 / 2.1*	**2.0** *1.5 / 2.2*	**1.8** *1.5 / 2.0*	**1.6** *1.2 / 1.8*	**1.4** *1.4 / 1.5*	**1.5** *1.3 / 1.6*	**1.3** *1.3 / 1.3*	**1.3** *1.5 / 1.2*
Deprived of necessary health care	**1.1** *1.3 / 1.0*	**0.9** *1.0 / 0.9*	**1.0** *0.9 / 1.0*	**1.0** *1.0 / 1.0*	**1.0** *1.0 / 1.0*	**1.0** *1.0 / 1.1*	**1.0** *0.9 / 1.1*	**1.0** *1.0 / 1.1*	**1.0** *0.9 / 1.1*
Child absent from home in danger	**2.7** *1.9 / 3.2*	**2.8** *1.9 / 3.2*	**2.1** *1.6 / 2.4*	**1.7** *1.5 / 1.8*	**1.4** *1.1 / 1.6*	**1.1** *0.9 / 1.3*	**1.0** *0.8 / 1.1*	**0.9** *0.8 / 1.1*	**0.6** *0.5 / 0.7*
Parent deceased: inadequate provision	**0.9** *0.9 / 0.9*	**0.8** *0.8 / 0.8*	**0.7** *0.7 / 0.7*	**0.7** *0.7 / 0.7*	**0.6** *0.6 / 0.6*	**0.7** *0.6 / 0.8*	**0.5** *0.5 / 0.6*	**0.6** *0.4 / 0.8*	**0.6** *0.4 / 0.8*
Parent refuses treatment of condition	**0.6** *0.5 / 0.6*	**0.5** *0.5 / 0.5*	**0.4** *0.4 / 0.3*	**0.3** *0.3 / 0.3*	**0.3** *0.4 / 0.3*	**0.3** *0.4 / 0.2*	**0.3** *0.5 / 0.2*	**0.3** *0.3 / 0.2*	**0.2** *0.3 / 0.2*

Notes: Data are from March of each year. Top figures are total percentages for all children; figures in italics are percentages of Aboriginal children; figures in roman are percentages of non-Aboriginal children. Individual cases can have up to three different reasons for service.

Source: Ministry of Children and Family Development, Decision Support Branch

Figure 2.9

Aboriginal children in care by health service delivery area, 2003

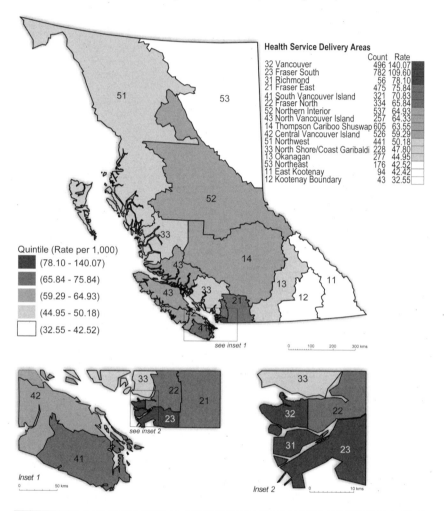

Source: Ministry of Children and Family Development, Decision Support Branch

the percentage that are in care based on the Spearman rank correlation coefficient ($r = -0.4$; $p < 0.05$). This suggests that Aboriginal families who have left their traditional supports back on the reserve for an urban environment are more likely to be struggling. Alternatively, Aboriginal families living on a reserve may be less likely to express concern about neighbours' children if they believe that the children will be removed from their community and placed in white foster homes. Anecdotal evidence suggests that

Figure 2.10

Non-Aboriginal children in care by health service delivery area, 2003

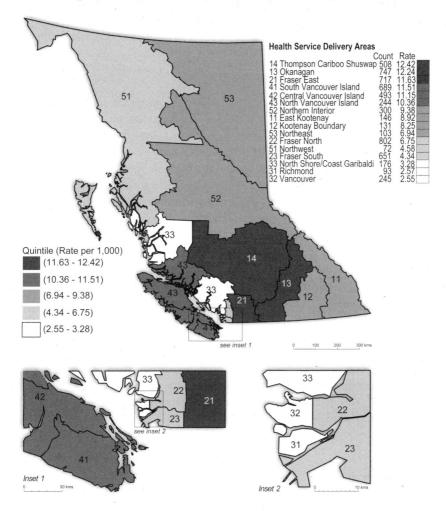

Health Service Delivery Areas

	Count	Rate
14 Thompson Cariboo Shuswap	508	12.42
13 Okanagan	747	12.24
21 Fraser East	717	11.63
41 South Vancouver Island	689	11.51
42 Central Vancouver Island	493	11.15
43 North Vancouver Island	244	10.36
52 Northern Interior	300	9.38
11 East Kootenay	146	8.92
12 Kootenay Boundary	131	8.25
53 Northeast	103	6.94
22 Fraser North	802	6.75
51 Northwest	72	4.58
23 Fraser South	651	4.34
33 North Shore/Coast Garibaldi	176	3.28
31 Richmond	93	2.57
32 Vancouver	245	2.55

Quintile (Rate per 1,000)
- (11.63 - 12.42)
- (10.36 - 11.51)
- (6.94 - 9.38)
- (4.34 - 6.75)
- (2.55 - 3.28)

Source: Ministry of Children and Family Development, Decision Support Branch

when Aboriginal agencies take over child welfare functions, Aboriginal children-in-care rates show an initial increase, perhaps reflecting more comfort within Aboriginal communities at the thought that the children will be looked after by their own people once they are placed in care.

An examination of the rates of non-Aboriginal children in care shows that the lowest rates occur in the Lower Mainland HSDAs of Vancouver, Richmond, and North Shore; all are less than three per thousand. This pattern is almost the inverse of the Aboriginal pattern. The highest rates for non-Aboriginal children in care occur in the East Fraser and the interior Okanagan and Thompson/Cariboo/Shuswap HSDAs. But these highest rates are still three times *lower* than the best (lowest) rates for Aboriginal children in care. This is a sad reflection on both federal and provincial child welfare policies and other social support policies currently available.

Conclusion

In the post-Second World War period, a driving force that accounts for the number of children in the care of the state has been the "boom, bust, echo" phenomenon of the birth rate and subsequent numbers of children in the province. Overlaying this was the increasing funding made available, first by the province to cover the costs of children in care that were borne mainly by municipalities and children's aid societies, and secondly by the federal government, which shared 50 percent of these same costs. In the 1990s, however, the federal contributions were reduced just as the number of children in care began to rise rapidly. A further major factor in the increasing numbers relates to the changes in the federal *Indian Act,* which enabled the province to assume responsibility for child welfare on reserves. The result was that massive numbers of Aboriginal children came into state care.

Changing policies in other welfare programs, such as the income assistance reforms in the 1990s that were necessitated by federal cutbacks, meant there were fewer programs available to support children outside state care. There was also increasing pressure placed on families receiving welfare as welfare cheques were reduced. Finally, specific incidents – in particular, the death of a child, the subsequent public inquiry, and the resulting government response – led to increased public scrutiny of the child welfare system, making workers more risk-averse and ending with more children entering care.

Acknowledgments
Thanks go to Jeannie Cosgrove, Thomas Godfrey, and Kim Denderfer for assistance in obtaining data for this chapter. All work with MCFD, and cheerfully responded to many requests.

References
Aboriginal Advisory Committee to the Minister for Children and Families. (2001). Draft memorandum of understanding. Retrieved 1 November 2005 from www.bcaafc.com/policy/aacmou.html.

Aboriginal Committee of the Community Panel on Family and Children's Services Legislation Review. (1992). *Liberating our children: Liberating our nations.* Victoria: Ministry of Social Services.

Allen, D. (1998). *Contract and program restructuring review: Report to the Honourable Lois Boone.* Victoria: Ministry for Children and Families.

Armitage, A. (1998, Summer). Lost vision: Children and the Ministry for Children and Families. *BC Studies, 118,* 93-108.

Badgley, R. (1984). *Report of the Committee on Sexual Offences against Children.* Ottawa: Government of Canada.

Bennett, M., and Blackstock, C. (2002). *A literature review and annotated bibliography focusing on aspects of Aboriginal child welfare in Canada.* Ottawa: First Nations Child and Family Caring Society of Canada.

Bennett, M., Blackstock, C., and De La Ronde, R. (2005). *A literature review and annotated bibliography focusing on aspects of Aboriginal child welfare in Canada* (2nd ed.). Ottawa: First Nations Child and Family Caring Society of Canada.

Blackstock, C., Clarke, S., Cullen, J., D'Hondt, J., and Forsma, J. (2004). *Keeping the promise: The Convention on the Rights of the Child and the lived experiences of First Nations children and youth.* Ottawa: First Nations Child and Family Caring Society of Canada.

Blackstock, C., Prakash, T., Loxley, J., and Wien, F. (2005). Summary of findings. In *WEN:DE. We are coming to the light of day* (chap. 1; pp. 7-59). Ottawa: First Nations Child and Family Caring Society of Canada. Retrieved 1 November 2005 from www.fncfcs.com/docs/WendeReport.pdf

British Columbia Association of Social Workers. (2006). *Submission to the BC Children and Youth Review.* Vancouver: Author.

British Columbia Statistics. (1998). "Focus on BC aboriginals: Living on-reserve/off-reserve: Fewer than one in three aboriginals live on-reserve." *1996 Census Fast Facts 13.* Victoria: BC Stats. Retrieved 20 October 2006 from www.bcstats.gov.bc.ca/data/cen96/facts/cff9613.pdf

–. (2002). *Evaluation of the Youth Agreement Program.* Victoria: Ministry of Management Services. Retrieved 16 October 2005 from www.mcf.gov.bc.ca/youth/yap.htm

Callahan, M., Brown, L., MacKenzie, P., and Whittington, B. (2004, Fall/Winter). Catch as catch can: Grandmothers raising their grandchildren and kinship care policy. *Canadian Review of Social Policy, 54,* 58-78.

Callahan, M., and Wharf, B. (1982). *Demystifying the policy process: A case study of the development of child welfare legislation in B.C.* Victoria: Sedgewick Society.

Canadian Institute for Health Information. (2004). *Improving the health of Canadians: Canadian population health initiative.* Ottawa: Author.

Clague, M., Dill, R., Seebaran, R., and Wharf, B. (1984). *Reforming human services: The experience of the community resource boards in B.C.* Vancouver: UBC Press.

Community Panel on Family and Children's Services Legislation Review. (1992). *Making changes: A place to start.* Victoria: Ministry of Social Services.

Cook-Fong, S.K. (2000). The adult well-being of individuals reared in family foster care placements. *Child and Youth Care Forum, 29*(1), 7-25.

Downing-Orr, K. (1996). *Alienation and social support: A social psychological study of homeless young people in London and Sydney.* Aldershot, UK: Ashgate Publishing.

Foot, D., and Stoffman, D. (2001). *Boom, bust and echo: Profiting from the demographic shift in the 21st century.* Toronto: Stoddart.

Foster, L.T. (2005). Youth in B.C.: Selected demographic, health and well-being trends and patterns over the last century. In R.S. Tonkin and L.T. Foster (Eds.), *Youth in British Columbia: Their past and their future* (pp. 15-37). Canadian Western Geographical Series, Vol. 39. Victoria: Western Geographical Press.

Foster, L.T., and Wright, M. (2002). Patterns and trends in children in the care of the province of British Columbia: Ecological, policy and cultural perspectives. In M.V. Hayes and L.T. Foster (Eds.), *Too small to see, too big to ignore: Child health and well-being in British Columbia* (pp. 103-40). Canadian Western Geographical Series, Vol. 35. Victoria: Western Geographical Press.

Gove, T. (1995). *Report of the Gove Inquiry into Child Protection in BC. Vol. 2. Matthew's legacy.* Victoria: Ministry of the Attorney General.

Hughes, E.N. (2006). *BC children and youth review: An independent review of BC's child protection system.* Victoria: Ministry of Children and Family Development.

Johnston, P. (1983). *Native Children and the Child Welfare System.* Canadian Council on Social Development. Toronto: Canadian Council on Social Development in association with James Lorimer.

Kempe, C.H., Silverman, F.N., Steele, B.F., Droegemueller, W., and Silver, H.K. (1962). The battered child syndrome. *Journal of the American Medical Association, 181,* 17.

Kendall, P.R.W. (2002). The health and well-being of Aboriginal people in British Columbia. *Report on the Health of British Columbians.* Povincial Health Officer's Annual Report, 2001. Victoria: Ministry of Health Planning.

Kershaw, P., Irwin, L., Trafford, K., Hertzman, C., Schaub, P., Forer, B., Foster, L.T., Wiens, M., Hertzman, E., Guhn, M., Schroeder, J., and Goelman, H. (2005). *The British Columbia atlas of child development.* Human Early Learning Partnership. Canadian Western Geographical Series, Vol. 40. Victoria: Western Geographical Press.

Leslie, B., and Hare, F. (2003). At care's end: Child welfare grads and street youth services. In K. Kufeldt and B. McKenzie (Eds.), *Child welfare: Connecting research, policy and practice* (pp. 239-47). Waterloo, ON: Wilfrid Laurier University Press,.

MacDonald, J.A. (1985). The child welfare programme of the Spallumcheen Indian band in British Columbia. In K.L. Levitt and B. Wharf (Eds.), *The challenge of child welfare* (2nd ed., pp. 253-65). Vancouver: UBC Press.

Merner, G. (1983). *Forecasting children in care counts.* Victoria: Ministry of Human Resources.

Ministry for Children and Families. (1999). *Aboriginal strategic plan.* Victoria: Author.

–. (2001). *Historic agreement signed with First Nations leaders.* Retrieved 15 October 2005 from www2.news.gov.bc.ca/archive/pre2001/2001/4609.asp

Ministry of Aboriginal Relations and Reconciliation. (2005). *The new relationship.* Victoria: Author. Retrieved 21 August 2005 from www.gov.bc.ca/arr/popt/the_new_relationship.htm

Ministry of Children and Family Development. (2002). *Memorandum of Understanding for Aboriginal Children.* Retrieved 21 August 2005 from www.mcf.gov.bc.ca/about_us/aboriginal/mou.htm

–. (2005). *2005/06-2007/08 service plan update.* Retrieved 15 October 2005 from www.bcbudget.gov.bc.ca/

Ministry of Human Resources. (1979). *Family support worker services evaluation: Program evaluation and planning support.* Victoria: Author.

Montgomery, H.M. (n.d.). *First Nations child welfare: Background and historical context.* Unpublished fact sheet. Victoria: University of Victoria, School of Social Work.

Morgan, J. (1987). *Native Indian autonomy: Historical overview, emerging trends and implications for the Ministry of Social Services and Housing.* Victoria: Ministry of Social Services and Housing, Corporate Services Division.

Morton, C. (1996). *Morton report: British Columbia's child, youth and family serving system; Recommendations for change. Report to Premier Glen Clark.* Victoria: Transition Commissioner for Child and Youth Services.

–. (2002). Learning from the past: Improving child serving systems. In M.V. Hayes and L.T. Foster (Eds.), *Too small to see, too big to ignore: Child health and well-being in British Columbia* (pp. 161-92). Canadian Western Geographical Series, Vol. 35. Victoria: Western Geographical Press.

Paliavin, I. (1993). The duration of homeless careers: An exploratory study. *Social Service Review, 67,* 576-98.

Petch, H., and Scarth, S. (1997). *Report of the task force on safeguards for children and youth in foster or group home care.* Victoria: Ministry for Children and Families.

Rippon, A.W. (1969). *Review of Indian caseloads: Research and standards division.* Victoria: Department of Social Welfare.

Roman, N., and Wolfe, P. (1997). The relationship between foster care and homelessness. *Public Welfare, 55*(1), 4-9.

Royal Commission on Aboriginal Peoples. (1996). *Report of the Royal Commission on Aboriginal Peoples: Vol. 3. Gathering strength.* Ottawa: Minister of Supply and Services.

Rutman, D., Hubberstey, C., Barlow, A., and Brown, E. (2005). *When youth age out of care: A report on baseline findings.* Victoria: University of Victoria, School of Social Work.

Serge, L., Eberle, M., Goldberg, M., Sullivan, S., and Dudding, P. (2002). *Pilot Study: The child welfare system and homelessness among Canadian youth.* Ottawa: National Secretariat on Homelessness. Retrieved 1 November 2005 from www.cecw-cepb.ca/

Sullivan, R. (1998, Summer). Commentary on 'Lost vision: Children and the Ministry for Children and Families.' *BC Studies, 118,* 109.

Trocme, N., Fallon, B., MacLaurin, B., Daciuk, J., Felstiner, C., Black, T., Tonmyr, L., Blackstock, C., Barter, K., Turcotte, D., and Cloutier, R. (2005). *Canadian incidence study of reported child abuse and neglect – 2003: Major Findings.* Ottawa: Public Health Agency of Canada. Retrieved 1 November 2005 from www.phac-aspc.gc.ca/cm-vee/index.html

Trocme, N., Knoke, D., Shangreaux, C., Fallon, B., and MacLaurin, B. (2005). The experience of First Nations children coming into contact with the child welfare system in Canada. In *WEN:DE: We are coming to the light of day* (chap. 2, pp. 60-86). Ottawa: First Nations Child and Family Caring Society of Canada. Retrieved 1 November 2005 from www.fncfcs.com/

Tweedie, A. (2005). *Youth leaving care – how do they fare?* Discussion Paper. Prepared for the Modernizing Income Security For Working Age Adults Project. Retrieved 1 November 2005 from www.laidlawfdn.org/cms/

Union of BC Indian Chiefs. (2002). *Creating a vision for the future: A provincial conference on Aboriginal child and family services governance.* Retrieved 16 October 2005 from www.ubcic.bc.ca/News_Releases/2002.htm

Vital Statistics Agency. (2004). *Regional analysis of health statistics for Status Indians in British Columbia, 1992–2000.* Retrieved 15 October 2005 from www.vs.gov.bc.ca/

Wade, A. (1996). Resistance knowledges: Therapy with Aboriginal persons who have experienced violence. In P.H. Stephenson, S.J. Elliott, L.T. Foster, and J. Harris (Eds.), *A persistent spirit: Towards understanding Aboriginal health in British Columbia* (pp. 167-206). Canadian Western Geographical Series, Vol. 31. Victoria: Western Geographical Press.

Walkem, A., and Bruce, H. (2002). *Calling forth our future: Options for the exercise of indigenous peoples' authority in child welfare.* Vancouver: Union of BC Indian Chiefs.

Welch, C. (2004). *A history of child welfare.* Unpublished report. Victoria: Ministry of Children and Family Development.

Weller, F., and Wharf, B. (2002). Contradictions in child welfare. In M.V. Hayes and L.T. Foster (Eds.), *Too small to see, too big to ignore: Child health and well-being in British Columbia* (pp. 140-59). Canadian Western Geographical Series, Vol. 35. Victoria: Western Geographical Press.

Wright, M. (2005). *Children in British Columbia: An overview of key trends.* Victoria: Ministry of Children and Family Development.

Zlotnick, C., Kronstadt, D., and Klee, L. (1998). Foster care children and family homelessness. *American Journal of Public Health, 88,* 1368-70.

3

The Community Resource Board Experience

Brian Wharf

> In almost every community we have a multitude of services that overlap and are duplicated or are inadequate or are just plain bad. In some areas there is even open warfare between agencies and there are defensive empires that have been developed over the years. There is an enormous amount of confusion. The sum total of this is that the consumer gets inadequate services and millions and millions of dollars are wasted every year. Certainly there are agencies that provide good services on an individual basis, but the system is not an agency. It is the system we have to improve. (Levi, 1973, p. 492)

This comment gives a sense of Norm Levi's contribution, as minister of rehabilitation and social improvement, to the debate over the New Democratic Party (NDP) government's first budget in 1973. The speech was laced with humour (responding to a comment from an opposition member regarding Mr. Levi's casual dress, the minister retorted, "Bright, beautiful and capable I might be, but not sophisticated"). More importantly, the speech made clear the minister's dissatisfaction with the ways in which services were provided to children and families and signalled his intention to bring about comprehensive changes, which were later announced under the rubric of the *Community Resources Act* (Bill 84).

This chapter describes these changes and examines their potential for improving the effectiveness of social services. Before outlining the objectives of the *Community Resources Act*, however, three important points require discussion.

The principle of integration is discussed in more detail below, but it should be noted that Levi was not alone in proclaiming the lack of integration of services a critical issue. Indeed, fragmentation was widely hailed as the pre-eminent problem facing the social services – not the absence of resources, not the quality and training of staff, not the appropriateness and effectiveness of practice approaches to deal with the problems faced by families, but the arrangement or, rather, the lack of proper arrangement of these services. For example, the influential report of the Commission on Emotional and Learning Disorders in Children (CELDIC), which surveyed services to children across the country over a period of three years, found that "the multiplicity of services seems to us to be the number one problem in providing assistance to children with emotional and learning disabilities" (CELDIC, 1970, p. 295). The conclusions of the CELDIC report were remarkably similar to those of the Seebohm Report in the United Kingdom (Committee on Local Authority and Allied Personal Social Services, 1968) and the Castonguay/Nepveu Report in Quebec (Commission of Inquiry on Health and Social Welfare, 1976).

The second point is that Levi had worked for many years as a social worker for the John Howard Society in Vancouver. He had served on United Way committees established to review fragmentation of services. In fact, the United Way had achieved some success in drafting and then implementing a local-area approach to services in selected neighbourhoods. But the time spent in seemingly endless discussions, and the rather slender outcomes of these deliberations, had convinced Levi that only legislation could bring about an end to this chaos and confusion. As minister of human resources – the first social worker to hold that position, with an avowed agenda of reform and supported by the premier, Dave Barrett, who was a former colleague and fellow social worker – Levi was in a position to translate his dreams into reality.

The third point is that there is no empirical evidence available to prove that the many actions taken under the act were effective. Vancouver's community resource boards, which were established under the umbrella of the Vancouver Resource Board (VRB), and the resource boards in smaller cities and towns, which had only funding and planning responsibilities, existed for a scant three years before being disbanded by the government that succeeded the NDP. Some bits and pieces of evidence are reported below, including favourable reviews of the community health and human resource centres (CHHRC) and the VRB. This chapter relies on these reviews, on interviews with individuals who were key actors in the reform, and on the comprehensive and detailed information contained in *Reforming Human Services: The Experience of the Community Resource Boards in B.C.* (Clague, Dill, Seebaran, and Wharf, 1984).

With the exception of the changes to health and social services that occurred in Quebec as a consequence of the Castonguay/Nepveu Report, the *Community Resources Act* was without doubt the most ambitious and comprehensive reform of the social services in Canada. Table 3.1 shows a brief chronology of significant events between 1972 and 1977. A detailed and comprehensive chronology of changes in child welfare is contained in Appendix 1.

Table 3.1

Timeline of key events in the Ministry of Human Resources, 1972-77

August 1972	Election of the NDP
September 1972	Norm Levi appointed minister of rehabilitation and social improvement (later minister of human resources)
July 1973	The Family and Children's Service Agency in Victoria dissolved and services transferred to the Ministry of Human Resources
February 1974	The Vancouver Resource Board (VRB) established on an interim basis
March 1974	The *Community Resources Act* introduced in the legislature
April 1974	The Children's Aid and the Catholic Children's Aid Societies in Vancouver dissolved
October 1974	Approval in principle given for the establishment of four community health and human resource centres (CHHRCs)
November 1974	The *Community Resources Act* proclaimed
October 1975	Orders-in-council passed to establish the VRB. Responsibility for child welfare and social assistance delegated to the VRB
November 1975	Local community resource boards established in Vancouver
December 1975	The Social Credit government elected
December 1975	First meeting of the VRB, with representatives of all local boards in attendance
February 1976	The new minister of human resources, William Vander Zalm, abolishes the non-urban community resource boards, but gives the VRB a one-year reprieve
February 1977	Following receipt of a favourable report, the CHHRCs are allowed to continue
October 1977	The VRB is dissolved and all programs are transferred to the Ministry of Human Resources

---

As noted in Table 3.1, three different types of agencies were created by the act: community resource boards (CRBs) in towns and small cities, which had no responsibility for providing direct services to families and children; the CHHRCs, which integrated outpatient health services with social assistance and child welfare; and thirteen CRBs in the Vancouver region. The latter provided child welfare, income support, and a variety of other locally relevant services. They were governed by boards of elected citizens and were the structures through which the principles of decentralization, integration, and citizen participation were to be achieved. These principles were implemented as intended, but, as noted earlier, the boards' short lifespan precludes evaluating their long-term viability.

The Vancouver Resource Board was created to serve as the umbrella structure for the local boards. It was governed by appointed officials and by representatives from the local boards. Partly because board members often disagreed with each other – in a very vocal fashion – and partly because the VRB was the most visible representative of the local boards, it became the lightning rod around which much of the controversy about the principles and objectives of the act swirled.

The different types of resource boards are described in some detail in the next section of the chapter; however, despite their differences, all were anchored in the principles of integration, decentralization, and citizen participation.

Taken together, these principles represented an expression of and commitment to a philosophy of democratic socialism – a philosophy that guided the work of the minister, the premier, and many other elected members of the legislature. When applied to the social services, democratic socialism holds that services to the public should be owned and controlled by the public; they should be readily accessible and arranged together in such a fashion that consumers do not have to run from agency to agency to obtain the services they require. Social services should be universally available as social utilities in the same way that health, education, and the public utilities of roads and transportation are available. According to Barrett, they "had found it was impossible to make the best use of funding with a proliferation of private agencies. It was necessary to integrate decision making with delivery and you can only do that with community participation" (Barrett, 1995, p. 86).

As noted above, integration was seen as a way to bring order to the chaotic arrangements that prevailed in urban communities. Integration required more than just voluntary agreements between a number of agencies to coordinate their services – that strategy had been tried for many years and found wanting. Rather integration required that separate agencies join together to form a new organization. Since Vancouver represented the most crowded interagency scene (and both the minister and the premier had worked in Vancouver as social workers for many years), it was the obvious choice for the first and most ambitious attempt to integrate services.

The other principles of decentralization and citizen participation were also crucial components of the *Community Resources Act.* The minister and the cadre of people who worked with him (Dick Butler, Raymond Wargo, Joe Denofreo, Ev Northrup, and Ron Willems)[1] had long been critical of the arrangement of social services agencies, particularly the lack of accessibility for clients. They were determined to bring services to the people, inspired by the immortal phrase from the Seebohm Commission, which recommended that "services should be available in pram pushing distance" (Committee on Local Authority and Allied Social Services, 1968). This was perhaps not entirely appropriate for British Columbia, where pram-pushing would certainly not be possible in rural communities, but the image conjured up by the phrase spoke to the vision of decentralization. As noted earlier, thirteen CRBs were established throughout the Vancouver area in locations with a distinct sense of community.

The third principle, citizen participation, was also a cherished notion in social democracy. It had gained strength during the War on Poverty of the 1950s and 1960s in the United States and Canada, although the Canadian version might be more appropriately termed a skirmish rather than a war. In addition, the principle had important academic credentials. One of the many scholars advocating local forms of democracy was Robert Dahl, a political scientist at Yale University who developed the principle of affected interests, which stated that "everyone who is affected by a decision of a government should have the right to participate in the decisions of that government" (Dahl, 1970, p. 64).[2] The principle of affected interests has worked for years to the advantage of the elites, especially with regard to rates of personal and corporate tax (see Newman, 1999, for a detailed and disturbing account of the influence of the National Council on Business Interests, now known as the Canadian Council of Chief Executives). But it has been noticeably absent in terms of the power exercised by the poor, particularly with respect to the institutions and agencies that serve them. For this reason, the CRB reform was designed, in the words of the act, to "encourage the participation and involvement of the general public in the region in defining its own requirements in respect of social services in the region and in the administration and operation of such community boards as are established within the region."

Taken together, these principles were seen by the minister and his staff as the means to provide more effective services to families and children. In the speech noted above, Levi stated that

> the main thrust of the department [at that time the provincial Ministry of Rehabilitation and Social Improvement] is directed towards our children and specifically, there were 7,000 children that we have in care under the Child Welfare Division. There are as you know, another 3,000 that are under the care of the Children's Aid Societies. The previous Government failed for three years to do anything about staffing in the department ... This Government's direction is to keep the child in its own home, and remove only as a desperate last resource. To help communities develop resources for children in their own communities and deal with the problems at that level. (Levi, 1973, p. 491)

After a brief description of the three structures created by the act, we will examine the adequacy and robustness of the principles of integration, decentralization, and citizen participation for guiding the development of social services.

The Community Resource Boards in Towns and Small Cities
Since the CRBs in towns and small cities did not provide direct services and, therefore, stayed away from the struggle over which services should be integrated, they represented the simplest and least troublesome of the three structures. In effect, these agencies were similar to social planning councils, which are found often in large centres but rarely in small communities. Their responsibility was to identify unmet needs in their communities and to provide funding for the needs deemed to be of the highest priority. However, their contribution to the development of social services should not be underestimated. Agencies like transition houses came into being as a result of a partnership between the women's movement and the funds made available by the CRBs.

The Vancouver Resource Board and Community Resource Boards
As noted earlier, the *Community Resources Act* was introduced in the legislature in March 1974, passed three months later, and proclaimed in November 1974. It took another full year to establish the Vancouver CRBs and the Vancouver Resource Board. It was not until October 1975 that orders-in-council were passed to establish the VRB as a formal agent of government and delegate to it the statutory responsibilities of child welfare and social assistance. In the end, the VRB and the local boards existed as fully functioning agencies for only a year before the Social Credit government ordered their dissolution.

The sheer magnitude of the changes taken during the brief life span of the VRB are captured in the words of the former director of the agency, who recalled that "on Friday, March 14, 1975, we closed the offices of the Vancouver City Welfare Department and the two Children's Aid Societies. We reopened the offices on Tuesday March 18. In the interim, moving trucks came in, all staff were reassigned and on the Tuesday we opened as a completely new integrated system. On Thursday of one week we were operating as three separate agencies, on Tuesday of the following week a complete transformation had occurred" (Schreck, quoted in Clague et al., 1984, p. 87). This transformation included interviewing fourteen hundred staff members of the dissolved agencies, phasing out seventy-one positions, creating sixty-eight new ones, assigning staff to these positions, negotiating contracts with four unions, identifying and deciding on the geographic boundaries of the local CRBs, organizing and carrying out elections for the CRBs and the VRB, and, at the same time, providing child welfare services and income assistance.

In December 1975, the NDP government was defeated, a Social Credit government was returned to power, and William Vander Zalm was appointed minister of human resources. Both before and during his campaign, Vander Zalm had been a strident and consistent critic of the reforms carried out under the *Community Resources Act*, particularly the establishment of the VRB. He ordered and obtained a review of the reforms, conducted by the Surrey city manager. The review identified some areas for improvement and recommended that the elected boards be dismantled, but concluded that the VRB showed sufficient evidence of effectiveness that it be given a reprieve of one year. The minister accepted the recommendation, but the reprieve was to be just that. A year later, despite a storm of protest (described below), the VRB was closed and services transferred to the Ministry of Human Resources.

The Viability and Effectiveness of the Community Resource Boards in Vancouver

There is some anecdotal information that points to the effectiveness of Vancouver's community resource boards. One study notes that

> when the first community board began to operate in South Vancouver, social services took on a new look. The counter that had previously served as a barrier between staff and people needing assistance was torn down. Chairs were placed in the lobby and toys were provided in the waiting room for children. Coffee was available for clients. Cheques which had previously taken three weeks now took three days. The staff focused on keeping families together and as a result the number of children in care in this area dropped from 143 to 77 in the space of approximately a year. (Clague et al., 1984, p. 96)

This assessment is correct only in part. Counters were certainly a prominent feature of the social assistance offices in Vancouver, but not in the children's aid societies' offices.

A further indication of effectiveness was the storm of protest aroused when the Social Credit government decided to disband the VRB. Support for the board came from no less than seventy-six organizations, including the Vancouver School Board, the Parks Board, the BC Federation of Labour, and, surprisingly, the Vancouver City Council. This was surprising because many members of council had originally viewed the VRB with suspicion, seeing it as an additional and unnecessary layer of government. Only the mayor abstained from the show of support for the VRB. In addition, a petition containing 27,000 names was sent to the government, urging it to reverse its decision to disband the VRB. The Vancouver newspapers, also early critics of the VRB, came out solidly in its favour.

All in all, the VRB "had proved that a citizen board could operate a social service system that was responsive to individual citizens and the community" (ibid., p. 211).

The Community Health and Human Resource Centres

The CHHRCs emerged in a different fashion than the CRBs. Norm Levi took office with a thorough understanding of the weaknesses and problems in the social service system. He did commission a couple of reports to deepen his understanding, but he had a clear idea of what changes were needed. Such was not the case for the newly appointed minister of health, Dennis Cocke, who had only limited experience in health care, having served for a time as a director of a hospital board. He needed background information on problems in health care, as well as specific recommendations for change. He, therefore, appointed Dr. Richard Foulkes to conduct a comprehensive inquiry into the state of health care in British Columbia. Following two years of study and research, *Health Security for British Columbians* was released in December 1973. The report was critical of the lack of connections between hospital and outpatient care. It recommended that all services be placed under regional authorities and called for increased resources for prevention and outpatient care. CHHRCs were seen as a principal structure for providing outpatient care and preventive programs.

Levi was mainly concerned with the Vancouver Resource Board, but he also supported the CHHRC concept, containing, as it did, the potential to integrate health and social services. He and Cocke established a development group with the mandate to help interested communities implement this ambitious concept. Communities, particularly those in rural areas, responded with alacrity to the challenge. To be sure, they were often motivated by the opportunity to recruit physicians and nurses to areas that had experienced enormous difficulties in recruiting and retaining medical personnel. Typically, physicians trained in medical schools in urban areas found the absence of colleagues and medical equipment in rural and remote towns a limiting, if not frightening, prospect. Even when they were recruited, they often stayed for very short periods of time. For these physicians, the prospect of working with a team in a relatively well-equipped outpatient clinic helped overcome the barriers of isolation and cold winters.

Ron Willems, a member of the team that developed the CHHRCs, firmly believes that communities were not interested in having social services in their centres, particularly when they discovered that the social services in question were child protection and social assistance (R. Willems, interview, January 2005). These were not the services outlined in the Foulkes Report, which portrayed "social casework services, counseling, etc."(*Health Security for British Columbians*, 1973, Vol. 5, p. 5). The intent of the Foulkes Report was to bring "all of the services ... together – one common waiting area, common rooms etc." However, the plan was redeveloped, as a result of managers' comments, so that all of the human resources services were on one side of the building and all the health services were on the other side. Managers said, "Well we would not want our clients to be in the same waiting room as those people waiting for welfare payments" (Pallan and Foster, 1994, p. 158).

However, a review of the CHHRCs reveals that social workers did contribute to the work of the centres. In the Houston centre, a physician noted a steady intake of young, married women complaining of depression. He brought this matter to a staff meeting, where a social worker with experience working in remote communities "diagnosed" the condition as cabin fever. These women were becoming depressed because they were left alone on isolated farms scattered around the area when their husbands went to work and their children went to school. Rather than treating them with medication, the team made it possible for the women to come to town on the school bus and attend programs and activities at the centre. The complaints of depression quickly faded away (Clague, Dill, Seebaran, and Wharf, 1984).

CHHRCs were located in the Queen Charlotte Islands, Houston, Granisle, and the James Bay neighbourhood in Victoria. They quickly established themselves as valuable community resources and proved resistant to calls for their disestablishment when the Social Credit government was elected. The new minister of health called for a review of the centres. When he received a favourable report, he decided to give the centres a one-year reprieve to allow for a thorough evaluation. A six-member audit team conducted the evaluation, looking at such criteria as community participation in elections, quality of services, integration of services, preventive services, and management and administration (Audit Committee on Health and Human Resource Centres in BC, 1976). The team concluded that the centres showed potential for delivering outpatient health and social services cost-effectively and recommended that they be established on a permanent basis.

Given such a positive recommendation and supportive evidence from all communities, the ministers of health and human resources decided that the centres would remain in place and that they would conduct a further evaluation in three years. However, the CHHRCs did not fit into the two ministries' tight organizational structures and soon came to be seen as maverick organizations with little support from senior bureaucrats. Faced with this indifference, the centres slowly faded away. Houston and Granisle transformed themselves into hospital societies, but in the process lost much of the interdisciplinary teamwork that had characterized them in the beginning. Only the James Bay centre exists in its original form, but it has struggled mightily in the past few years to obtain adequate funding and has had to relinquish community development, formerly an integral part of its work.

In Retrospect: Are the Principles Valid and Useful Today?

All of the individuals interviewed for this chapter thought the principles of integration, decentralization, and citizen participation were sound and appropriate for guiding the development of social services. However, some interesting differences of opinion emerged as to each principle's relative importance. Some individuals thought that integration was the most important, and it should be noted that this principle has retained its appeal as the most promising way to improve social services. Thus, as will be noted in Chapter 7, the Gove Inquiry strongly criticized the fragmentation of services and recommended that programs for children and families be brought together under the auspices of the Ministry for Children and Families (Gove, 1995). Other interviewees pointed to the problems created when programs are integrated.

Integration

Ev Northrup, an associate deputy minister during the NDP era, pointed out some of the limitations of integration (E. Northrup, interview, December 2005). He noted that all organizations develop a culture that may be expressed in the form of a vision statement, but which more often shows up as an understanding shared by staff about the organization's procedures, priorities, and receptiveness to change. If organizations share a similar culture, a merger may well occur smoothly and without problems. On the other hand, if cultures differ, especially if they differ markedly, the path of integration will be rocky and the clash of cultures not easily resolved. This is particularly true if the cultures are not articulated and the points of similarity and difference are not noted.

A clash of cultures emerged in the CRB reform when the three children's aid societies were disbanded and the staff were transferred either to the ministry's offices or the Vancouver Resource Board. The societies in Vancouver and Victoria were well resourced, and most staff were graduates of schools of social work. They viewed themselves as social caseworkers offering services to individuals and families. The culture of these agencies was formal and professional, and interviews were usually carried out in agency offices. In contrast, the managers of the VRB sought to establish informal work arrangements, as illustrated by the example of the South Vancouver office that was described above.

A second consequence of integration is that collapsing separate agencies into a single structure results in a large organization. Many years ago a British scholar commented that, "on social grounds, bigness is on most counts a disaster – it makes sharing in decision making and responsiveness to community interests much more difficult because of the remoteness in human relationships which it inevitably creates and bureaucracy reinforces" (Child,

1976, p. 447). This observation about the consequences of size in the human services remains pertinent today.

Ev Northrup pointed out yet another consequence when he noted that all organizations develop a chain of command with an executive director at the apex (E. Northrup, interview, December 2005). Such directors are often influential in establishing the culture and, almost without exception, are interested in retaining and extending their control. When agencies or ministries of government are integrated, it means that some executives lose their positions and power. Hence, plans to integrate are usually resisted by those who stand to lose. Finally, integration can smother differences and innovation, all in the name of bringing effectiveness and efficiency to the social services.

Yet, when viewed from a practice perspective, integration brought about improvements. For Northrup, integration of services is best achieved at the line level when workers and their supervisors meet to ensure that gaps in services do not exist. Raymond Wargo concurs, stating: "For me, it was integration of income assistance and child welfare services that helped to put a more human face on service delivery. Social workers and financial assistance workers were now colleagues not adversaries as had been the case before. Social work principles were the guidelines. Integration allowed for more flexibility and better support for the food and shelter issues that were so often an issue for families caught up in child protection issues" (R. Wargo, notes on the draft chapter, August 2005).

However, Norm Levi remains convinced today, as he was in his days as minister, that informal means of creating integration have never been entirely satisfactory, and their lack of effectiveness is precisely the reason for ensuring integration through legislation and policy (N. Levi, interview, December 2004).

Both views have merit, and the argument is perhaps impervious to a resolution satisfactory to all. It may well be that effective integration requires both informal co-operation between line staff and, in certain instances, the amalgamation of agencies composed of staff who share common objectives, values, and ways of working. To impose integration where cultures clash and a large, complex organization is created is a recipe for failure.

Decentralization
Dick Butler, a key individual in the creation of the VRB, argued that decentralization was the most important principle (D. Butler, interview, November 2004). By decentralization he referred not just to the geographic distribution of offices, but also to the delegation of authority to the local level. He based his argument on the conviction that local offices know their communities and, therefore, can identify their needs and plan appropriate services to meet these needs. This approach is supported by a study of public services

in the federal government, which asked: "Why can't policy and administrative changes originate in field offices? After all, if they are going to be implemented in field offices eventually why not allow them to originate in field offices in the first place?" (Carroll and Siegal, 1999, p. 208). However, it should be stressed that the delegation of authority to the CRBs was limited by the provisions of the *Community Resources Act*, which specified minimum levels of service and required CRBs to conform to the levels of social assistance established by the minister and cabinet.

Indeed the Butler/Northrup vision of decentralized services, with local offices given a considerable degree of autonomy in decision making, characterized social services in British Columbia following the repeal of the *Community Resources Act*. The province was divided into regions, with regional managers having responsibility for a number of district offices, each of which was headed by a supervisor. With the exception of the costs allocated for statutory programs in social assistance, regions were assigned a global budget and had some ability to apportion funds according to the needs of their local communities. For some staff who had previously worked for the VRB, the new provincial structure had much to commend it. The lines of reporting and decision making were clean and uncluttered. No longer were there protracted discussions, first at the community level, then with the VRB, and finally with the ministry; instead, a straight line of accountability ran from the regional manager to the deputy minister and minister.

However, this positive situation did not endure. The ministry assumed responsibility for social assistance from urban municipalities; it also increased the number of ministry offices and launched into extensive contractual arrangements with voluntary agencies. All of these changes required additional staff both in the field and at head office. Perhaps unintentionally, the ministry became a large and complex organization with control increasingly centralized in Victoria.

Although the argument for decentralization is attractive, it contains seemingly intractable dilemmas. First, though there are exceptions, many ministers and deputy ministers enjoy and, indeed, cherish the control they exercise over the affairs of their organization. Most of them do not wish to relinquish their control over departmental budgets and programs. Second, while the *Community Resources Act* charged regional and local boards with the responsibility of fine-tuning services to meet the particular and, in some instances, unique needs of the communities they served, a contrary objective pervades all public services – namely, that the same level of services will be provided to people regardless of their geographic location, race, and sex. While this goal cannot be attained completely (for obvious reasons, specialized medical services are always found in large cities), it remains a highly regarded expectation.

Nevertheless, the question remains: Can a degree of control over certain programs like child welfare or mental health be delegated to local offices, whether these offices are managed by civil servants or, as was the case for the CHHRCs and the CRBs in Vancouver, governed by locally elected citizen boards? And if the answer is yes, how much control can be delegated and over what? A final response awaits the insights from other chapters in this book, but a preliminary answer is noted in the concluding section of this chapter.

Citizen Participation

Citizen participation was, without doubt, the most troublesome of the three principles. From the beginning, many people believed that establishing citizen control over social services introduced an unnecessary level of bureaucracy into the already crowded scene of local government. For other, more politically oriented, critics, the principle was seen as nothing less than a way to recruit citizens into the NDP fold and train them for future careers in either municipal or provincial government.

There were debates within the NDP over the importance of the principle of citizen participation. Levi and Barrett clung firmly to the belief that citizens had a right to participate in decisions that affected them – and there is no doubt that the policies and actions of social service organizations impinge directly and severely on the lives of people who are poor and who have been accused of neglecting or abusing their children. While not discounting its importance, others, like Joe Denofreo, who was largely responsible for tackling the union issues related to the social service reforms, believed that this principle was so contentious it hindered the work of establishing the Vancouver Resource Board: "In retrospect I would have focused on integration and decentralization and let the ramification of that cataclysmic change percolate and stabilize before attempting to introduce elected CRBs. The concept of elected boards tended to become a political lightning rod so that the principles of integration and decentralization were submerged in the heated political discussions provoked by the elected boards issue" (J. Denofreo, personal communication, 30 January 2005). Raymond Wargo noted that the first attempt to hold an election "was a disaster," and he stated his belief that "citizens, particularly clients, can get more safely involved through community development initiatives aimed at developing preventive/support services that are not perceived as child protection initiatives. On balance, though, the public in general isn't much interested" (R. Wargo, personal communication, 5 March 2005).

Given the size and scale of the changes required, particularly in Vancouver, the points made by Denofreo and Wargo are cogent. Perhaps a strategy focused on integration and decentralization should have preceded the election of citizens to govern the services, especially since elections take time and are expensive to organize. In addition, although reformers hoped that clients and other marginalized individuals would be elected to the boards and bring their particular perspectives and experience to the discussions, this did not occur. With more time, this objective might have been achieved.

Yet despite the problems described above, Butler expresses a contrary view: "I have asked myself many times if there were more people knowledgeable about the social services after the CRB structure than before. My answer has always been – absolutely! My conclusion is supported by the fact that more people turned out to vote for the CRB boards than for the general municipal elections, that citizens went to the streets in support of the VRB, and that 27,000 signed a petition to maintain the VRB" (D. Butler, personal communication, 5 July 2005). Obviously participants in the reform have come away with different perceptions of the relative importance of the principles, although all would agree that they were crucial for anchoring plans for reforming the social services. They differ, too, in their view of whether all three principles should have been implemented at the same time or in a staggered pattern.

What Was Learned from the CRB Experience?

The signal accomplishment of the *Community Resources Act* was to establish a set of principles designed to increase the accessibility and responsiveness of social services. These principles provided a framework that could have been used by social service and health ministries for further experiments in the search for coherent and effective patterns of service. Unfortunately, no subsequent government, whether Social Credit or NDP, took advantage of the opportunity. Instead they retreated into the familiar organizational structures and patterns. Chapter 9 examines whether Gordon Hogg, the first minister of children and family development in the Liberal government elected in 2001, benefited from the CRB experience or was completely divorced from that reform when he attempted to create regional structures for the child welfare system.

In this writer's view, the three principles are valid and useful, particularly if they are used selectively. Thus, integrating agencies and programs can reduce confusion and bring order into the social services, but if the consequence is the establishment of large, complex, rule-bound organizations, integration may create more problems than it solves. However, integration of relatively small agencies dedicated to common values and with common ways of working would be a most positive development. For example, locating child welfare services in elementary schools would have been another way to implement the principles. Elementary schools are geographically decentralized and are accessible to citizens. They are governed by elected boards, and many, especially community schools, make deliberate efforts to involve citizens in their programs and activities. Such a form of integration would have been entirely possible under the act and would have provided an alternative structure for the delivery of services.

Again in this writer's view, decentralization of location and authority is best used with respect to non-statutory services, such as family counselling, daycare, and community development. This would require that the ministry take the courageous step of separating the functions of protecting children and providing support to families. It would also require the ministry to renounce the egregious practice of off-loading responsibilities to communities without providing appropriate financial resources. The same argument applies to citizen participation: trying to insert this principle into the statutory services is exceedingly difficult because it interferes with the line of accountability from the legislature to the minister and ministry staff. In Chapters 11 and 13, after we have gathered the insights from other chapters, I revisit these issues and propose comprehensive reforms for the social services.

Before concluding, however, a word about practice – the day-to-day work of social workers – seems appropriate. The architects of the CRB reforms were principally preoccupied with structural reforms, with amalgamating agencies and dealing with the inherent union and seniority issues. As a result, reforming practice was not their first priority. However, some significant changes in practice did occur. First, as already noted in the example of the South Vancouver resource board, by locating offices in neighbourhoods and creating comfortable waiting rooms, the architects and managers of the CRB reforms strove to improve the relationships between clients and workers. Second, each resource board employed a community development worker who worked with residents to identify community needs and propose ways of meeting these needs. Third, in keeping with the principle of integration, families were assigned to a single worker rather than having to report to a number of staff members.

Yet even these positive efforts allowed most staff to continue functioning as caseworkers – a practice modality that encourages workers to view problems as the responsibility of individuals and to extend problem-solving efforts on a one-to-one basis. Such practice is a far cry from the group/community work that is discussed in some detail in Chapter 6. In this latter mode of practice, workers spend little time in their offices, but see families in neighbourhood houses and other community institutions. They bring clients together on a regular basis, and in group discussions, clients learn that their problems are known and felt by others. Because of their life experiences, clients often suggest creative remedies to problems that might not have occurred to them in a casework mode. The local offices under the VRB umbrella and the CHHRCs would have provided a most congenial arena in which to practice community social work.

Notes

1 The list of references below contains a brief note on the background and positions held by these individuals during the planning of the CRB reform.

2 Other prominent academics pushing for the rights of clients were Frances Fox Piven and Richard Cloward. See, among their many publications, *Poor People's Movements: Why They Succeed and Why They Fail.* And while he would not have welcomed the label of academic, the best-known organizer for the poor was Saul Alinsky.

Persons Interviewed

David Barrett. Former social worker, MLA and premier of BC, and member of Parliament. Interviewed December 2004.

Dick Butler. A regional manager in Prince George prior to the election of the NDP. Appointed to plan the development of the Vancouver Resource Board. Prior to retirement was a deputy minister in the Ministry of Social Services and Housing. Interviewed November 2004.

Joe Denofreo. Former executive assistant to Norm Levi. Now retired after working as a union organizer for many years. Interviewed March 2005.

Riley Hern. Former social worker in the Family and Children's Service Agency in Victoria and in the Ministry of Human Resources. Interviewed February 2005.

Norm Levi. Former social worker and minister of human resources. Interviewed December 2004.

Ev Northrup. A supervisor in the Dawson Creek office of the Ministry of Human Resources and executive director of the BC Association of Social Workers prior to his appointment as associate deputy minister of the Ministry of Human Resources. Interviewed December 2004.

Deryck Thomson. Former director of the Family Service Agency in Vancouver and the Pearkes Centre for Children in Victoria. Interviewed February 2005.

Ron Willems. A social worker in the Dawson Creek office before being chosen to be a member of the development group establishing the community health and human resource centres. Interviewed January 2005.

References

Alinsky, S. (1972). *Rules for radicals.* New York: Vintage Books.

Audit Committee on Health and Human Resource Centres. (1976). *Report of the Audit Committee on Health and Human Resource Centres.* Victoria: Ministries of Health and Human Resources.

Barrett, D. (1995). *Barrett: A passionate political life.* Vancouver: Douglas and McIntyre.

Carroll, B., and Siegal, D. (1999). *Service in the field.* Montreal and Kingston: McGill-Queen's University Press.

Child, J. (1976). Participation, organization and social cohesion. *Human Relations, 25,* 429-51.

Clague, M., Dill, R., Seebaran, R., and Wharf, B. (1984). *Reforming human services: The experience of the community resource boards in B.C.* Vancouver: UBC Press.

Commission of Inquiry on Health and Social Welfare. (1976). *Report of the Commission of Inquiry on Health and Social Welfare* (The Castonguay/Nepveu Report). Quebec City: Government of Quebec.

Commission on Emotional and Learning Disorders in Children. (1970). *One million children: A national study of Canadian children with emotional and learning disorders.* Toronto: Leonard Crainford.

Committee on Local Authority and Allied Personal Social Services. (1968). *Report of the Committee on Local Authority and Allied Personal Social Services* (The Seebohm Report). London: Her Majesty's Stationery Office.

Dahl, R. (1970). *After the revolution.* New Haven, CT: Yale University Press.

Gove, T. (1995). *Report of the Gove Inquiry into Child Protection in BC* (2 vols.). Victoria: Ministry of the Attorney General.

Health Security for British Columbians (The Foulkes Report). (1973). 2 vols. Victoria: Ministry of Health.

Levi, N. (1973). Speech to the legislature, 16 February. *Debates of the Legislative Assembly, 2nd sess., 30th Parl.,* 490-94.

Newman, P. (1999). *Titans: How the new Canadian establishment seized power.* Toronto: Penguin Books.

Pallan, P., and Foster, L. (1994). Integrating health determinants into policy: Barriers and prospects. In M.V. Hayes, L.T. Foster, and H. Foster (Eds.), *The determinants of population health: A critical analysis.* Western Geographical Series, Vol. 29. Victoria: Western Geographical Press.

Piven, F.F., and Cloward, R.A. (1979). *Poor people's movements: Why they succeed and why they fail.* New York: Vintage Books.

4

Child Welfare in the 1980s: A Time of Turbulence and Change

Sandra Scarth and Richard Sullivan

A residual approach to child welfare dominated the philosophy of the Social Credit government during most of the 1980s. "We don't do it all for you," a quote attributed to John Noble, deputy minister of human resources, epitomizes the overall approach, which focused on targeting services and resources to those families experiencing difficulties raising their children rather than presuming to know, or to deal with, the underlying causes of their distress. Despite the tensions between those who favoured the residual approach and those who favoured a broader, more universal, family support model, there were significant efforts to improve services and supports to children and families in need throughout this period.

From 1980 to the beginning of 1992, the frequently renamed ministry responsible for child welfare had six ministers and six deputies (see Appendix 2). Beginning in 1980 with Grace McCarthy, whose deputy was John Noble, a series of cabinet shuffles placed Jim Nielsen in the minister's chair for a short spell, followed by Claude Richmond, with deputies John Noble, Jim Carter, Isabel Kelly, and Dick Butler in charge. Richmond was followed by Peter Dueck and Norm Jacobsen. Dick Butler was deputy for both of them until he retired before the 1991 election that ended the Social Credit era. In the brief interim, Lynn Langford served as deputy until she was replaced by New Democratic Party (NDP) minister Joan Smallwood's own choice, Bob Cronin, in early 1992.

Differences between these key actors were evident in their styles of policy development and management, as well as in their priorities. The era was shaped by three main events: the 1981 *Family and Child Service Act*, the 1983 restraint program, and the emergence of the push for Aboriginal communities to control Aboriginal child welfare.

New Legislation: The Focus on Child Protection

The *Family and Child Service Act* was introduced in August 1980 during Grace McCarthy's term as minister. (McCarthy's term, which lasted for nine years, was the longest for any minister with responsibility for BC's child welfare portfolio.) Her deputy minister, John Noble, described the act as a significant change in approach from the old *Protection of Children Act*: "Although the safety and well-being of children continue to be paramount in the new legislation, the act moves beyond the traditional approach of treating the state and parents as adversaries in the process of protecting children. The Act makes provision for the state and parents to work together in maintaining the integrity of the family and caring for children with special problems or needs" (Ministry of Human Resources, 1981).

Noble recently stated that he was particularly proud of the section that, for the first time, dealt specifically with child sexual abuse (J. Noble, interview, 2005). It represented an attempt by the ministry to educate the public about sexual abuse and affirm that it actually happens. It seemed to Noble that the courts often sided with the parents, recognizing their rights over those of the child. The new act established the rights of the child as paramount, and the health and well-being of the child definitely overrode the rights of parents. He noted that Chief Justice Allan MacEachern of the BC Supreme Court supported the act and quoted it several times in judgments.

The act was the culmination of several years' work, which included the review of more than 1,200 submissions. The key people who put together the act's main features were Associate Deputy Minister Ev Northrup and Senior Public Servant Mike Thomas. The act replaced the 1939 *Protection of Children Act* – essentially legislation dating from 1901 that had survived with a few amendments (see Appendix 1) – which included outdated references to mendicancy and immorality in clauses that had long since fallen out of use. However, the updated language and inclusion of the section dealing with child sexual abuse did not shield the *Family and Child Service Act* from criticism.

Child welfare practitioners and advocates were disappointed that the new legislation ignored many of the recommendations from the Royal Commission on Family and Children's Law, initiated by the NDP government in 1973 and headed by Justice Thomas Berger, that would have broadened support to families and institutionalized the rights of children in care. Most notable was the observation that there were no references to the role of the community anywhere in the act. The legislation was shaped by the philosophical underpinnings of the Social Credit government, which favoured volunteerism and a more active role for churches and other non-governmental organizations. It was also influenced by a ministry culture that reflected the income assistance mandate – a mandate with a narrow view of "entitlement" and an emphasis on control and eligibility processes. The statute was focused on child abuse, silent on support services, and dissimilar to the broader child welfare statutes of the time. The contemporary language of capacity building was a long way off.

In the early 1980s, there was a deep philosophical divide between the views of government members and those of field staff and external critics in the universities, social work profession, First Nations community, and unions, who were seen as, and sometimes acted as, "enemies" rather than potential allies in the process of change. John Noble explained that his initial reluctance to be interviewed for this chapter was due to his memories of being under attack by a politicized press and feeling undermined, particularly by the schools of social work, which seemed to see themselves as an unelected opposition when government tried to do things the schools did not agree with. He went on to note that child welfare was always controversial. For her part, Grace McCarthy described the politicized state of the ministry as the principal challenge of her early years as minister (G. McCarthy, interview, 2005). She identified the professionalization of the field service as her primary initial objective, and she lauded the ability of administrative staff within the ministry to support this objective. Changes to the act itself were intended not only to remove outdated and value-ridden language, but also to hold professionals culpable for failing to report child abuse, to enable others to report anonymously, and to support the professional discretion of staff.

In effect, the *Family and Child Service Act* did not move beyond a traditional focus on parental acts of commission and omission as these related to the living conditions of the children the act was intended to protect. However, there were some significant improvements over the earlier legislation, and some innovative practices emerged during this period. Leslie Arnold, who served in a number of senior roles in the ministry and ultimately was Superintendent of Child Welfare – at the assistant deputy minister level – recalled a number of innovations (L. Arnold, interview, 2005). As deputy minister, John Noble initiated a process of case reviews by senior officials of the ministry. Traditionally, these had been undertaken by field supervisors. This ultimately led to the establishment of the Inspections and Standards Branch. The branch's objective was to adopt a set of child welfare practice standards based on contemporary research in the field and to move to implement a systematic approach to periodic caseload audits to assess compliance with the standards. The Inspections and Standards Branch eventually became responsible for reviews of high-profile child welfare cases, such as those that ended up in the appeal-court system.

Several appeal cases in the courts brought attention to state intervention in cases where families did not want ministry involvement. For example, in some cases involving severely disabled children, the ministry intervened to assume guardianship in order to provide medical services contrary to the wishes of parents. These cases resulted in a major debate between the interventionist and non-interventionist approaches, and cast voluntary and non-voluntary or mandated services as diametrical opposites rather than separate points on a continuum of services. In a residual, as opposed to universal, approach to services, the principle of first apportionment of services to those in greatest need is exaggerated to rationalize an approach that positions "public" provision as a last resort. When private capacity cannot address the problems that place vulnerable family members in harm's way, then late and reluctant public service is presented as an intrusive but necessary evil violating the boundaries of private family life.

This is in contrast to a view of child welfare that frames family support needs as the defining conditions for a right to services provided on a voluntary, preventive basis. By denying rights claims to minimal levels of voluntary, normative, and supportive developmental services, a residual approach inevitably constructs mandated services as involuntary and intrusive. This construction of a binary approach to social services is extended to the mandated response itself, which is depicted as governed by the discretion of service providers who are either interventionist or non-interventionist. Responsibility for the purported violation of family boundaries is then assigned to the services and professions associated with the provision of these residual services and not to the policy decisions that determine the parameters of public provision. This construction of child welfare as "interventionist" capitalized on public ambivalence about anything approximating the adjudication of private life and legitimized further government distancing from this unpopular function. It fit conveniently with an ideological disposition toward government downsizing in the 1980s, and it fit just as conveniently a decade later when NDP minister Joan Smallwood sought to distance herself from a ministry that had fallen out of public favour prior to the NDP winning power in 1991, as a result of media attention given to a couple of children's deaths and parental objections to ministry involvement in controversial removals of children from their families.

As deputy minister in the early 1980s, John Noble wanted to be certain that he had all the facts before he made controversial decisions. As noted earlier, this resulted in the comprehensive case-review process that is still in place. In turn, case reviews revealed that the ministry could not exercise its protective mandate in isolation. The *Inter-Ministry Child Abuse Handbook* was one outcome of this revelation and marked the first step in developing a protocol for the investigation of complaints in daycare and other institutional settings. The Badgley Report (Badgley, 1984), released by the federal government in 1984, shocked the nation with its high estimate of the number of sexual offences against children and provided a strong push for the creation of new services and co-ordinated processes to respond to the needs of the children affected. The allegations of sexual abuse at the Jericho Hill School for the Deaf in 1982, 1983, and 1987 (Ombudsman of British Columbia, 1993), and the class-action suit launched by former residents in 2001, which named the province as a defendant, gave further impetus to these developments.

Noble felt that, until the early 1980s, senior managers had been responsible only for their own ministry, and other ministries saw child welfare as the responsibility of the Ministry of Human Resources alone. One of his major concerns throughout his tenure was the lack of co-ordination of services with schools, courts, and the mental health system. Although he worked hard to achieve co-ordinated services, setting up inter-ministry committees at the deputy minister and regional director level and in the community, he was never satisfied with the amount of co-ordination achieved. He saw the *Child Abuse Handbook,* which has been updated periodically and is still in use today (Ministry of Children and Family Development, 2003), as a major accomplishment that created greater understanding of the impact of child abuse and the necessity to co-ordinate services among different ministries. Regional child abuse teams, the provincial child abuse phone line, and other inter-ministerial activities were implemented because of the essential interest, leadership, and support of Grace McCarthy and the cabinet.

Dick Butler, who was a regional director in the ministry in the 1980s before becoming deputy minister later in that decade, also remembers the early 1980s as a time of positive practice, with the Family Support Worker program and the use of community-based service contracts providing strong support services to vulnerable families (D. Butler, interview, 2005). The regions co-ordinated training for social workers. Quality supervision of social workers was a priority and was implemented through a contract with Lawrence Shulman of the School of Social Work at the University of British Columbia.

The Restraints of 1983

A major budget deficit drove the Social Credit leadership's determination to downsize the scope and scale of government. This downsizing culminated in significant reorganization and program cuts in 1983, which met with large-scale labour and community opposition and mobilization in the form of the Solidarity Movement. The Ministry of Human Resources reduced its full-time staff complement by 599 people and eliminated or reduced several programs. Almost 90 percent of the staff who were laid off worked directly with children and families. Cuts to the child abuse teams, which consulted with field staff involved in complex cases, and to the family support workers, who provided intensive in-home support to families facing possible separation as a result of family court orders, were seen as particularly regressive and hurtful to poor children and families at risk of residual involuntary entry to the child welfare system. Although many of these services were no longer offered by the public sector, others, as will be noted later, were moved to the contract sector so that they could be maintained at some level.

Child advocates predicted that the deep cuts to welfare would result in higher rates of children in care and that those in care would stay longer.

This was a reasonable concern, since British Columbia had a history of post-ing consistently higher percentages of children in foster or institutional care than most other provinces. The difference was dramatic. In 1981, British Columbia's rate of children in care was twice that of Ontario, Nova Scotia, and Prince Edward Island. Compared to children in Ontario, those in gov-ernment care in BC stayed there longer. These high numbers may be partly due to the fact that BC spent considerably less money on each child in gov-ernment care than other provinces did – about one-third less than Ontario or Manitoba, for example. Ron Yzerman, director of Welfare Services for Health and Welfare Canada, carried out a comparison with Alberta. It indi-cated that with three thousand fewer children in care, Alberta received over $10 million more than BC from the Canada Assistance Plan, which indi-cates that Alberta spent more on child welfare than BC (Callahan, 1984).

Despite the child advocates' dire predictions, however, the number of children in care continued to drop throughout the 1980s, continuing the trend started at the beginning of the 1970s (see Chapter 2). Ministry offi-cials were perplexed by this, as the demographic changes – namely the start of the "echo" baby boom – had suggested there would be an increase (Fos-ter and Wright, 2002; Merner, 1983). One possible explanation for the contin-ued decline in numbers is that, because of the economic downturn in the early 1980s, families that might have split up, leaving single-parent house-holds, found it more advantageous, at least in the short run, to stay together. Evidence has shown that lone-parent families headed by women, especially those on income assistance, are often seen as neglectful, resulting in chil-dren being taken into care (Foster and Wright, 2002; Weller and Wharf, 2002). Even with the decline, though, the numbers in care remained high compared to those in other jurisdictions across Canada. At the end of the decade, the rate of children in care per thousand children was 7.6 in British Columbia, compared to 4.3 in Ontario and 5.0 in Alberta. The national average was 6 per thousand (Child Welfare League of Canada, 1992).

The services of family support workers, who had been laid off following the introduction of the 1983 restraint program, were gradually replaced quiet-ly and in significant volume by contracts with community agencies begin-ning in 1985, when senior bureaucrats recognized that research supported the efficacy of providing support to vulnerable families. Such community-based non-profit agencies proliferated in the years immediately following the 1983 restraint period; through them, services could still be provided without using valuable but highly controlled government employee resources known as full-time equivalents (FTE). Each ministry was constrained not only by its financial budget but also by its FTE budget. A decade later, the Korbin Commission found that both personnel numbers and costs associ-ated with providing services through the non-governmental sector had in-creased significantly (Korbin, 1993).

The decentralization that characterized the transition from children's aid societies to community resource boards in the 1970s (see Chapter 3) was reversed in the late 1980s with a move toward centralization and standardized approaches to practice. Leslie Arnold remembered that when he was deputy minister, John Noble was concerned about the response time from child protection complaint to first interview. Once a complaint concerning a child protection matter had been received, it was important for the system to respond quickly, lest a child be left in a high-risk or dangerous environment. Providing standards for response time and training workers to follow the standards ensured that workers would focus on attaining these goals. Centralization of control also ensured that standards were met, and resources made available. These initiatives bumped up against arguments that front-line social workers should be allowed to exercise professional judgment and discretion, but some of those serving with Noble during this period gave little credence to the idea that social workers were capable of exercising clinical judgment. This is not surprising given the ministry's minimal requirements for professional and clinical qualification at that time. There were differences of opinion at the senior management table that were as significant as any argued in the corridors of the legislature. Leslie Arnold recalled that Terry Pyper, assistant deputy minister for field operations, fundamentally disagreed that there was a legitimate role for social workers to intervene in family life (L. Arnold, interview, 2005).

Dick Butler, who served as deputy minister during the latter part of Claude Richmond's tenure and continued to serve under Peter Dueck, had come up through the ranks and was respected by fieldworkers, but he was unable to resolve these differences of approach. He remembered how difficult it was to convince the cabinet that the most important people in child welfare were the child protection workers, whom he wanted to provide with better working conditions and a career path (D. Butler, interview, 2005). Although he was originally an integrationist and favoured the generic model, he soon realized that supervisors could not manage a hundred or more programs effectively and began to see the value of specialization. Leslie Arnold noted it was a credit to Butler that, during his time as deputy minister, senior executives in the ministry undertook a strategic planning process to establish a vision of what the ministry should seek to achieve. They arrived at the goal that all children in the province should be safe from harm. Although she acknowledged that they fell short of their goal, Arnold thought it was significant that this was the first time the ministry had attempted to go beyond its normal narrow mandate (L. Arnold, interview, 2005).

More tension among senior bureaucrats arose from the changed reporting structure within the ministry. From 1981 to 1986, John Noble was Superintendent of Child Welfare as well as deputy minister, which meant all staff members were accountable to him. Grace McCarthy announced her intention to separate the functions without Noble's knowledge or agreement. He was not in favour of this approach, which gave the superintendent responsibility for delegated field staff acting on his or her behalf, but without the authority for staff management or policy direction. This tension explained, in part, the shortness of Andrew Armitage's tenure as superintendent. The rotation of ministers may also have been a factor, as Armitage was McCarthy's choice for the position, but it was Jim Nielsen who announced the appointment before being shuffled out of the minister's position a short while later. The philosophical approaches of Noble and Armitage could not have been more different. They embodied the broader issues of the intervention/non-intervention, residual/universal arguments described earlier.

Andrew Armitage had been the assistant deputy minister responsible for housing in the Ministry of Lands, Parks, and Housing, and he came to his new position with high hopes of bringing an open, consultative approach to the development of policy and professional practice. He had no idea how deeply the former superintendent opposed the change. His approach and his views were antithetical to those of Noble (who was still the deputy minister), whose achievements were facilitated by his considerable management and control powers. There were significant differences of opinion that became public, and Armitage's appointment was abruptly terminated without explanation. However, during his brief tenure as superintendent, Armitage promoted the profession of social work for front-line workers, many of whom did not have training in that field. He encouraged the employment of professionally trained social workers, and brought in Leslie Arnold as associate superintendent to develop the Inspections and Standards Branch. Like Noble, he wished to achieve a consistent, timely response to complaints by centralizing efforts to establish a reliable standard of common practice from the point of intake.

After Claude Richmond became minister, John Noble went to the Ministry of Health, and Jim Carter moved from the education portfolio to become deputy minister of human resources, with Leslie Arnold as Superintendent of Child Welfare. In a direct and prescient move, Richmond explained to her that an order-in-council appointment as superintendent meant that she would inevitably be replaced, as Andrew Armitage had been before her (and as has been the case with nearly everyone since). The superintendent's role, with its attendant separation of responsibility and authority, was essentially that of a "flack catcher" whose job was to get the ministry out of the bunker. If it served government, the superintendent's "head would roll" in the service of political survival. In this sense, the centralization of decision making within the ministry paralleled the political process by which government sought to dissociate itself from the political risks associated with a controversial ministry.

An example of such controversy involved the superintendent's responsibility for authorizing abortions when provincial wards became pregnant at an age when their physical immaturity would make delivery dangerous. As deputy minister, Jim Carter concurred with Premier Bill Vander Zalm's opposition to abortion and felt the superintendent should find another solution for such pregnancies. Claude Richmond consulted with the deputy Attorney General, Ted Hughes, and sought independent legal counsel for Leslie Arnold to ensure she would not be liable for doing her job as the guardian of these children's interests. Vander Zalm had cut hospital funding for abortions, but Arnold continued to approve them as medically indicated procedures for young children. This was a test of the intended quasi-independence of the superintendent, originally designed to shield the person in that role from political pressure. Arnold faced this test within her first two months as superintendent and survived it, owing in part to a legal opinion, conveyed to the premier, that she could be criminally charged or civilly sued if she failed to do her job, irrespective of the political popularity of her decisions. The provincial chief justice, Allan MacEachern, also ruled that the premier could not arbitrarily cut funding to hospitals (Thomson, 2004).

Claude Richmond, who was appointed minister of human resources in August 1986 while retaining responsibility for Expo 86, took over a ministry that had a troubled history with the media. He felt one of his first tasks was to "get it off the front page" and let the staff get on with their important work. He was able to do this, he believed, because in John Noble, Dick Butler, and Leslie Arnold he had good people and he let them do their job without letting the roles of politician and public servant get mixed up. Policy direction during his term was clear – the first priority was always the welfare of children – and he felt good about two programs that were introduced while he was minister. One was the Reconnect Program for runaway youth; the other was the At Home Program, which provided a variety of services that made it possible for parents of children with severe disabilities to care for their children in their own homes. At Home was an inter-ministry initiative, funded and delivered by the ministries of health and of social services and housing, along with the BC Lotteries Corporation. Richmond has said that he felt the ministry was quite stable during his tenure and that it was "running like clockwork" when he left (C. Richmond, interview, 2005).

It is easy to cast differences in policy orientation along party lines, but there was considerable diversity within parties as well. Leslie Arnold recalled that the development of professional standards and best practices was a priority during Claude Richmond's tenure as minister. The Inspections and Standards Branch began conducting practice audits proactively rather than reactively, keeping field offices apprised of their compliance levels with practice standards. Understandably, this met a mixed reaction in the field. Some workers were concerned about continuing surveillance of their documentation (the raw data for practice audits) when they were not receiving a commensurate commitment of additional financial and staff resources. The case review and practice audit process led to only one dismissal during this period, but that one incident took on what Leslie Arnold described as a "living memory" that produced anxiety, resistance, and dissent at the front lines (L. Arnold, interview, 2005). These concerns grew over the following decade as the number of people and government bodies involved in oversight operations grew. In the mid-1980s, ten people in the Inspections and Standards Branch were responsible for service monitoring. They were joined by a special section of the Ombudsman's Office and, later, by staff from the offices of the Children's Commissioner and the Child, Youth, and Family Advocate, which were both established in the 1990s. (The issue of oversight/service monitoring is discussed in greater detail in Chapter 7.)

The emphasis on the professionalization of field services was given a further push during Jim Carter's and Dick Butler's terms as Claude Richmond's deputy ministers. At this time the ministry aligned itself with the Child Welfare League of America and sought accreditation in order to meet the league's standards in administration and practice. Jim Carter also initiated the process of making grants to the schools of social work at the University of British Columbia and the University of Victoria so they could develop research projects with the ministry.

It was during this period that the minister introduced an amendment to the *Adoption Act*, removing the words "as if born to" in the definition of the relationship between adoptive parents and their children. This language was an impediment to recognizing the right of adopted people to information about their origins, which was a precondition to establishing the Adoption Reunion Registry. The ministry had first sought permission to introduce the amendment in 1980, and it was finally passed in 1987. The registry's success in satisfying the needs of adoptees, birth parents, and adoptive parents set the stage for a major reform of the *Adoption Act* a decade later.

The Push for Aboriginal Communities to Control Aboriginal Child Welfare Services

In 1980, members of the Spallumcheen Band took a number of steps to preempt provincial government control of child welfare services for their children. The band aimed to achieve control over child welfare decisions by asserting its jurisdiction and passing a "By-law for the Care of Our Indian Children" that gave the band exclusive jurisdiction over any custody proceeding involving a band child, whether the child was located on or off the reserve (see Chapters 2 and 5). Despite concerns at the federal level about the constitutionality of the bylaw, the band signed a formal, negotiated agreement with the federal government in 1981.

This was followed by political action to persuade the provincial Ministry of Human Resources to respect the bylaw and the band's authority over child welfare matters. The culmination of the action was a very public protest march, including a children's caravan that camped on the lawn of the minister, Grace McCarthy. McCarthy was not home at the time, but' she returned the next day to discover dozens of signs on her lawn and a very interested press and neighbours awaiting her return. McCarthy phoned Spallumcheen chief Wayne Christian and opened the Vancouver cabinet offices for an immediate meeting. She recalled that only her executive assistant was with her at the meeting, and she had no deputy minister or other senior staff to advise her. McCarthy acknowledged that, at the time, she had not thought about whether she had jurisdiction to enter into such an agreement without federal participation. Rather, she was motivated by the conviction that this was "the right thing to do" and that First Nations' people should assume responsibility for the care of their own children. In her view, the handwritten agreement produced at that historic meeting was never intended to put political self-determination ahead of the paramount right of First Nations' children to protection from abuse and neglect (G. McCarthy, interview, 2005). Provincial and federal authorities were initially left scrambling in the wake of McCarthy's meeting with Christian, but within a year the Spallumcheen Band was operating its own child welfare program.

Other distinct Aboriginal services emerged through tripartite agreements negotiated during this period, first with the Carrier Sekani under the leadership of Ed John (who served as minister for children and families in 2000-1), and also with the Nuu-chah-nulth Tribal Council in 1986. The following year, the Nuu-chah-nulth commenced child welfare operations.

Adoption policy was changed to require ministry workers to consult with the bands, and this slowed the rate of placing children in adoptive families outside their cultural traditions. While this fell short of the later moratorium on the adoption of First Nations children by non-Aboriginal people, it marked an attempt to balance the best interests of these children by recognizing their need for timely and secure placements as well as the imperative of cultural continuity. Chapters 2 and 5 provide more detailed descriptions of the evolution of Aboriginal child welfare services, but it is important to note that Aboriginal peoples' push to regain control over their own services emerged strongly during this decade.

Norm Jacobsen, who was appointed minister in 1990, supported these initiatives in the area of adoption on the advice of his deputy minister, Dick Butler, and the Superintendent of Child Welfare, Leslie Arnold. The latter recalled that the minister based his support for the Adoption Reunion Registry on the contention that all members of the public had the right to information about themselves. By the end of the decade, the ministry had extended the term limit of services for youth in care to the age of twenty-one when the youth were involved in educational or vocational programs that would be disrupted if guardianship were terminated when they reached the age of majority (L. Arnold, interview, 2005).

Jacobsen received approval from cabinet to begin a review of the *Family and Child Service Act* and agreed to a community consultation process as a prelude to the development of new legislation. Ted Hughes, who was later responsible for a review of the BC child welfare system (see Chapter 9) was asked to direct this process with the assistance of Leslie Arnold. The election called in 1991 put this review on hold. With the election of the NDP, and appointment of Joan Smallwood as minister, it was left to her to put into place her own community review process and implement changes (see Chapter 6).

Residualism and Managerialism: Effective Approaches for Child Welfare?

John Noble had an enormous influence on child welfare for almost a decade. He is described by many of those interviewed as a quintessential public servant, implementing the policies put forward by the government of the day. One senior civil servant who declined to be identified said the Noble era was "epitomized by a strong executive committee structure, with cohesive teams that acted corporately and began to break down the silos within and outside the ministry." He described a period of stability without constant internal reorganization and thought that the greatest achievement was the belief in a strong public service and the ability to manage or accommodate change – i.e., manage through the constraints. "John managed with a strong and relatively supportive and unified group of senior executives for much of this period. He was definitely seen as in charge, as was Leslie Arnold when she worked with him."

Suzanne Veit, a regional director during this era, described Noble as a dedicated professional who, nonetheless, had a particularly well-developed opinion that social workers did not need to be trained as social workers. Rather, they needed to be intelligent, hard-working types who could learn on the job. Because there were so few social workers with bachelor's or master's degrees in social work, the ministry relied on an extensive set of policy manuals that tried to cover every imaginable situation, assuming that most of the workers needed such detailed instruction. After working in many northern offices, Veit realized how poorly this reliance on a bureaucratic system of authority worked in practice. She could not recall a single Aboriginal child welfare worker, although most of the caseload in the north involved Aboriginal children. While workers were dedicated, on the whole, they came from urban middle-class families and their views of what was acceptable conflicted deeply with the majority of the population they worked with. Veit felt that the ministry needed to set up a professional approach instead of micro-managing a bureaucratic system. It needed to get rid of the policy books, rely on a clear set of standards that would provide guidelines for practice, and anticipate the use of judgment in assessing individual situations, with built-in accountability provisions. She appreciated Joyce Rigaux's approach, short-lived though it was (S. Veit, interview, 2005; also see Chapter 7).

Toward the end of the era there occurred what Andrew Armitage described as a "mellowing" process, and some of the rigidities that had been built in through the residual (narrow) approach to child welfare became open to re-examination (A. Armitage, interview, 2005). In spite of the external criticisms of the ministry during this period, and the "bunker mentality" that developed in response, a number of positive programs were begun, some of which continue to this day. The inter-ministry initiatives established early in the decade helped pave the way for the development of a broader children's ministry that incorporated other ministries responsible for children's services.

Fifteen years into her political retirement, Grace McCarthy still believes inter-ministerial co-ordination and budget planning are important objectives essential to child welfare and the development of services to support children and families. Competition among senior bureaucrats for limited resources should not be an impediment. While still a self-styled "free enterpriser," McCarthy noted the importance of population-based estimates for budgetary planning. She also emphasized the role of professional interdisciplinary education for child protection and the crucial role of child care and early education to augment the efforts of parents to rear the "best and brightest." The politicization that she observed as an obstacle at the beginning of her tenure as minister has never been entirely eradicated, perhaps because, as she noted, those drawn to the social services want to change the world, while those elected to office may only seek to manage it (G. McCarthy, interview, 2005).

There is perhaps no other period in British Columbia's history that illustrates the consequences of a vacuum at the political centre as clearly as the 1980s do. The pattern of alternating construction and deconstruction that has followed the social policy pendulum was amplified in the 1980s by a number of factors including fiscal priorities, labour unrest, discontinuous leadership, and tension between the political and public service arms. The long arc of incrementalism eventually produced some innovations in long-stagnant adoption policy, some recognition of the increasing skill requirements and diminishing labour pool associated with foster care, a nod of recognition to the needs of youth aging out of provincial guardianship, and some unintended revitalization of community interest in the wake of privatization and service reductions.

There have been moments of innovation and inspiration in BC's child welfare policies and programs. Comparisons with other provinces are only useful to the extent that they reveal unique patterns in response to common problems. BC has had both centralized and decentralized approaches to the problems of child abuse and neglect. In this sense, it has experimented with approaches adopted by other provinces. Unfortunately, these approaches have not been sustained, nor have they been informed by evaluation and research, but rather by prevailing and often contradictory political philosophies. In that sense, BC has differed little from other provinces except, perhaps, in the speed and frequency of the pendulum's swing.

Persons Interviewed

Leslie Arnold. Former deputy superintendent and superintendent of Child Protection, 1986-92. Interviewed 2005.

Dick Butler. Former regional director and deputy minister of the Ministry of Social Services and Housing. Interviewed 2005.

Grace McCarthy. Former deputy premier of British Columbia and minister of human resources, 1977-86. Interviewed 2005.

John Noble. Former deputy minister of human resources, 1976-87, and superintendent of child protection, 1979-86. Interviewed 2005.

Claude Richmond. Minister of social services and housing, 1986-89; currently minister of employment and income assistance. Interviewed 2005.

Suzanne Veit. Regional director, Ministry of Human Resources, and later deputy minister of municipal affairs, before retirement in 2001. Interviewed 2005.

References

Badgley, R. (1984). *Report of the Committee on Sexual Offences against Children.* Ottawa: Government of Canada.

Callahan, M. (1984). The human cost of restraint. In W. Magnusson, W. Carroll, C. Doyle, M. Langer, and R. Walker (Eds.), *The new reality: The politics of restraint in British Columbia* (pp. 227-41). Vancouver: New Star Books.

Child Welfare League of Canada. (1992). *The number of children in care by province: A statistical report.* Ottawa: Author.

Foster, L.T., and Wright, M. (2002). Patterns and trends in children in the care of the province of British Columbia: Ecological, policy and cultural perspectives. In M.V. Hayes and L.T. Foster (Eds.), *Too small to see, too big to ignore: Child health and well-being in British Columbia* (pp. 103-40). Canadian Western Geographical Series, Vol. 35. Victoria: Western Geographical Press.

Korbin, J. (1993). *Commission of inquiry into the public service and public sector.* Victoria: Ministry of the Attorney General.

Merner, G. (1983). *Forecasting children in care counts.* Victoria: Ministry of Human Resources.

Ministry of Children and Family Development. (2003). *The B.C. handbook for action on child abuse and neglect.* Victoria: Author.

Ministry of Human Resources. (1981). *Annual report: Report of the deputy minister John Noble.* Victoria: Author.

Ombudsman of British Columbia. (1993). *Public report no. 32: Abuse of deaf students at Jericho Hill School.* Victoria: Author.

Thomson, A. (2004). *Winning choice on abortion: How British Columbian and Canadian feminists won the battles of the 1970s and 1980s.* Victoria: Trafford Publishing.

Weller, R., and Wharf, B. (2002). Contradictions in child welfare. In M.V. Hayes and L.T. Foster (Eds.), *Too small to see, too big to ignore: Child health and well-being in British Columbia* (pp. 141-59). Canadian Western Geographical Series, Vol. 35. Victoria: Western Geographical Press.

5

Witnessing Wild Woman: Resistance and Resilience in Aboriginal Child Welfare

Maggie Kovachs, Robina Thomas, Monty Montgomery, Jacquie Green, and Leslie Brown

When given the opportunity to contribute a history of Aboriginal child welfare in British Columbia, we decided to approach our chapter as a collective endeavour. We are instructors of the First Nations Specialization Program at the School of Social Work, University of Victoria, and we have engaged with Aboriginal child welfare from a professional, community, and personal vantage point. Currently we all live on Coast Salish territory – though we represent a continuum of cultures including Coast Salish, European, Haisla, Micmac, Plains Cree, and Saulteaux. In our conversations about what to include in this chapter, we felt it was important not only to put forward an analysis of the barriers (including structural racism) that affect Aboriginal children, families, and communities and out of which the Aboriginal child welfare movement has arisen, but also to highlight the resiliency of Aboriginal communities in protecting Aboriginal children from the insidious intervention of colonization with all of its subsequent state impositions. To that end, the contributors in this chapter have put forward, in their own voices, their unique perspectives on protecting Aboriginal children. As the title suggests, each is an account of Aboriginal communities' acts of resistance and resiliency to keep Aboriginal children, families, and communities safe.

Our chapter is structured in four key sections, each offering a viewpoint on a distinctive aspect of Aboriginal child welfare from a different member of our team. Tansi and greetings. My name is Maggie and I am of Saulteaux and Plains Cree descent. My role is to guide you through our chapter and introduce you to the contributors.

Before we start this journey, we would like to share with you the intent behind our choice of title. We have used the term "Witnessing" because the act of witnessing has relevance to many indigenous cultures, including the Coast Salish peoples. To show how it applies to this chapter, we want to tell you about a recent cultural activity that we organized as a part of our First Nations Social Work Specialization Program. In spring 2005, our program held a ceremony to honour the contributions of community members who assist our program, including Elders, indigenous healers, and local social service agencies that provide practicum placements for the First Nations specialization students. We have a tradition of hosting an honouring feast to carry out the important work of giving thanks and recognition to the community for its contributions. At our feasts we follow a traditional Coast Salish practice of witnessing. Feasts are significant events where community members gather and share a meal, but they also have a purpose. In our case, the purpose was to honour individuals. Prior to the work being done at a feast, specific individuals are selected from the gathering and called to witness this work. Individuals who are called to witness have a significant role. It is their responsibility to hold the memory and retell the activities of the event. The act of witnessing is an integral part of the oral tradition as it is the means by which a public accounting of the work being done will live on in the oral history of the community. We chose to use the phrase "Witnessing Wild Woman" as our chapter title because it is our way of recognizing those who have been part of protecting our children (the meaning of the term "Wild Woman" is outlined in the following section). By choosing to share each of our perspectives on Aboriginal child welfare, we give witness – an accounting – of the work that has and is being done. While this chapter is written in a textual form, these accounts began with the act of orally sharing, among ourselves, our stories of Aboriginal child welfare, acquired through our personal experience, thought, and engagement.

In reflecting on Aboriginal child welfare, we recognize that the creation of First Nations and Aboriginal child and family services under the mandate of provincial authorities (whether delegated or through other arrangements) is not ideal. As we write this chapter, we are at a specific time in history with a situation that is far from perfect. Yet the provision of child and family services by Aboriginal people for Aboriginal people is, arguably, far preferable to no services at all, as was historically the case, or services administered solely by local mainstream authorities. Given our mixed feelings about the current state of Aboriginal child welfare after years of witnessing its evolution, we were left with the challenge of finding something to say that could honour this important work while simultaneously expressing caution. The quandary was soon evident: We had been given an opportunity to write about Aboriginal child welfare, but what did we want to say? Through several circle discussions, we came to our decisions.

We knew that we wanted to cast light on Aboriginal peoples' successes in wrestling back control over the protection of our children, while tempering these victories with the acknowledgement that it is not yet smooth sailing. However, before launching into this discussion we needed to pay respect to our culture(s) by highlighting the traditional ways of caring for children that predate Aboriginal child protection services. We wanted to make clear that protecting Aboriginal children did not start with a provincial ministerial department. In fact, much of the Aboriginal communities' work in child welfare has been about protecting Aboriginal children from the ministry. To this end, we begin our conversation with "Tul ti lew Slheni (Wild Woman)," a Coast Salish teaching story that describes how one of the Hul'qumi'num Mustimuhw communities traditionally protected children. Robina Thomas offers us a rendition of this story as told to her by a *s'alqwen* (an elder or old person). Robina reveals an intriguing link between the traditional teaching story and state-sanctioned child protection services. She tells this story as a caution about the formal Western child welfare systems and as a reminder of the need to tell Aboriginal children about this history so it will not be repeated.

From the time of contact with Europeans, indigenous peoples have endured the battering force of colonialism, so systematic and effective that it has nearly obliterated indigenous cultures. Social workers have been complicit in this act, most often through the power of mandated child welfare practices. Aboriginal child welfare service models, which are funded by government and follow provincial jurisdiction, are very much a product of the European colonial system. That being said, they offer services every day at a practice level that, in the context of Aboriginal communities, are more relevant and meaningful to clients than those being offered through a mainstream authority. Monty Montgomery gives a brief overview of the current Aboriginal child welfare models that exist in British Columbia and offers an analysis of the difficulties of practising child welfare, even under an Aboriginal service delivery model, that is rooted in policy frameworks based on a Western model of protecting children. Monty's contribution to this discussion circle is another caution, this time about Aboriginal child welfare systems, and he shares with us his perspective on both the risks and opportunities of Aboriginal child welfare models. Monty affirms that while the professionalization of protecting children is a significant component of Aboriginal child welfare, the values inherent in our Aboriginal cultures continue to be the foundation upon which protecting children is carried out. While Aboriginal communities have entered into constricted service-provision agreements to provide protective services to children, he points out that the traditional, pre-contact values of protecting children, such as we see in the story of Tul ti lew Slheni, have not been lost. If anything these teachings are experiencing a cultural renaissance and this gives us hope.

In introducing the next person to contribute to our compilation of Aboriginal child welfare perspectives, I see, in my mind's eye, Chief Seattle standing on his sacred land as he looks upward to watch a storm brewing in the dark sky. He senses a foreboding for indigenous people, and to prepare us, possibly to protect us, he offers his words. He tells us to remember that we belong to each other; he says that this world is a web of relationships and that our individual actions have the ability to harm or help others. The old chief tells us to hold fast to community because we will need each other. In Jacquie Green's accounting of Aboriginal child welfare, the focus is on the importance of community involvement in child and family service work. Jacquie shares with us the experience of the Spallumcheen First Nation's child and family service program, which operates under a band bylaw model. She speaks with Wayne Christian, one of the founders of this program, about the lessons of their journey. She reminds us that the voice of our communities needs to be integrated into child welfare programs and offers some insight into the Spallumcheen's experience of holding to these values. Interwoven throughout her account of a community-based Aboriginal child welfare program is a reminder of the important role that leadership plays in the delivery of Aboriginal child welfare services. Leaders, with their power to act (or not), have the ability to build trust (or not) between differing communities.

Our first three perspectives highlight the cultural, policy, and community aspects of Aboriginal child welfare. Additionally, as a group, we wanted to make explicit the complexity of the human and structural relations that underlie Aboriginal child welfare. As with many Aboriginal/non-Aboriginal attempts at reconciliation, there has been a move toward increased understanding, cross-cultural partnerships, and trust building. We questioned whether it is necessary or even possible to have trust between mainstream and Aboriginal child welfare forces – particularly in the form of institutional trust. We did not want to discount the personal, individual relationships that Aboriginal and non-Aboriginal social workers share, which are necessary if child welfare is to be done in a positive fashion, but we questioned why Aboriginal peoples would trust mainstream child welfare. In an interview with Debbie Foxcroft, a long-time advocate of Aboriginal child welfare, Leslie Brown reviews the experience of the recent provincial shift to create Aboriginal child welfare authorities in British Columbia. Leslie's piece provides a critical analysis of the interplay between politics, leadership, and Aboriginal child welfare and highlights the complexities of building trust between Aboriginal and non-Aboriginal organizational structures given the history, politics, finances, and differing values of the two parties. It illustrates how easily exercises in trust building can go sideways.

So let us start this work with the story "Tul ti lew Slheni (Wild Woman)."

Tul ti lew Slheni (Wild Woman)

My name is Qwul'sih'yah'maht (Robina Thomas), and I am Lyackson of the Hul'qumi'num-speaking people (Coast Salish). Presently I reside on the traditional territory of the Lekwungen people in Victoria, BC. Traditionally, indigenous children were taught through storytelling, and I believe that it is critical to incorporate storytelling into our teaching practices. For indigenous people, stories carried teachings, culture, tradition, names, values, beliefs, and history (to name a few of the contents). I would like to share one story that the Hul'qumi'num Mustimuhw (respected Hul'qumi'num people) used to tell their children. This version of "Tul ti lew Slheni (Wild Woman)" was told to me by Auggie Sylvester a *s'alqwen* (elder or old person) from Penelakut (Kuper Island, BC).

A long time ago before there was Canada, the Hul'qumi'num Mustimuhw resided in various locations throughout southern Vancouver Island and the Gulf Islands. The Hul'qumi'num people lived in their *tum'huytl* (winter) villages during the *tum'huytl* months, but during the *tum'kwe'lus* (summer), families moved about to fish and gather medicines, fruit, and vegetables in preparation for the long *tum'huytl*. It was not unusual for the Hul'qumi'num Mustimuhw to cross the Strait of Georgia in canoes and travel up the Fraser River to fish.

Children were a big part of this process as this is how they learned the skills they needed to survive. Traditionally, storytelling was the primary source of educating our children. Our children were seen as gifts from the Creator and, as such, were protected by all in our communities. One way that we protected our children was through storytelling. This is the story of Tul ti lew Slheni.

Tul ti lew Slheni was a very ugly, hairy, and smelly woman who lived in the mountains. She could fly, and as dusk set in she would fly close to the villages, searching for children who were still wandering about and not yet safely back in the village with their families. It is said that Tul ti lew Slheni would try to bribe the children with smoked salmon and other food they enjoyed. Tul ti lew Slheni carried a cedar-bark basket on her back, and she used to collect the children in this basket as she caught them. Once her basket was full, she would fly far, far away into the mountains and feast on the young ones.

Children were taught that the only way they could protect themselves from Tul ti lew Slheni was by paying careful attention to the signs and signals that dusk was setting in. They were taught to always watch the position of the sun. They were taught to listen for the "hoot" of the owl as it only came out at dusk. They were also taught to pay particular attention to how far they were from the village and how to return home quickly. These examples illustrate a few of the lessons that this story teaches the children; there were many more.

As Ṭul ti lew Slheni was relentless and kept returning to the villages, the Hul'qumi'num Mustimuhw realized they needed to take drastic measures to stop her from stealing any more children. The men devised a plan. They decided they would follow her home one evening and find out where she lived. One night, after Tul ti lew Slheni had left the village with her cedar-bark basket bulging with their children, the men followed her into the mountains. They knew that after she ate all the children she would fall into a deep sleep. As she slept, the Hul'qumi'num Mustimuhw sneaked up on her and covered her eyes with pitch they collected from the trees. They also covered her stinky, dirty body with pitch. When she woke she was very agitated and startled because her vision was blurred from the pitch. She was so frightened she tried to flee by flying away, but she could barely fly enough to leave the ground. As she tried to flee, the Hul'qumi'num Mustimuhw shot her with burning arrows, and the pitch caught fire. That was the last they ever saw of Tul ti lew Slheni.

Now this may seem like a very scary story to be telling young ones. Some might even say that it is too traumatic to scare children this way. Years ago, however, the biggest concern that parents and communities had was protecting their children from the natural environment, the very rugged terrain, wild animals, and the dark. It was the natural elements that posed the biggest risk for children's safety. Today we need different stories to keep our children safe as the natural environment is not the biggest threat to their safety.

Unfortunately, as time went on, Tul ti lew Slheni did return, but she came back in such a vastly different form that we could not even recognize her at first. As a result, we were unable to teach and prepare our children to protect them from her. Tul ti lew Slheni came back in the form of paper and ink. She came back in the form of legislation – the *Indian Act,* residential school legislation, and child welfare legislation. These policies were developed without the input of First Nations people. In fact, First Nations people were not even aware of the implications of these policies, which were being presented as policies to "protect," "civilize," and "Christianize" First Nations people when in fact they were and are policies of genocide. These policies have devastated and nearly annihilated generations of First Nations people. The most tragic point of this story is that we never had an opportunity to create stories that would protect our children from Tul ti lew Slheni – Wild Woman – in her modern-day form. However, we must now create new Tul ti lew Slheni stories that will protect our children. Our new story will include the traumatic experiences children endured in residential schools and child welfare systems. Now that we have recognized Tul ti lew Slheni in her modern-day form, we must once again figure out a way to combat her and protect our children.

Community Responsibility and Aboriginal Child Welfare

My name is Monty Montgomery, and as a person of European and Aboriginal ancestry (Micmac) who lives and works as a professional social worker in First Nations territories that border the Pacific Ocean, I am aware of the multiplicity of genuine Aboriginal voices striving to reassert themselves in the field of child welfare in British Columbia. In this chapter I put forward my observations of the current state of the various community-driven initiatives that are emerging in response to the enduring effects of oppression that so many still struggle with today.

In British Columbia there are nearly two hundred designated Indian bands and numerous other Aboriginal and First Nations communities consisting of individuals with indigenous ancestry who reside within metropolitan and urban areas of the province. Each of these communities differs from the others culturally and historically, even if they are located only a few kilometres apart and have members who speak the same traditional language. Yet regardless of the historic dissimilarities, First Nations residents of British Columbia share a common history in terms of the alienation of our children from our traditional cultures.

Successive amendments to the *Indian Act* regarding the education of Indian children have done much harm to our ability to pass our traditions on to our children. Indeed, federal and provincial legislation and policy governing both voluntary and involuntary child welfare services has seen many more of our youngest citizens forcibly dissociated from their ancestral heritages. The common values shared by all our communities have been unalterably affected by the multitude of oppressive and assimilationist ideologies and policies that have been forced upon us (Kline, 1992). This is an unquestionable historical fact, one that cannot be denied and that must always preface any discussion of First Nations control of child welfare.

In order to exercise our inherent cultural responsibilities to those who will carry our traditions to the generations still to come, we have been forced to work within the restrictive and arbitrary policy frameworks set out by both the federal and provincial governments. Under the auspices of the *Constitution Acts* of 1867 and 1982, First Nations and Aboriginal peoples have been subjected to federal and provincial policies of denial, assimilation, integration, indigenization, and devolution (Powderface, 1984). These impositions on our families and communities have tested the limits of our resiliency, and many of our relatives have not survived this onslaught. We need look no farther than the sheer numbers of Aboriginal children in the legal care of the state for evidence that mainstream social policies have not served First Nations citizens well.

However, as professionally trained First Nations social workers, we owe a debt to those in our communities who live with the destructive effects of well-intentioned mainstream social policies. Through education, we have become the holders of the tool of specialized knowledge that is required to successfully navigate through the unfamiliar institutions of mainstream society (e.g., the justice, child welfare, and educational systems, etc.). This specialized tool, when used in concert with the compass provided by our traditional values, laws, and histories, is enabling First Nations to chart a variety of culturally appropriate courses through the dangerous jurisdictional waters of child welfare services that have already capsized the canoes of too many families within our communities.

In historic times, many coastal First Nations had stories that spoke of the dangerous supernatural creatures who lurked under the sea, waiting for unsuspecting or unprepared individuals to unwisely venture near enough to fall victim to their destructive powers. These stories spoke to the need to respect local traditional knowledge and to follow culturally and geographically specific protocols when preparing for a potentially dangerous journey. Each First Nation had unique protocols for honouring the power of the supernatural creatures that were specific to its territory, and each had its own cultural means of doing things in a good way.

Accordingly, when faced with the challenge of acting responsibly to the families and individuals who have been wounded by malevolent mainstream social policy, each First Nation will draw on its unique traditions to develop a course of action that is appropriate for its specific territory and traditional ways. Not surprisingly, given the cultural diversity of the First Nations residing in the territories now known as British Columbia, many different service delivery structures have emerged as each First Nation attempts to chart its own course through the known dangers of child welfare social policy. To some extent, many of the models that have been developed are seen by First Nations as capacity-building measures that enable a limited range of services to be delivered until such time as the nation is sufficiently prepared to respectfully resume the journey back to autonomy that the ancestors set out centuries ago.

The diversity of self-determined interests among indigenous communities, and the variety of funding mechanisms, has led to a range of models for the delivery of child welfare services to Aboriginal people in British Columbia. The range of jurisdictional options associated with the various service delivery models is represented in Figure 5.1. This diagram illustrates the three levels of authority – federal, provincial, and inherent Aboriginal – recognized in the 1982 *Constitution Act* by placing these spheres of authority in relation to each other in the form of overlapping circles. There are currently four different models of delivering child welfare services to Aboriginal people in place in British Columbia, indicated by the letters in the centre of the diagram.

As shown by Figure 5.1, First Nations child welfare policy is in a complicated situation in British Columbia at this time. Many First Nations and several urban Aboriginal and Métis communities have established formal relationships with the Province of British Columbia for delivering services to their members. In most situations, the relationships are codified in bipartite delegation enabling agreements, which delegate authority flowing

Figure 5.1

Jurisdictional options for child welfare

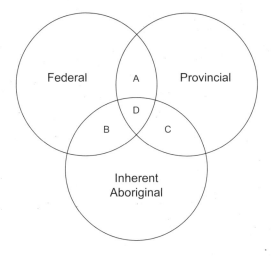

from the provincial child welfare legislation – the *Child, Family and Community Service Act* – to individuals employed by Aboriginal organizations based on the organizations' adherence to established standards. Additionally, some First Nations have also established bipartite agreements for the funding of child welfare services with the Government of Canada. This federal funding flows to the agency that employs the individuals who have received authority delegated from the province. The agency itself is an entity that has been legally empowered by one or more First Nations bands specifically to provide child welfare services to the constituent band members.

The delegated model of service delivery (represented by the letter "D" in Figure 5.1) is the most widespread model of Aboriginal-controlled child and family service delivery in British Columbia. This model is supported by policy developed by Canada (Department of Indian Affairs and Northern Development, 1990) and standards developed by British Columbia (Ministry of Children and Family Development, 1999). Since the 2003 BC Treaty Principles Referendum, the delegated service delivery model has been entrenched as the provincial government's official policy for addressing Aboriginal aspirations to self-governance. Although these organizational frameworks do advance capacity-building within Aboriginal communities, they do not genuinely reflect the interests of First Nations and are seen by many groups as interim measures on the journey to self-determination for First Nations.

According to the First Nations Congress, "it is expected that First Nations will continue to fall under the jurisdiction of existing Canadian law and related statutes and government regulations. As such, Aboriginal child and family services will be bound, for the time being, by existing child welfare legislation until corresponding Aboriginal legislation replaces it" (1992, p. 60).

Although the three-way delegated model is the most prevalent model for First Nations–administered child welfare services in British Columbia, there is a significant variant for urban Aboriginal and Métis communities in British Columbia. This is represented by the letter "C" in Figure 5.1. In this case, the federal government is not a party to the delegation agreement, and both legal authority and funding for child welfare services flow to the Aboriginal organization entirely at the discretion of the Province of British Columbia. Child and family service agencies operating under this model must also meet the standards established by the province (Ministry of Children and Family Development, 1999), but they do not have the same degree of financial and practice autonomy as agencies operating under the three-party delegation agreements.

The Spallumcheen agreement (represented by the letter "B" in Figure 5.1) is a model of service delivery that does not involve provincial standards or legislation. This situation, which is unique in Canada, arose in 1980 when the chief and council of the Spallumcheen band passed a resolution regarding the band council's authority to assume responsibility over the band's children. When the federal minister of Indian affairs did not disallow the band council's resolution, it became a regulation of the *Indian Act* of Canada. This meant the federal government, rather than the province, now had jurisdiction over child welfare service delivery for the Spallumcheen band members, and because, constitutionally, federal law takes precedence over provincial statutes, provincial child welfare legislation no longer applied to Spallumcheen band members. A separate agreement for operational funding for this service was later arranged directly between the Government of Canada and the Spallumcheen band. Although other Indian bands have attempted to pass similar resolutions, no other resolution of this type has been permitted to become a regulation of the *Indian Act*. This model is unique in Canada, although it does bear some similarity to the *Indian Child Welfare Act* in the United States. It is discussed in more detail in the next section.

For those communities of Status Indians who are members of an Indian band that is not eligible for federal funding or is not interested in participating in a delegated service delivery model, child welfare services are provided through a federal-provincial bilateral agreement (represented by the letter "A" in Figure 5.1). The Canada-BC bipartite *Memorandum of Understanding for the Funding of Child Welfare Services,* signed in 1998, allows British Columbia to bill Canada for the provision of child welfare services (including a per diem rate for the cost of children in care) to eligible Status Indians by

Ministry of Children and Family Development social workers. In this situation, Canada is empowered through the *Indian Act* (Section 88) and BC through the *Child, Family and Community Service Act* (Section 93). Agreements similar to this MOU exist between Canada and every other province.

Finally, each circle of jurisdiction represented in Figure 5.1 also provides child welfare services directly to the Aboriginal individuals over whom they have a duty of care. Canada provides funding to Indian bands and Indian or Native friendship centres that run family support service programs for Aboriginal families who are experiencing crises. British Columbia provides a full range of child welfare services to individuals regardless of their ancestry. These services include such activities as arranging and solemnizing adoptions, which have yet to be delegated to the staff of Aboriginal child and family service agencies.[1] First Nations continue to provide services to their members through the natural helping systems that have existed since time immemorial. Grandmothers and aunties continue to provide residential care for their young relatives as they have in the past. Community members still make arrangements for the guardianship and upbringing of children who become orphaned. Young parents receive guidance on the responsibilities of being a parent from compassionate elders. These actions are not financially motivated, but are simply normal examples of what must be done in order to live in a respectful way.

Interestingly, actions deemed to be professional child welfare services by mainstream social policy definitions are still important elements of the "informal" natural helping system of First Nations. Just because institutional care homes, homemaker services, child care worker programs, and licensed adoption agencies have been created to service needs manufactured by mainstream society, it does not mean that First Nations need exact duplicates of the formalized helping services that exist for the culturally and socially fragmented mainstream population. Our traditional ways still do exist, and though we do need help in some very specific areas, our systems of care are not broken despite the decades of actions of the often well-intentioned agents of mainstream. Indeed, it is this very professionalization of our traditional caring functions that has done much to disempower our citizens and foster a cycle of dependence on those who are purportedly assigned the task of helping our most disadvantaged citizens.

Despite the professionalization of the "helping professions" and the development of models for child welfare service delivery that centre on arcane funding mechanisms and legalistic principles of best interests, First Nations ways of helping have survived. Decades of oppressive social policy designed to minimize and devalue the range of traditional child welfare services has not replaced the traditional knowledge that has always charted the course for the intergenerational transmission of cultural practices that are necessary to sustain First Nations into the future. The mainstream policy frameworks are now known dangers on the charts of First Nations child welfare – obstacles that need to be respected for their power to affect our citizens' lives in very damaging ways. We are now cognizant of these dangers, and the voyages back to self-determination that we are charting for ourselves as First Nations and Aboriginal peoples are sensitive to the hazards around us. The range of routes can only expand as more and more groups regain confidence in their inherent ability to set their own course and propel themselves forward with their own strength.

The Spallumcheen Experience

Jacquie Green is my English name; my traditional name is Kundoque, originating from the Tsimshian peoples. I am also Kemano from my father's side and have been born and raised in Haisla territory. I currently live, learn, and teach in traditional Lekwungen territory and have been here for ten years. I bring with me teachings from my traditional places of knowing and incorporate these teachings into the classroom. It is important to bring to students and other people the importance of understanding our histories and the stories of our places of being. Particularly for child welfare, understanding our stories will indeed break the cycle of colonialism and oppression for all children and families.

The Spallumcheen band has operated its child welfare services under the only bilateral agreement in Canada for twenty-five years. In 1980, a caravan of Spallumcheen people marched to the home of Grace McCarthy, then the minister of human resources, and demanded that the province delegate the delivery of protective child welfare services to their community (see Chapter 4). Since the agreement was signed, the Spallumcheen have provided child welfare services to their people using paradigms designed and implemented by their leadership and voices of their community. Based on a discussion with Wayne Christian, who was instrumental in developing and implementing this agreement, I reflect on their vision at that time and on whether revisions may be necessary in the future. After twenty-five years of working with their model of child welfare, the Spallumcheen continue to be approached by other First Nations communities and asked to share their vision so others can implement a bilateral agreement. I will look at what worked and what could be done differently. And, importantly, I will look at how relationships among their community and government remain challenging.

Community members who had experienced tragedies within their own families began the process of developing the bilateral agreement. Some of their family members had committed suicide, while others had been apprehended by the ministry and placed in white foster homes with no opportunity to return home. When Wayne Christian and I reflected on the process, we noticed that at the time of dialogue and development, no one mentioned the issue of residential schools. During that time, issues such as suicide, apprehension, neglect, and alcoholism were recognized, but residential schools were not spoken of, even though it was well known that many families had experienced severe trauma arising from the time spent in the schools (W. Christian, interview, March 2005).

Nonetheless, through their trauma, the Spallumcheen community used an ancient philosophy of First Nations peoples, the philosophy of oral tradition. Those who were developing policies for their people listened to countless stories about events in their lives that affected parenting, community relationships, and community dialogue. Overall, the evolution of the new policy was community driven rather than imposed by provincial legislation. The community legislation was developed over a year, section by section. Within this document the sections are written in Spallumcheen as well as in English. For Spallumcheen people, it was difficult to translate some of their language into English, which had an effect on the "meaning" of the policy section.

As they were taking on the responsibility of governance over child welfare, it became apparent that the psychological effects of their time in residential schools were emerging. Community members became dependent on their chief and council to oversee most aspects of their lives in regards to child welfare. Historically, extended family members had provided support to children and their parents, but this was no longer possible because of the impact of the residential school experience. Many individuals had lost touch with their culture and their families; they experienced feelings of alienation and lacked self-confidence.

Additional challenges for the Spallumcheen stemmed from their relationships with the provincial and federal governments. In the beginning, the provincial ministry was most reluctant to relinquish its governance over child welfare. However, once the document had been signed, the relationship became "How do we work together?" rather than "This is how you will provide child welfare services." It was evident that the federal government felt the Spallumcheen agreement was not legal, and it did not want to assume responsibility for child welfare, which it saw as under the jurisdiction of the province. In turn, the Spallumcheen people reminded the federal government of its financial obligations under Section 35 of the Constitution. Although relationships with both levels of government have been difficult, the Spallumcheen have been able to provide evidence that their child welfare governance has worked because the agreement has been developed and driven by the community rather than imposed from outside the community.

Within provincial practice standards and policies, the principle of "best interest of the child" guides how social workers will work with children and families. While this is an important principle, it is based on Eurocentric policies and practices and requires modification in order to meet the needs of First Nations communities. Based on First Nations traditions, the principle of best interests might be revised to reflect the "best interest of families" or, even more importantly, "best interest of communities." For example, the Eurocentric version of "best interest of the child" requires that children be with their biological parents and remain in school from September to June. This differs markedly from the best interest for First Nations families, which means that the oldest child will live with Grandma and Grandpa, and all the children in the home will travel with the family for one month during the spring oolichan-fishing season to learn indigenous ways. First Nations children are not protected, and their best interest is not served, when they are apprehended and moved out of their homes and communities. Moreover, when children are removed from their parents, who may have attended residential school, it triggers feelings of abandonment and isolation in the parents, which often serve to further decrease their ability to parent effectively. The result is that parents are unlikely to have their children returned to them.

The authority delegated to child welfare workers by the *Child, Family and Community Services Act* must be revisited and renewed. The relationships between government and First Nations peoples must come from a place of understanding historical implications, and history must inform how practice and policies are implemented. All those involved in dialogue must also recognize the importance of learning to agree to disagree. This form of dialogue is healthy and will benefit children and families. When in dialogue regarding the welfare of children, it is critical that we not let bureaucracy continue to abuse children, families, and communities because different value systems, historical issues, trauma, and leadership around child welfare tend to infuse harm rather than protect families and communities. For First Nations people, it is important to return to protection of families and communities while relearning and renewing traditional values that could enrich lives.

Presently, the number of children in First Nations communities is increasing. Many young people continue to fluctuate between living on-reserve and off-reserve on a regular basis. Youth who are unsure about their identity and their traditional place are using drugs and alcohol to numb their pain and their anger. Many of our young people are living on the streets, not only of the larger cities, but also in many of the small towns throughout British Columbia. It is critical for our leadership and child welfare programs to address youth needs. For almost fifty years the current practice standards have not benefited our people. It is time for our programs, our leaders, and other leaders to think outside their "policy box" and outside our circle and to be creative in child welfare development. We must include our youth and ensure that their voices are heard, implemented, and visible in our practices, our policies, and, more so, our legislation.

So, as leaders, the question remains: "How do we provide protection for our children?" From Wayne Christian's experience, change is created and cycles broken when we learn by lived experience and learn from mistakes to move forward (W. Christian, interview, March 2005). Leadership must return to the community to ask children what kind of service works for them and what does not work. As leaders, it is important to hear the people's truth, even though it hurts and is difficult to hear. Moreover, when revisiting the past practices and policies, we must adhere to and implement the voices of the people. By incorporating the voices of our people, families will be able to ask for support. They will want to understand their identities and will want to know about their traditional places. In contrast, what currently happens is that they are afraid to ask for family support in case their children are removed.

In order to keep the spirit of the Spallumcheen child welfare vision alive, it is important to reflect on the last twenty-five years of child welfare. Wayne Christian spoke to the importance of remembering the event in ceremony and remembering the origins of their intent at that time. He spoke to the importance of child-centred practice and suggested that we should look at removing parents rather than children (ibid.). As First Nations people, we claim that children are our future and are our next seven generations, yet when it comes to trauma and community issues, we remove our children from our communities, which weakens them culturally and spiritually. It is important to recognize trauma in our communities, such as that arising from the impact of residential schools, and have the ability to see through alcoholism in order to truly protect our children and begin healing.

Aboriginal Regional Authorities in BC – A Case of Trust-Building Gone Sideways

My name is Leslie Brown. I am the non-indigenous member of our writing team. I have strong personal and professional ties to the Aboriginal community, most particularly in Saskatchewan and on the West Coast. My interest in writing about the proposed innovation of Aboriginal authorities stems from my work with First Nations, urban Aboriginal organizations, and Métis groups over the years. The model discussed in the following piece intrigues me because of its ambitious attempt to bring together all Aboriginal groups in an effort to wrestle some control of child welfare from the settler government.

Aboriginal governments, communities, and families have long recognized that the provincial child welfare system does not serve Aboriginal children well. This disservice threatens the health and future of Aboriginal peoples and communities. As articulated by the Union of BC Indian Chiefs (UBCIC), self-determination cannot happen without authority and jurisdiction over child welfare (Walkem, 2002).

In 2001, British Columbia's newly elected Liberal government announced its intention to regionalize the delivery of child welfare, and Aboriginal and non-Aboriginal planning committees were established in each of the five regions of the province to develop local child welfare authorities. These committees began working with their communities to figure out how services might be offered and what resources were needed to achieve their objectives. Aboriginal people saw in these actions an opportunity for progress toward Aboriginal control of Aboriginal children. However, the initial government proposal sought to blend Aboriginal and non-Aboriginal authorities – a direction clearly against the wishes of Aboriginal communities.

On 10 and 11 June 2002, a meeting of First Nations, Métis, and urban Aboriginal organizations produced a recommendation for the development of regional Aboriginal child welfare authorities. This "Tsawwassen Accord," drafted by Stewart Phillip of the UBCIC, came out of resistance to the BC government's pursuit of a blended approach to the establishment of regional authorities. The accord had the support of the First Nations Summit, the Métis Provincial Council of BC, and the United Native Nations, making it a historic moment in relations among Aboriginal groups in the province. Despite the structural and political realities of the different interests, Aboriginal leaders and service providers from First Nations, Métis, and urban communities around the province shared the view that continuing to blend Aboriginal and non-Aboriginal child welfare would only further the assimilation of Aboriginal peoples. On 11 June 2002, having clearly presented a unified stance, the groups issued a press release stating that "the Aboriginal community now requires a clear commitment from the Minister [of Children and Family Development] to work in partnership to develop and implement these Aboriginal authorities in a timely and respectful manner." In September 2002, the leadership of the four Aboriginal political organizations and the Government of British Columbia signed a memorandum of understanding (MOU) that reflected the substance of the Tsawwassen Accord. A month later, the government passed legislation that gave the regional Aboriginal planning committees the legal and financial authority necessary for the work that lay ahead.

The regional Aboriginal planning committees continued their work, engaging with communities to determine how the development process for regional authorities should proceed. The intention was that the communities should be part of the process and that development of the authorities should be driven by the Aboriginal communities, not by the politicians (whether they were Aboriginal or in the BC government) or the bureaucrats. Understandably, because of the respect for a community-based approach, the process differed in each region of the province. The relationships between the Aboriginal and non-Aboriginal planning committees in each region were also unique to their local realities.

In March 2004, Christy Clark, the minister of children and family development, announced that the plan to establish regional authorities was postponed indefinitely. The non-Aboriginal planning committees were disbanded. The Aboriginal committees were allowed to continue, although with significantly reduced funding. Clark felt that the Aboriginal authorities were not all at the same level of development and so wanted to slow down the process. Many people in the communities, planning committee members, service delivery workers, and others who were "on the ground" felt betrayed by their leadership when the four Aboriginal political leaders met with Christy Clark and agreed with her that everyone should be working off one plan. Debbie Foxcroft, chair of the Vancouver Island Aboriginal Transition Team (the regional planning committee on Vancouver Island), observed that the Aboriginal leaders' involvement in this postponement has strained relations between the political leaders and the people involved in the development of the authorities (D. Foxcroft, interview, February 2005).

It is ironic that when the minister thought the Aboriginal authorities were not ready to take on the responsibility of child and family welfare, her response was to cut two-thirds of the funding to the planning committees working to develop the authorities. This decision causes one to question the sincerity of the BC government's intention to establish Aboriginal authorities.

Funding has not been the only challenge to the development of Aboriginal authorities. Racism and colonization continue to plague the process. "Indians don't pay bills" was the reason one financial officer gave for his refusal to delegate spending authority to one of the regional planning committees. Others charge that this initiative is a money grab by Aboriginal people. However, according to Foxcroft, the Aboriginal planning committees and leadership have been clear: the issue is not about having control of resources, but about ensuring that Aboriginal values are front and centre in both the planning and the delivery of Aboriginal child welfare services (D. Foxcroft, interview, February 2005).

The BC government stalled the authority process with the excuse that the Aboriginal authorities were not ready. The arrogance of this stance is palpable. The provincial government has clearly and persistently demonstrated that it does not have the answer for Aboriginal children. So how are the Aboriginal authorities less prepared to care for Aboriginal children than the current non-Aboriginal system? Accusing Aboriginal groups of being unprepared validates the erroneous impression that the reason there are social problems in Aboriginal communities is because Aboriginal people have made poor choices. The historical context often goes unexplored. Aboriginal people are often told to "Move on, put it behind you," but this is hard to do when the assault continues.

When the concept of Aboriginal authorities was first discussed, Gordon Hogg was the minister of children and family development. He urged the planning committees to move quickly to implement the idea because, he cautioned, once the bureaucracy got hold of the process, it would get dragged down in bureaucratic procedures. This warning turned out to be true. The government has backed away from its initial zeal because the bureaucracy has started studying, managing, financing, and regulating the process. Now it moves at a snail's pace, with inadequate funding and ever-increasing control from the bureaucracy and provincial politicians. In one of the community dialogues that occurred, an individual commented: "I hope that this process is the beginning of true empowerment for First Nations people and our children." With the increasing control by the bureaucracy, this hope is fading.

The authority model is also encountering increasing resistance from the directors of First Nations' delegated child welfare agencies. This resistance reflects the colonial constructions of Aboriginal peoples and groups, and the mistrust of colonial governments' participation in Aboriginal child welfare. First Nations do not want to jeopardize treaty rights and negotiations by buying into the authority model. Aboriginal leaders have not given child welfare the priority attention that issues of land and resources have received, so the directors of the First Nations' delegated agencies have not had a lot of political support. Now, however, these directors have garnered influence because child and family services are increasingly seen by political leaders as a step to sovereignty. The regional planning committees will need the support of the delegated agencies in order to move ahead with the development of authorities.

Debbie Foxcroft sees the authorities taking on a broader responsibility than child protection alone. They have the potential to integrate all services that affect children and families, including early childhood development, adoptions, community living, youth justice, and youth mental health. Foxcroft sees them as a conduit for Aboriginal service providers. But she readily acknowledges the limitations of the model. Regional Aboriginal authorities, like delegated agencies and other proposals, such as a First Nations directorship model, are constructs of a non-Aboriginal government. They must, therefore, be seen as only interim measures, and Aboriginal people must remember that creating our own legislation to keep our children and families safe, through our own governments, is the ultimate goal (D. Foxcroft, interview, February 2005).

Given the number of starts and stops in the process, and the various threats the authorities have faced, Foxcroft feels it is amazing that Aboriginal groups have stayed together (ibid.). The concept of regional authorities is complex and, as most people agree, is not a sufficient response to the need to transform the way in which Aboriginal children are kept safe. Authorities remain a creation of the non-Aboriginal government, yet to some they still provide an opportunity to transform our current child welfare system. The caution is that we do not want to cut off future opportunities or be dissuaded from our goal of sovereignty, of Aboriginal responsibility for Aboriginal children – lock, stock, and barrel.

While not a complete success, the regional authority development process has moved things ahead. It has raised awareness and has caused the Ministry of Children and Family Development to focus on its own practices (e.g., through the file reviews of practice with Aboriginal children). In the Interior region, interdisciplinary service teams have been created that are focusing on Aboriginal operating practice standards. Some of these teams have been placed in delegated First Nations agencies. Caring for First Nations Children Society, an agency in Victoria, is providing training to ministry workers. Schools of social work and of child and youth care have responded to the need for Aboriginal child welfare education. A few minds and hearts have been changed.

The strength of regionalization is that Aboriginal people have not given up. There is still a commitment to making changes for our children. So where do we go from here? Debbie Foxcroft challenges us all to look at the past and move forward (ibid.).

Conclusions

This chapter's commentary on Aboriginal child welfare is indicative of the persistent, unified message that Aboriginal people have been offering throughout our engagement with state child welfare services – it is our values that matter most in protecting children. To reiterate an important comment by Debbie Foxcroft, the process is not just about having control of the resources, but also about including Aboriginal values. Our chapter has been a compilation of voices presenting this same theme in different words, contexts, and stories. Throughout British Columbia – and Canada – myriad Aboriginal voices offer differing perspectives on protecting and keeping Aboriginal children safe. While there have been attempts by federal and provincial governments to standardize Aboriginal child protection (e.g., the delegation model), Aboriginal people continue to resist this "one size fits all" approach. Distinctive Aboriginal communities each have their own vision and values for protecting their children that incorporate their own culture, community, and ways of being. In this sense, there is no one story, no one standard account, no singular perspective, nor one all-encompassing model for Aboriginal child welfare – but there is a commonality of vision about values. Because no one person owns the discourse, it has a fluidity that allows the dialogue to shift and resettle. Periodically our communities may get absorbed in the distractions (government funding, jurisdictional promises, etc.), but they are distracted only so long before we return to what matters in ensuring the well-being of our children and families: culture, community, values, and self-governance. This is akin to the creation story about the earth resting on the turtle's back. In his book *The Truth About Stories,* Thomas King tells the story of a little girl who, on hearing this story, asks the storyteller a question: "If the earth rests on the turtle, then what is below the turtle?" The storyteller tells the little girl that all he can say for sure is "it's turtles all the way down" (King, 2003, p. 1). It is much the same with Aboriginal child welfare – for Aboriginal people and their allies it's Aboriginal values all the way down.

It is from the place of values, worldview, and ways of being that we see resistance to oppression happening every day in Aboriginal communities, and we need to take time to notice. So to summarize our intent for this chapter is simple: we chose to notice – witness – the work being done within Aboriginal child welfare from our own stories, and in doing so we offer this chapter as one small act of reclamation.

Acknowledgements
We would like to acknowledge David Stevenson, Auggie Slyvester, Debbie Foxcroft, and Wayne Christian, who contributed their time and knowledge to help us prepare this chapter.

Note
1   Under the terms of the *Nisga'a Final Agreement* (Canada, British Columbia, and Nisga'a Nation, 2000), the Nisga'a Lisims government has the legal ability to create child and family service legislation (including adoptions) applicable to Nisga'a citizens, but at this time the Nisga'a are delivering services and developing organizational capacity employing authority delegated by, and funding provided solely by, the Province of British Columbia in accordance with provincial standards.

Persons Interviewed
Wayne Christian. Executive director, Community Health Associates of BC. Interviewed March 2005.
Debbie Foxcroft. Chair, Vancouver Island Aboriginal Transition Team. Interviewed March 2005.

References
Canada, British Columbia, and Nisga'a Nation. (2000). *Nisga'a final agreement.* Ottawa/Victoria: Federal Treaty Negotiation Office/Ministry of Aboriginal Affairs.
Department of Indian Affairs and Northern Development. (1990). Policy directive 20-1. Ottawa: Department of Indian Affairs and Northern Development.
First Nations Congress. (1992). *Indian Child and Family Services Project final report.* Vancouver: First Nations Congress.
Government of Canada. (1964). Treasury Board minute #627879. Ottawa: Minister of Supply and Services.
King, T. (2003). *The truth about stories: A Native narrative.* Toronto: Anansi Press.
Kline, M. (1992). Child welfare law: "Best interests of the child" ideology and First Nations. *Osgoode Hall Law Journal, 30*(2), 375-425.
Ministry of Children and Family Development. (1999). *Aboriginal operational and practice standards and indicators.* Victoria: Crown Publishing.
Powderface, S. (1984). Self-government means biting the hand that feeds us. In L. Little Bear, M. Boldt, and J.A. Long (Eds.), *Pathways to self-determination: Canadian Indians and the Canadian state* (pp. 164-68). Toronto: University of Toronto Press.
Walkem, A. (2002). *Calling forth our future: Options for the exercise of indigenous peoples' authority in child welfare.* Vancouver: Union of BC Indian Chiefs.

6

The Community Advocate Minister: Attempting Major Changes

Riley Hern and John Cossom

Joan Smallwood was well-informed when she arrived in her inaugural cabinet appointment as minister of social services, but she had an abundance of issues to deal with. Before entering politics, she was known in her local community as an anti-poverty advocate and a strong proponent of family support services. Her background provided her with a keen interest in the Ministry of Social Services (MSS), a passion for social justice, and a mission to serve this ministry's clients. More than this, her community development and social service experience led her to place great emphasis on listening to people's concerns.

Smallwood was first elected as a New Democratic Party (NDP) member in 1986 and was re-elected for Surrey-Whalley in 1991. She describes herself as a working-class feminist, a perspective that gave her an analytical framework with which to understand power relationships and do political work. Premier Mike Harcourt appointed her to cabinet on 5 November 1991. In opposition she had been critic of Social Services and Housing – at that time the ministry with responsibility for child welfare, income assistance, and services to developmentally delayed people. Over the years she had been in contact with many of the ministry's clients and contractors, and she now strongly advocated rewriting the child protection legislation. As a member of the shadow cabinet, she had consulted a wide range of people and was supported by an NDP social policy committee that included ministry insiders, university professors, and leaders of special interest groups with strong lobby interests. While the membership of this committee represented diverse ideas and directions, Smallwood was a unifying force for it in opposition. When her party came to power and she was appointed minister, the committee expected quick, decisive action on her part to deal with its litany of concerns.

Minister Smallwood, then, was well versed in the failings of the ministry that was now her domain. The press, critics, and special interest informants had no difficulty assembling a long list of issues to be addressed and wrongs to be righted. But she inherited a ministry with resistance to change – some would say it had a secretive approach – and a history of avoiding public input to, and discussion of, its operations and issues. Critics portrayed it as a brick wall – a closed system. This ministry was a frequent target of media criticism and had suffered through some high-profile cases that battered its public credibility. There was public skepticism that the "Ministry of Misery," as the press referred to it, could organize a coherent and reasonable response to the social problems it was mandated to address. However, in the early days of her appointment, Smallwood gave critics every reason to believe that the MSS would be open to community input, that she would be attentive to what people wanted, and that significant change was in the cards. Just how this change was to be orchestrated was not clear.

What Smallwood Inherited: The 1987-88 Reorganization

Major structural change occurred in the ministry before Smallwood's arrival. Bill Vander Zalm's Social Credit government set the stage for important changes in 1987-88 with the appointment of Jim Carter as deputy minister. Carter had been deputy minister of the education ministry, where, with patience, persistence, and innovation, he re-established credibility and restored public confidence. This deputy minister's manner was accessible, confident, and easygoing. In the social services ministry, Carter's leadership style helped soften management's cantankerous relationship with the BC Government Employees Union (BCGEU). However, he remained as deputy minister for only a short, if active, period before opting for early retirement.

Carter proposed that any change process be characterized by values of quality leadership, innovation, and professionalism and by setting employment requirements with basic professional credentials. He wanted to develop a culture in which the organization could learn from service breakdowns rather than blaming staff for problems. He stressed that these characteristics were critical for restoring public confidence in the ministry, and he emphasized the importance of involving front-line workers in planning and decision making. His aim to create a "learning culture" and a consultative process was seen as a breath of fresh air by most staff and many outside the system. Of course, although there was considerable enthusiasm for change, there was also substantial skepticism, both inside and outside the ministry.

With assistant deputy ministers Dick Butler and Terry Pyper, Carter launched an ambitious reorganization that was, in our view, larger and more significant than the ministry's shift to community resource boards under the 1970s NDP government (see Chapter 3). This restructuring affected each and every office, department, and position, from file clerk to minister, and radically altered structure, policy, and practice in all corners of the ministry.

Butler and Pyper brought considerable experience and credibility to this job. Butler was knowledgeable about big change processes because he had also been a key manager in developing community resource boards. These two assistant deputies assembled a group of approximately forty employees chosen from every level and department of the ministry, including headquarters staff, managers, field staff, and administrative support staff. They were organized into sixteen special focus groups that moved their operations into a Vancouver hotel for three months. With creativity, consultation, and debate, they rebuilt the ministry from a generalist organization into one with three separate divisions – Community Living, Child and Family Services, and Income Support.

Substantial autonomy was delegated to regional administrations to design service delivery systems and structures (e.g., the degree of centralization or dispersal of services). In all three divisions, further specialization units were encouraged to develop expertise in specific service delivery. The expectation was that, wherever possible, specialized practice areas such as child protection, foster care recruitment and training, youth services, job training, etc., would be developed. This separation of services and move to specialization was a radical change for most areas outside Victoria and the Lower Mainland, and it required a major redistribution of staff, budgets, and resources from large urban areas to more sparsely populated rural ones. Naturally, a transformation of this magnitude was greeted with some resistance, but Butler and Pyper, with the support and enthusiasm of the core planning and implementation teams, forged ahead. Extensive reclassification of staff at all levels, improved job descriptions and salaries, and the creation of new opportunities for advancement accompanied this structural change. Also included was a vast improvement in the systems operations of the ministry, including rapid enhancement of the ministry's computer and technical systems, which was sorely needed and long overdue.

For the first time in the ministry's history, income assistance (IA) was split into a separate service stream with its own management system. It was the main driver of new technical and computer-based developments, and its policy development was now divorced from family and child welfare services. Family and children's services staff no longer supervised IA and could no longer use IA policy to protect vulnerable children. The three new service streams competed vigorously with each other for money, resources, and policy influence. Not surprisingly, they came to be separated by gaps in service and philosophy.

The ministry sought to create an organizational culture in which management personnel were comfortable with business thinking and the principles of private enterprise management. The new structure led to the appointment of approximately fifty field managers who were almost exclusively promoted from within, including many who were members of the reorganization team. New managers faced high expectations to perform. Innovative professional practice and experimental community development were expected, along with strong management of budgets and resources. These new emphases brought a new organizational jargon, which was not always well understood.

The changes were enormous and very quickly implemented. Results were mixed. Change was resisted for a variety of reasons. Some managers were loath to make changes; loss of budget and staff, reluctance to move to new styles of service delivery, and lack of adequate or fully trained staff were some of the contributing factors. Politicians, worried about their re-election, were aggressive with executives about the continuing extensive public media coverage of ministry problems and case breakdowns.

While there were areas of significant innovative success and projects of excellence, relentless media attention and public criticism fostered a milieu of continued secrecy. For example, when the executive director of the BC Association of Social Workers arrived to address an assembly of ministry managers, there was great tension in the room about the possibility of "leaks." Every document that had been out on the tables, being worked on, was hidden before the outsider was allowed to enter the room. This ongoing atmosphere of conflict and tension once again overwhelmed the atmosphere of goodwill and optimism that the deputy minister had engendered. After the period of reorganization, both Butler and Pyper took early retirement. This was the ministry that Smallwood inherited.

Ministry Leadership and Organizational Culture

Despite Carter's short period of leadership, style and creativity are not words that usually spring to mind when describing government leadership in a heavily regulated ministry like social services. Expectations of conformity tend to rule policy making and personnel. This approach admirably suits automobile licensing, but it tends to frustrate the work of strengthening children's and families' well-being.

Employees were expected to study policy thoroughly and absorb its essentials. Their big challenge was to combine policy detail with what education and experience had taught them was "good social work" and to blend it all together in an attempt to respond positively to their caseloads' human demands. This was a difficult task, to say the least, and contributed to the loss of many a competent ministry employee to the private sector or some other less-regulated realm of practice. For employees pursuing a career in the ministry, the rewards of promotion seemed to favour those who played policy close to the vest. One comment about creative practice that is heard from time to time in the civil service is "You can risk your career if you want to, but I'm not doing that with mine!"

Joan Smallwood wanted to change the ministry. Damage control had been a preoccupation of a series of Social Credit ministers who preceded her. In contrast, Smallwood brought passion and an understanding of the clients being served by this powerful and seemingly impenetrable bureaucracy. She was determined to open up the system; be receptive to people's concerns and ideas, including those of clients and their advocates; and work with the community, to which she was well-connected.

The minister sometimes visited district offices without advance warning and with little ministerial fanfare. She came across as an interested and questioning thinker as she went about learning her ministerial responsibilities. She was very sure of the service tone she wanted and clear about her distaste for what she saw as some workers' oppressive behaviour toward clients. Workers were not accustomed to a minister who was in tune with their clients and who had this level of engagement with their work. They found her advocacy and client-centredness challenging.

Smallwood decided that the incumbent deputy minister – a woman who had arrived with a reputation in the premier's office as a "fire fighter" – did not have the confidence of the executive staff or a good grasp of the issues. As problems mounted, she eventually appointed Bob Cronin, capable, respected, and a long-time ministry executive with whom she developed a good working relationship. He was the well-informed, strategic partner she needed to help her tackle the complex task of redirecting MSS values and changing the way families and children were served.

The minister also replaced the Superintendent of Child Welfare. The incumbent, Leslie Arnold, was a sometimes feared but effective advocate and guardian of the thousands of ministry children for whom she was responsible. Unfortunately, she did not reflect Smallwood's philosophy and style. A superintendent's decisions are difficult ones, calling for extensive experience, clear articulation, and a full understanding of complex legal issues. The office holder has to be competent, rock-solid, and seen as totally reliable to make decisions in children's best interests. Whoever holds this position is under constant public scrutiny, so he or she must also be able to withstand the inevitable criticism the position attracts. Smallwood appointed Joyce Rigaux, a newcomer to the ministry, as her new superintendent. Rigaux, a highly respected social worker, did not have recent BC child welfare experience, although in the 1970s she had been manager of a Vancouver community resource board office.

Making Changes: The Community Panels

Prior to the election and Smallwood's arrival, the ministry had begun a review of its child protection practice and child welfare legislation (the *Family and Child Service Act,* which governed child welfare, had been in place since 1981) under the leadership of the Superintendent of Child Welfare and the deputy minister. The review was initiated because of the pressure that the Social Credit minister at the time, Norm Jacobsen, was receiving in the legislature, led by critic Smallwood. When she became minister, Smallwood was all in favour of a review, but she clearly indicated that the ministry would not review itself. As a result, the review committee membership was dramatically changed to embrace outside experts, activists, a BCGEU representative, ministry personnel, and critics of child welfare practice. The new members were Pat Chauncey, co-chair of End Legislated Poverty, from Vancouver; Jane Cowell, MSS area manager, Kamloops; Iain Cunningham, social agency director, Prince George; Michael Eso, the BCGEU's elected representative for social workers, Victoria; Patsy George, MSS Vancouver; Brent Parfitt, children's ombudsman, Victoria; Joyce Preston, co-chair and director of social planning for the City of Vancouver. Many observers viewed the composition of the panel as radical, given the well-established pattern of internally led, top-down change in the organization. Not surprisingly, when panel process and selection of panel members were announced, they caused controversy in some quarters (C. Haynes, interview, February 2005).

To reinforce Smallwood's stance that the ministry had to change direction, the tasks of the committee were also drastically changed. Instead of conducting an internal review, the committee, which was officially known as the Community Panel – Family and Children's Services Legislation Review, was charged with travelling the province to listen to ideas, solicit opinions, and hear critiques from any and all interested parties. All constituencies, including service recipients and ministry staff, were invited to participate. Based on this prolonged outreach to the BC community, the panel was to submit a major report that would provide a blueprint for future child welfare policy and practice.

The decision was made very early, following heavy pressure from Aboriginal communities, to split the group into two travelling panels, with one panel focused solely on matters of Aboriginal child welfare. The seven non-Aboriginal members of the community panel visited thirty-six BC communities, with multiple meetings in larger communities, and four simultaneously interpreted sessions with ethnic communities. It heard 550 oral presentations, all taped and transcribed, and received 579 written submissions from individuals and groups. Its report was entitled *Making Changes: A Place to Start* (Community Panel, 1992).

The two Aboriginal panel members, Lavina White (Haida Nation) and Eva Jacobs (Kwakiutl Nation), held meetings in thirty-three different communities throughout the province, hearing 424 presenters and receiving forty-one written submissions. They also held four regional conferences in major centres for feedback after their draft report was written. Their report was called *Liberating Our Children, Liberating Our Nations* (Aboriginal Committee of the Community Panel, 1992).

While this consultation process proceeded, the everyday business of the ministry continued and had to be dealt with using existing policy and legislation. With little directional clarity coming for a year while the two panels completed their work, opinion fluctuated inside and outside the MSS as to the likely new policy and practice focal points. Workers speculated about what the next blueprint would bring. Superintendent Rigaux, while often sitting in on the panel process and building community contacts, tended to keep her thoughts about the future to herself. There was regular media coverage, and internal ministry reports appeared regularly as the panels moved through their arduous province-wide schedules.

The MSS had long suffered from push and pull between experts at headquarters and the regional directors responsible for field performance. The people Joan Smallwood was relying on to bring about a new practice vision needed to speak out loudly and clearly to influence the dedicated staff in local offices of the ministry. But, given the minister's choice of this protracted community-consultation process, Smallwood's leadership team had to follow a holding pattern instead. While Joan Smallwood was very effective in reaching out to the community at large, she needed to work harder to build trust and relationships within her ministry, particularly with senior staff. They, in turn, had to work hard to gain confidence from her, and they struggled to show they were committed to the work and to working with her. This commitment seemed to develop in the latter stages of her tenure, but it came too late (R. Pollard, interview, March 2005).

For the front-line fieldworkers, the change process seemed to take a very long time. Those supporting Smallwood wanted to get on with the needed changes, while those holding back on their endorsement of the new values appeared to use the hiatus to muster their resistance. The large number of undecided workers, who Smallwood thought could be won over, were left in limbo for the better part of her term. There was little question about the general direction in which she would ultimately go, but the complex, yearlong, community-consultation process she initiated caused a costly delay.

Following many meetings, with a mountain of submissions to sift through and translate into a report and recommendations, the *Making Changes* panel moved into a Victoria hotel for thirty days. Its report was exhaustive, covering thirteen major areas and providing 103 recommendations, which are summarized below.

1. Poverty

There were seven wide-ranging recommendations aimed at the elimination of poverty, covering issues from increased social and co-op housing to school meals and more adequate minimum wage and IA levels.

2. Community Development

The report recommended that community development occupy a central position in child welfare work, and more broadly at an inter-ministry level, and that adequate resources be allocated for this. (A later section of this chapter will describe the community development program that emerged from this part of the report.)

3. Access to Information

The report addressed important principles of child welfare recording, information accuracy, privacy, and information access.

4. Advocacy

A central recommendation was for an independent Family and Child Advocacy Office to be established. It also recommended that the role of staff advocacy and external advocates be supported and that resources be provided to support independent advocacy groups.

5. Support Services

This section called for provincial funding for family and child support personnel and resources so that communities could develop a range of services relevant to their local needs.

6. Youth Services

Seven recommendations focused on the need for a wide range of programs for youth, whether in or out of care, from IA to institutional and community corrections services, programs for street youth, youth health clinics, sex education programs, and services for young parents.

7. Service Delivery Structure

The main thrust of three recommendations was that relevant government ministries must work together in a compatible, comprehensive way when developing and delivering services for children and families. The prime medium recommended to accomplish this was the neighbourhood-based integrated service centre.

8. Guardianship

In this section, the report recommended fundamental legislative revision of concepts related to guardianship, such as kinship, custody, care, shared parenting, adoption, self-custody for youth, and group custody.

9. Dispute Resolution

The central recommendation was for community tribunals to replace the court system when it came to making decisions in child protection cases. Other recommendations stressed the use of non-adversarial dispute-resolution mechanisms, mediation services, and collaboration with natural family support networks to resolve disputes.

10. Child Protection

There were thirty-one recommendations for changes in BC's child welfare legislation and child protection practice. Some of these aimed to introduce more checks and balances into the system's practice of removing children from their parents, particularly by using community tribunals and family conferencing processes.

11. Alternative Care

This group of seven recommendations focused on continuity and stability of care for all children served by the ministry, including those apprehended, those leaving care, and those looked after in their own family and community networks.

12. Staff

Twenty-one recommendations dealt with matters of staff planning, recruitment, and selection; staff education and in-house training; development of a certification program for staff; simplification of administrative requirements; changes to audits of staff decisions; promotion policies; and so on.

13. Legislating Change

Rather than making specific recommendations in this area, the report listed principles and general directions for new child welfare legislation. The panel wanted the new legislation to be called the *Family and Community Service Act,* and it asked that all provincial acts relating to families and children be consolidated by 1995.

The *Liberating Our Children, Liberating Our Nations* report also focused on thirteen areas, incorporating 102 individual recommendations. Its sweeping agenda for change is summarized below.

1. Transition Back to Aboriginal/First Nations Law – Colonial Legislation and the Inherent Right to Self-Government

This section asserted the need for Aboriginal self-government. It stressed the need for recognition of the paramountcy of Aboriginal rights and of Aboriginal jurisdiction over all child welfare matters. Any provincial child welfare legislation was to be seen as interim until Aboriginal family law was recognized.

2. Aboriginal Family and Children's Services

Aboriginal nations should be given the right to define citizenship; to take responsibility for all matters of child welfare, including the formation of child welfare agencies; and to assume decision-making authority under the *Family and Child Service Act*.

3. Appeal Mechanisms

Where Aboriginal nations or communities develop alternatives to provincial Family Courts for family dispute resolution, appeals of decisions made under the *Family and Child Service Act* must be referred to the Aboriginal dispute-resolution structure.

4. Healing the Wounds – Principles of Financing

Governments must provide legislatively guaranteed, adequate, ongoing finances for Aboriginal communities to meet child welfare responsibilities at a level of service comparable to non-Aboriginal communities. Federal and provincial governments must compensate Aboriginal communities for the negative effects of residential school programs and for removing Aboriginal children from their communities. Governments must guarantee the availability and accessibility of services when they are required by judicial order to reunite or keep a family intact.

5. Preventative Services

All services must be available as determined by the specific Aboriginal nation or community and delivered by them. Legislation must guarantee that an Aboriginal child not be removed solely because of the need for support services. While eighteen should be the maximum age at which guardianship may be exercised, the age at which a child is eligible for services must be flexible, based on the child's needs. Aboriginal communities must have ongoing financial resources to implement a wide range of culturally appropriate, integrated, preventative services, including family support, daycare, homemaker, respite, parenting, counselling, addictions treatment, and suicide prevention. For single-parent Aboriginal families, respite and homemaker services must be universally available on demand, and daycare for Aboriginal children must be universal, both off and on reserves.

6. Acquiring and Sharing Knowledge

Governments must make resources available to Aboriginal communities to replace non-Aboriginal standards with culturally appropriate methods of sharing knowledge and providing care. The Ministry of Continuing Education must consult with Aboriginal communities to determine educational needs and the optimum ways of meeting them with accredited educational programs.

7. Internationally Recognized Rights of the Child

This section affirms the primacy of the birth parents as providers of a child's care, with the extended family the next most appropriate source. When a child is removed, the goals must include reunification of that family wherever possible. Where it is not possible, the relationship between child and birth parents must be maintained, except in situations where such a relationship will result in physical harm to the child. In cases where neither birth parents nor extended family can provide care for the child, other members of the child's Aboriginal nation shall be the next most appropriate source of care. When judicial bodies make guardianship decisions, the birth parents, any member of the extended family, and the political body representing the child's Aboriginal nation or community shall be part of those deliberations. When an Aboriginal child is taken into care, all records shall be given to the political body representing that child's nation. The provincial government must negotiate with other provinces, the United States, and any other country, where applicable, to establish protocol agreements that facilitate the return of all Aboriginal children not in care of members of their families. In reunification, government must provide resources to assist the child, family, and community.

8. Ending the Legalized Abduction of Aboriginal Children – Paramountcy of Aboriginal Law

Upon request from any Aboriginal nation or community, all jurisdiction vested in the Superintendent of Child and Family Services must be vested in that Aboriginal nation or community. When Aboriginal nations enact their own laws with respect to families and children, provincial legislation must acknowledge the paramountcy of these laws. In each Aboriginal nation or community where the ministry exercises jurisdiction under the *Family and Child Service Act,* the ministry must enter into an agreement with that nation or community. That agreement must acknowledge the areas of jurisdiction and responsibility that the Aboriginal nation or community wishes to exercise. It must detail a plan by which temporary jurisdiction exercised by the ministry over certain areas will be transferred to the Aboriginal nation, and it must include a timetable for the transfer. It must also detail the non-Aboriginal government's provision of financial resources to the Aboriginal nation or community to enable it to undertake its responsibilities.

9. Children in Need of Protection

The *Family and Child Service Act* definition of "children in need of protection" must differentiate between children who are in immediate danger and children who would suffer in the long term if intervention did not occur. This is to ensure that a family can receive due process or alternative mediated intervention where this does not endanger the child. Unless there is immediate danger, a child cannot be removed from the home without a judicial order. Judicial bodies must be able to order the removal of the person presenting a threat to the child, rather than removing the child. Unless birth parents present an immediate danger to an apprehended child, they must be allowed unsupervised access.

10. Complaints and Investigations

In the case of a complaint of an Aboriginal child in need of protection, the ministry must turn over information received to the relevant Aboriginal nation or community. When a report of child abuse or neglect is found to be malicious or frivolous, the ministry must initiate civil litigation on behalf of the persons negatively affected by the report.

11. Apprehensions

All family courts must have duty counsel available to families. Also, when an Aboriginal child is apprehended, a mediator must be appointed within seven days to work with the apprehending authority and the family. Within forty-five days of the child's removal, the family's response to the apprehension must be heard by a judicial body. If an authority applies for child custody, it must demonstrate that all other options have been fully explored, including the option of having the offender removed rather than the child. Before a court can award custody to an authority, the mediator's report must be considered. In seeking a custody order, the authority must submit a plan for the child, including details of how the family may be reunited or reasons why it cannot be done. It shall also state how the child's connection with his or her Aboriginal culture will be sustained. Any Aboriginal nation or community that has an alternative dispute-resolution structure or a council of elders shall be asked to appoint an advocate for a child for whom removal is proposed.

12. Placement of Children

All extended family members of an Aboriginal child coming into care shall be considered approved foster facilities unless there are reasons this is not appropriate. In child placement, the parents' views shall be given weight.

All legislation must be removed that would allow a judicial body to place a child permanently outside the care of his or her extended family. Legislation must provide for the voluntary placement of children in the care of the superintendent for as long as it takes for the family to resolve its problems. The *Adoption Act* must be amended to eliminate all possibilities of a child being denied knowledge of his or her identity and extended family. When an Aboriginal child is removed from his or her natural parents and placed in another home within the nation, it must be possible to extend the order of temporary care in one-year (maximum) increments for as long as is necessary for the natural parents to resolve the problem resulting in the child's removal. Legislation must recognize no other forms of adoption of an Aboriginal child other than custom or open adoption by an Aboriginal family.

13. Family Violence and Abuse of Children

When custody decisions are made, traditional matrilineal and clan structures shall be considered. Where violence by an estranged husband against his estranged wife has been a factor, the physical well-being and safety of the wife shall take precedence over the father's right of access to any of the children. If a child is conceived as a result of involuntary intercourse, the child's father shall have no rights to access or custody. However, he may be held financially responsible for child maintenance. Each Aboriginal nation or community shall receive resources necessary to create a safe haven for women and children who are victims of abuse. Where it endangers a woman or her child, the requirement to seek maintenance from her estranged spouse as a condition of eligibility for financial support must not compromise the anonymity of her whereabouts. Aboriginal nations and communities must have resources to address problems that result from disclosures of sexual abuse. If a child victim of sexual abuse is of an age to form a valid opinion, and if the expression of that opinion will not negatively affect the victim, the victim's views must be considered when deciding whether criminal charges will be laid and in sentencing. If the victim is not of an age to form an opinion, or if the expression of that opinion will negatively affect the victim, then the victim's parents' views must be considered. If one of the parents is the offender, then the views of the parents of the non-offending parent must be considered. The videotaped disclosure of a child victim of sexual abuse should be admissible as evidence in a child sexual abuse trial.

Smallwood had received a multiplicity of sweeping, all-encompassing recommendations from her two community panels, but, as events unfolded, she had less than a year remaining in her position to deal with them. Sadly, very few of the recommendations found their way directly and concretely into the new legislation which was to come several years later. Nevertheless, we should not underestimate the impact of this extensive community-consultation process. Policy makers certainly relied very heavily on the two reports and struggled to incorporate and act on their key concepts.

Community Development

As noted above, the *Making Changes* panel made a series of recommendations that strongly urged the ministry to engage in community development. This was one area that was acted upon quickly, though there was considerable opposition to, and skepticism about, the MSS's move in this direction. However, Smallwood now showed her hand, and in this realm the ministry's new direction became clear.

Normally the ministry contracted out innovative activity like this. It was a bone of contention for staff that creative, interesting work was typically contracted out, while ministry employees were left with routine child welfare work, along with loads of frustrating accountability and paperwork. However, in this instance the ministry chose to advertise its new community development positions internally.

The minister turned to an experienced hand to direct this initiative, and it was hard to fault the appointment of Patsy George. She had a detailed understanding of the ministry from long employment in several different positions and had just completed a year as a *Making Changes* panellist. She also brought multicultural experience, a strong personality, confidence, and a potent dedication to community development principles and practice. Her values were closely in sync with the minister's, and she had the ability to skilfully handle the change process that was envisioned and communicate the kind of messages the minister wanted transmitted to the field.

Any mapping of child protection work shows that it occurs primarily in poor neighbourhoods (Foster, 2005; Foster and Wright, 2002). Communities where the poor gather or are forced to live have far fewer assets than the communities in which most people choose to raise a family. Housing is not good. Affordable recreation is unavailable. For the poor, shopping is often limited to second-hand stores and expensive corner groceries. Many residents have little to do and limited discretionary income. Poor communities typically need physical renewal, social resources, stronger institutions, injections of positive energy, and family- and child-centred activities to reverse the downward spiral they follow when devoid of development capital. There was no shortage of BC neighbourhoods where a community development worker could find many potential avenues for action, and where child protection workers saw families in need.

A neighbourhood that fit the foregoing description was situated just west of Victoria, contained in a one-square-mile area near the local MSS office. While the income support office and the child welfare team were set up to serve four expansive communities, the neighbourhood immediately surrounding the office was home to 80 percent of its clients. It was a natural fit for the Community Development Project, and we use it as an example of this ministry initiative.

Peter Scott, a child protection worker on the local team, with a background that included income support work, enthusiastically chose this task. He joined Patsy George and twenty other newly minted community development workers as they began to plan their future endeavours, but they received little support from their office teammates, who were preoccupied with child protection issues. The ministry milieu was hardly an ideal setting for the community development program. There were questions from within the ministry and from the community that challenged the choice of civil servants to do this work. Comments from the Ombudsman's Office and later the Gove Report (Gove, 1995) asked why the ministry devoted scarce full-time positions to this enterprise when child protection workers were still overburdened. Many protection workers themselves were angry that the program existed when they could not find enough time to do their work adequately. Income assistance workers viewed the program as a child welfare pipe dream with little chance of producing positive outcomes for the families they served who lived on sub-poverty-level incomes.

Peter Scott, however, who was back in the community in a new role, with new enthusiasm and a growing confidence buoyed by being part of a strong program team, focused on the clients and the support from advocates in the local community. He quietly worked away at cultivating groups, helping parents take a stand on their needs, and prioritizing initiatives. Scott described his community development approach as defining problems in solvable terms. He avoided paralyzing terms like "lack of resources," calling them "copouts." He saw poverty as a complex problem he could do nothing about as a whole, but when he broke the problem down to some of its local impacts, things began to happen. Lack of food meant creating a community kitchen; socially isolated people were linked to support groups; collectives responded to the need for hard-to-find childcare; and for some families, distance from or absence of supportive relatives led to involvement with local seniors.

Remembering the number of parents from his protection work who complained about their children's behavioural problems, Scott mentioned to one frustrated mother the possibility of forming a support group. She contacted other parents, put up a poster, and, with his help, set up a series of meetings with speakers at the local neighbourhood house. At the first meeting the community development worker sat back, not saying a word, as eighteen parents came together. For over three years this group stayed together as a resource for parents who came into contact with child protection services.

A large First Nations group also evolved with the help of a First Nations partner and some funding from the ministry. It supported parents dealing with child-rearing problems and linked them with parents doing well.

It was a shock to statutory workers to see the community publicly honour this worker for his quiet achievements and to hear people speak about development activities that over two years had strengthened the local neighbourhood.

This program lasted two years beyond Smallwood's tenure as minister. However, as pressure on the ministry increased under the scrutiny of the Gove Inquiry, and as evidence and criticism of the inadequacy and break-downs of protection services mounted (see Chapter 7), community development positions disappeared and the ministry converted its scarce staff resources back to child protection positions.

Innovative Practice

Few critics would argue that "innovative practice" is a prominent feature of BC child welfare. Child welfare innovation is more often seen as something done in progressive parts of Ontario, the United States, and the United Kingdom. New child welfare practice approaches are generally not attempted in British Columbia until they are well-established and proven elsewhere. The ministry's typical approach to innovative practice has been to take a good idea; apply tight protocols, rules, and regulations; and monitor its progress with an executive-led committee.

"Innovative practice" is, perhaps, a complimentary term for what ministry policy makers view as risky, questionable approaches proposed in a paper emanating from a school of social work. Social work schools typically see part of their mission as preparing students to enter the ministry generically armed with skills in critical thinking and progressive policy analysis and practice, with the long-term goal of converting fieldwork operations and administration into less oppressive, more caring, client-centred processes. However, BC social work curricula had paid little attention to the practice of child welfare up to the early 1990s. On the other hand, there was no shortage of BC social work professors criticizing ministry practice and pointing out its lack of originality. Academics were usually seen as the enemy and harshly spoken of in ministry circles, and workers were warned not to collaborate with them for fear of inadvertently sharing information about government operations.

BC child welfare, with its swings in practice emphasis from circumscribed child protection to family support interventions, has always presented a dilemma of balance for the professional practitioner. Under the regime of Joan Smallwood, practitioners faced a choice between sticking with the previous administration's protective approach to child welfare or buying into the ministerial challenge to get more involved in helping clients with their problems.

Many workers believed that moving away from a protection-oriented way of doing child welfare work and toward a family-centred emphasis would put children at potential risk in vulnerable situations. De-emphasizing investigations, removing fewer children, and spending scarce resources to support parents so they could keep children in the community was viewed as a recipe for disaster. Many ministry workers were uncomfortable taking these risks, especially in light of recent experiences of being in the media spotlight or dealt with harshly by administration for protection mistakes.

While it is inaccurate to suggest that practice innovation flourished in the brief Smallwood era, there were some workers who shifted their practice, and some formal practice innovations. One example is "Empowering Women," a project initiated by Marilyn Callahan and Brian Wharf (Callahan and Lumb, 1995). They proposed it to Joyce Rigaux, who was interested in this kind of initiative and approved it as a time-limited project with a Vancouver intake office, a semi-rural Fraser Valley office, and offices in Nanaimo, and Parksville as demonstration locations. This project was approved because its values and intent seemed to be in tune with Joan Smallwood's vision of what a child welfare ministry should be about.

The project's purpose was to demonstrate a different way ministry workers could approach clients and the problems they faced. Some women, if they felt oppressed by the investigation process, would fight fiercely to retain their parental role, using legal processes to keep the ministry at bay. Unfortunately, in a legally contested scenario, their children often remained in care for years. The "Empowering Women" project aimed to support child protection workers who were trying to shift to a more egalitarian place with their clients, with the goal of allowing the clients to think differently about themselves and their parenting capability. Group work – long out of fashion as a ministry practice modality – was used as the main empowering and change medium. The hypothesis was that if mothers valued themselves more and saw themselves as people with some power, they would be able to make better decisions about their children's well-being. If they were treated with respect and invited into the decision-making process, they would be able to make more thoughtful decisions about parenting, instead of being trapped in a fight with the ministry.

It was initially difficult to introduce this approach into policy-driven ministry offices, but the approach did have supporters and a number of successes by the time it concluded. Again, the project continued beyond Smallwood's tenure, but because it had only project status, it was an easy victim of later funding cuts. The project leaders regret the time-limited nature of the project, which put constraints on the inevitably slow process required to consolidate project gains into more general practice (M. Callahan, interview, March 2005). It is hard to disagree with this assessment.

There were some other innovative thrusts underway in the ministry offices, such as the Youth-in-Care Network. This network was very much part of Minister Smallwood's vision of how people in need should be treated in British Columbia. Set up as a self-run support organisation made up of fourteen-to-twenty-four-year-old ex-wards of the state who provided advocacy, support groups, rights awareness, and independence training to their peers, with minimum but useful guidance from the ministry, it is now a national and international movement of twenty years standing. Had they remained in leadership positions, it is likely that Joan Smallwood and Joyce Rigaux would have encouraged further similar projects.

We believe that BC child welfare sorely needs the experimentation and continued learning that flows from innovative demonstration practices, the participation of researchers, and creative involvement of social workers and their clients. Projects that operate in fits and starts and are prone to cancellation because of changes in ideology and funding restraints are rarely helpful. Also, importing innovation from other jurisdictions and applying it indiscriminately in BC has a poor record of success. Change almost always calls for local application, testing, and carefully applied research. Innovation that bears fruit can then be integrated into general practice. Polar shifts in BC political winds almost always prevent this from happening.

The End of the Smallwood Era
Smallwood's brief ministerial era began full of aspirations for significant child welfare policy change. These hopes flowed from the new minister's social advocacy orientation and her experience with family issues in the community, and it was strengthened by her further exposure as opposition family and child welfare critic. She was the opposition watchdog at a time when child welfare services received little sustained government attention, few resources, and much bad press, despite the fact that the ministry had undergone one of the most major structural reorganizations in its history.

Joan Smallwood's appointment seemed sound and logical, her background relevant and more than appropriate. She was better informed and much more eager to fill this role than most previous ministers, with strong expectations and endorsement for innovation and reform from her colleagues and an assortment of left-wing advocates and supporters. When her tenure ended less than two years later, it was a crash landing for a brief period of attempted major reform.

Was Smallwood's strong alignment with community, and her client-centred preoccupation, troublesome to those in power? Did she fail to select the right people for some of the key positions in her ministry quickly enough? Did her critics, particularly those in the opposition party and the media, contribute to her ministerial demise by portraying her as negligent in tackling welfare costs and fraud?

The NDP's allegedly loose control of expenditures on income assistance had been used to attack the party since its first taste of power in BC in the 1970s. After the Social Credit Party defeated the NDP in 1975, it kept the NDP's "overspending" on IA programs on the financial books for years, even though the debt could have been retired. This albatross re-emerged as a major public issue during the party's second term in the early 1990s. The Fraser Institute, a right-wing think tank in BC, quoted an analysis which stated that Joan Smallwood made it clear to staff that they were "to serve clients, not police welfare use" (Richards, 1997, p. 160). Premier Harcourt received criticism from all sides on this issue. Political observers knew trouble was brewing when the normally moderate premier used derogatory words to describe fraudulent welfare clients. For ministry clients and staff alike, it felt like time to duck for cover. The IA time bomb contributed more than any other factor to Joan Smallwood's departure.

During Smallwood's tenure as minister, the pendulum swung once again between protecting children and supporting families, with the oscillation moving hard to the support-prevention side. Smallwood did not pay nearly enough attention to the major area of her ministerial responsibility – the protection of children from abuse and neglect – while she championed her primary agenda of supporting families and strengthening communities. However, leadership for this significant paradigm shift was inconsistent, and the necessary buy-in by a staff majority did not happen. It was also essential for the minister to ensure that the child protection mandate was supported and well served while her favoured community support initiatives were put back on the child welfare map. Perhaps, in her passion to push change, she fell into the trap of forgetting that, in order to be effective, a child welfare ministry must balance its two primary responsibilities. Most observers would agree that the Smallwood era was not a high point in helpful conceptualization of this bifocal nature of child welfare. Sadly, it meant a significant opportunity to organically reshape child welfare in BC was missed.

Smallwood's own appraisal is that during her term of office, one-third of her ministry staff were with her, one-third were against her, and the other third were "thinking about it." It is hardly surprising that there was such a division of opinion about a minister who brought a distinct change in philosophy and emphasis in child welfare practice. Her staff was confronted with yet another sharp swing of the child welfare practice and policy pendulum. They were weary of labouring in a field that was so vulnerable to criticism and that could so readily be dissected under the public microscope. Soon, with the Gove Commission's penetrating scrutiny, they were subjected to scathing, relentless, public criticism as never before.

Our position is that striking the right balance between family and child welfare practices and staying the course can bring stronger results for this ministry. We believe that strong consideration should be given to separating and protecting the funding for these two essential, parallel, child welfare activities. This would go a long way to stabilizing unproductive swings in one direction or the other, when both activities are necessary for long-term progress to be made.

Whatever the combination of factors that precipitated her removal as minister of social services, Smallwood takes full responsibility for what happened. She feels she was making the necessary changes at an appropriate pace. Yes, there was bad press for child welfare, but isn't there always?

On a warm September weekend in 1993, Joan Smallwood was told to remain available. Premier Harcourt called her to his office, and as part of a large cabinet shuffle, she was reassigned. She hit the roof, said a number of angry, forceful things, and marched out. This had been the best time of her working life, but after only twenty-two months, it was over.

Smallwood recovered from her disappointment and went on to other cabinet portfolios. However, the MSS certainly did not go on to better things. In 1994, the NDP government was faced with what became BC's most infamous child welfare case. Five-year-old Matthew Vaudreuil died tragically at his mother's hands. The cabinet appointed Judge Thomas Gove to undertake an independent inquiry into, and report on, the adequacy of child protection services, policies, and practices (see Chapter 7). While Matthew was killed on Smallwood's watch, his troubles and involvement with the ministry's staff began long before she became minister. The MSS had been working with both Matthew and his mother for years. Nevertheless, Joan Smallwood remains deeply troubled by his death, and she finds Judge Gove's critical comments on her policies hurtful. It certainly does not reflect how she wants her ministerial tenure to be remembered.

There is no doubt that, under Smallwood, the BC child welfare system was opened to community input as never before. Extensive consultation took place, problems were debated and identified, and a very ambitious set of directions recommended. But, as is often the case, change did not follow directly from this. Very few of the community panels' sweeping recommendations were acted on concretely. When the new legislation arrived, it did not explicitly reflect the strong recommendations in the panel documents. Much of their content was trumped by the demands of the Gove Report.

While Smallwood's community consultations garnered a wealth of often contradictory opinion about directions for family and child welfare, the Gove Report focused on an examination of system and procedural errors that led to the tragic death of Matthew Vaudreuil. Given the severe political embarrassment of the Gove Inquiry, this report pushed the work of the community panels into the background, despite their range and depth of important content. The cabinet had no political choice but to incorporate many of the Gove Report recommendations into new policy and legislation. Sadly, the *Making Changes* and *Liberating Our Children, Liberating Our Nations* blueprints for child welfare, produced from very broad constituencies, were forced into the shadows.

Acknowledgments
The authors are grateful to all those who contributed to this chapter by participating in interviews. They also greatly appreciate Ron Pollard's detailed, thoughtful responses to chapter drafts.

Persons Interviewed
Marilyn Callahan. Co-investigator of the Empowering Women Project and emerita faculty member at the University of Victoria School of Social Work. Interviewed March 2005.

Jane Cowell. Member of the Making Changes Community Panel and MSS area manager in Kamloops. Interviewed March 2005.

Michael Eso. Member of the Making Changes Community Panel, former child welfare social worker, and, since 1985, the BCGEU's elected representative for social workers. Interviewed February 2005.

Patsy George. Member of the Making Changes Community Panel and director of the Community Development Project. Interviewed March 2005.

Chris Haynes. Former MSS regional manager for North Vancouver Island. From March 1993, MSS assistant deputy minister, and from 2001 to 2004, MSS deputy minister. Interviewed February 2005,

Marjorie Martin. Former faculty member, School of Social Work, University of Victoria, former member of the NDP social policy committee, and a friend of Joan Smallwood. Interviewed March 2005.

Ron Pollard. Former area manager of MSS Family and Children's Services in Victoria West. Interviewed March 2005.

Peter Scott. Former MSS social worker, hired as a community development project worker. Interviewed February 2005.

Joan Smallwood. Minister of social services from 5 November 1991 to 14 September 1993. Interviewed March 2005.

References
Aboriginal Committee of the Community Panel on Family and Children's Services Legislation Review. (1992). *Liberating Our Children: Liberating our Nations.* Victoria: Ministry of Social Services.

BC Auditor General. (1992). *Managing professional resources: An assessment of the Ministry of Social Services' human resource management processes for its social workers.* Victoria: BC Auditor General.

Callahan, M., and Lumb, C. (1995). My cheque or my children. *Child Welfare, 74*(4), 796-820.

Community Panel on Family and Children's Services Legislation Review. (1992). *Making Changes: A Place to Start.* Victoria: Ministry of Social Services.

Foster, L.T. (2005). Youth in B.C.: Selected demographic, health and well-being trends and patterns over the last century. In R.S. Tonkin and L.T. Foster (Eds.), *Youth in British Columbia: Their past and their future* (pp. 15-37). Canadian Western Geographical Series, Vol. 39. Victoria: Western Geographical Press.

Foster, L.T., and Wright, M. (2002). Patterns and trends in children in the care of the province of British Columbia: Ecological, policy and cultural perspectives. In M.V. Hayes and L.T. Foster (Eds.), *Too small to see, too big to ignore: Child health and well-being in British*

Columbia (pp. 103-40). Canadian Western Geographical Series, Vol. 35. Victoria: Western Geographical Press.

Gove, T. (1995). *Report of the Gove Inquiry into Child Protection in BC. Vol. 2. Matthew's legacy.* Victoria: Ministry of the Attorney General.

Richards, J.G. (1997). *Retooling the welfare state: What's right, what's wrong, what's to be done.* Toronto: C.D. Howe Institute.

Swets, R., Rutman, D., and Wharf, B. (1995). The community development initiative of the Ministry of Social Services: A review of the experience and a framework for practice. Victoria: University of Victoria, School of Social Work, Child, Family and Community Research Program.

Wharf, B. (1993, September). A comparative analysis of three policy documents: *Making Changes: A Place to Start, Liberating our Children, Liberating our Nations,* and *Making Changes: Next Steps.* Unpublished article. Victoria: University of Victoria, Faculty of Human and Social Development.

7

Thomas Gove: A Commission of Inquiry Puts Children First and Proposes Community Governance and Integration of Services

Andrew Armitage and Elaine Murray

In 1994, Joy MacPhail, NDP minister of social services, appointed Judge Thomas Gove to conduct a public inquiry into the circumstances of the death of Matthew Vaudreuil and the lessons to be learned for the administration of child protection in British Columbia. The inquiry's conclusions had far-reaching implications for policy, administration, and practice, and it took time to implement them all, but by 1998, many of the changes that Gove had recommended had been made. This included replacing the former Ministry of Social Services with a new Ministry for Children and Families that had significantly different responsibilities. Key events related to this chapter are summarized in Table 7.1.

Verna and Matthew's Life
The events that resulted in the Gove Inquiry began much earlier, in 1966, when Verna Vaudreuil, Matthew's mother, was born to Kenneth Vaudreuil and Florence Cummings in Estevan, Saskatchewan. In 1968 the family moved to Taylor, BC, and by the early 1970s the family was in regular contact with the child protection staff from the Ministry of Human Resources. In November 1974, Verna and her sister, Claudine, were apprehended under the *Protection of Children Act* on the grounds that their parents were unable to care properly for them due to marital strife, and the children were suffering severe emotional rejection. Verna was then eight years old (Gove, 1995a).

Verna Vaudreuil was in continuous contact with the ministry from 1974 until Matthew Vaudreuil died in 1992. Between 1974 and 6 April 1985, the day she was discharged from care at age nineteen, Verna was nearly always a child in care. During the first seven years, Verna lived in eight different foster homes. From age fifteen to eighteen, she lived in a ministry-supported Skills Development Community Residence in Fort St. John. Finally, she lived independently while being supported financially by the ministry's independent-living program. When she was returned home to her parents in 1978 for one year, she was sexually abused by her older brother. A 1981

Table 7.1

Timeline of key events surrounding the Gove Inquiry

August 1992	Matthew dies of neglect and abuse
March 1994	Verna pleads guilty to manslaughter
March 1994	Ministry of Social Services' internal inquiry into Matthew's death begins
May 1994	Joy MacPhail, minister, tables Superintendent Joyce Rigaux's report in the legislature
May 1994	Justice Thomas Gove appointed to inquire into the circumstances of Matthew's death and make recommendations on "the adequacy of services, and the policies and practices, ... of the Ministry of Social Services" in the area of child protection
March 1995	Interim Report of the Gove Inquiry released
November 1995	Report of the Gove Inquiry released
January 1996	Transition Commission established, Cynthia Morton appointed commissioner
February 1996	Dennis Streifel appointed minister of Social Services
September 1996	Transition commissioner's report on ministry reorganization and policy changes released
September 1996	Penny Priddy appointed minister for Children and Families
September 1996	Bob Plecas appointed deputy minister
November 1996	Katie Lynn Baker dies in Nelson; manager, supervisor, and social workers are suspended without pay
March 1998	Lois Boone appointed minister and Mike Corbeil appointed deputy minister

assessment noted that Verna was developmentally delayed and emotionally insecure, and she displayed such behavioural problems as lying and stealing (ibid.).

By the time she was discharged from care, Verna was in a common-law relationship with Kenneth Hutchins. In October 1986, Matthew Vaudreuil was born. From 1985 until 1992, she was again in continuous contact with the ministry, receiving services provided by the ministry's income assistance, child protection, and child care divisions, as well as associated health care services. Ministry records reviewed by the Gove Inquiry show that the Fort St. John office saw itself dealing with a chronic situation in which Verna's inability to care for Matthew, and her abuse of the child, were under continuous review, with the ministry seeking to supplement Verna's caring abilities, and alleviate Matthew's abuse, by providing child care and support services to Verna (ibid.).

In March 1992, Verna and Matthew moved to Vancouver. Shortly afterwards, in July 1992, Matthew was killed by Verna. He was five-and-a-half years old. The autopsy report showed that he weighed thirty-six pounds and had been starved, bound, and severely beaten, resulting in a fractured arm and eleven fractured ribs. Death had been caused by asphyxiation, apparently by covering his mouth and nose. By the time he died, "21 social workers had been responsible for providing him with services ... 60 reports about his safety and well-being had been made ... he had been taken to the doctor 75 times and had been seen by 24 different physicians" (ibid.). Verna was charged with second-degree murder and, following the preliminary hearing, pleaded guilty to manslaughter.

Inquiry into Matthew's Death

The first inquiry into Matthew's death was an internal ministry inquiry, initiated and managed by Joyce Rigaux, the Superintendent of Family and Child Services. The report was tabled in the legislature on 17 May 1994. Chris Haynes, the assistant deputy minister, told the Gove Inquiry "that the Superintendent made a 'fundamental decision' that the report should look for themes rather than individual culpability" (Gove, 1995a).

However, following opposition challenges, the minister, Joy MacPhail, decided that an independent inquiry should be conducted. On 19 May, she appointed Judge Thomas Gove to conduct the inquiry with the following terms of reference:

> To inquire, report and make recommendations on the adequacy of services, and the policies and practices, including training and workload, of the Ministry of Social Services respecting:
>
> - receipt and investigation of reports that a child is in need of protection,
> - decision making concerning provision of services to the child and the child's family,
> - case management and monitoring of these services, and,
> - case coordination, and documentation and sharing of information on the case, within the Ministry and among ministries, professionals and agencies having contact with the family
>
> as they relate to the apparent neglect and abuse, and the death, of Matthew Vaudreuil. (ibid., pp. 274-75)

The Gove Inquiry report (Gove, 1995a, 1995b) was released in November 1995 following exhaustive investigation, public hearings, and receipt of sworn testimony from 115 witnesses. Transcript evidence covered more than six thousand pages, and thirty-two background papers were prepared to support and inform the inquiry.

Findings and Recommendations of the Gove Inquiry

Judge Gove found that Matthew had not been provided the protection to which he was entitled: "Overall an unmistakable pattern emerges of a boy routinely neglected, and emotionally and physically abused. Through it all, he was not protected – not by his mother, not by his community and not by those charged with protecting British Columbia's children" (Gove, 1995a, p. 153).

Gove made 118 recommendations. They fall into six principal categories: case practice (recommendations 1-28); quality assurance (recommendations 29-54); education and training (recommendations 55-67); legislation (recommendations 68-92); a new child welfare system (recommendations 95-111); transition and implementation measures (recommendations 112-118). (Recommendations 93 and 94 dealt with administrative details concerning the child, youth, and family advocate.) A consistent theme throughout Gove's recommendations is that the safety and well-being of the individual child must be the primary consideration in child welfare legislation, administration, training, and organization.

Implementing Gove's Recommendations

The government accepted Judge Gove's recommendation to appoint a transition commissioner, and it appointed Cynthia Morton to the position in January 1996, initially with a three-year mandate. However, her terms of reference differed from those proposed by Gove: "For Gove, the role was to oversee implementation of his proposed changes. For government, the role was to test the 'do-ability' of the proposed changes and report back to the premier with recommendations for implementation" (Morton, 2002, p. 165). Morton found that Gove's recommendations for a new system, including the establishment of a new ministry for children and youth, were not welcomed outside the Ministry of Social Services (MSS), and she began to explore alternatives. However, the Gove Inquiry had succeeded in focusing media attention on the failings of the MSS and had created an expectation that change would follow.

During the 1996 debate on the MSS estimates, opposition questions about the numbers of children who were "known" to the ministry and who had died "either went unanswered or responses changed daily" (ibid., p. 167). The impression that the ministry was not able to fulfill its mandate or implement the changes proposed by Gove deepened. As a result, in September 1996 the premier asked the transition commissioner to submit her report much earlier than originally anticipated, and she did so that month.

The commissioner's report endorsed most of Gove's recommendations, with the exception of the regional governance proposals for the new system (Morton, 1996).

On receipt of the commissioner's report, the government established a new ministry – the Ministry for Children and Families – with Penny Priddy as minister and Bob Plecas as deputy minister. The appointment of Plecas as deputy minister was particularly significant. He had held a number of senior posts in the bureaucracy when the Social Credit Party had been in power, but had been fired following the election of the NDP government in 1991. Bringing him back on a two-year contract as deputy minister of the new ministry put all parts of the government and ministry on notice that Gove's recommendations were going to be implemented.

Plecas adopted a hands-on approach to the task of establishing the new ministry. Many of the child-serving responsibilities of other ministries were transferred to the Ministry for Children and Families. The new ministry was simplified and decentralized, with no more than four reporting levels between client and deputy; the staff resources at head office were cut, and some resources were sent to the field; computer systems were modernized; and management was held professionally accountable for services. In November 1996, the mother of Katie Lyn Baker, a ten-year-old with Rett syndrome, allowed the child to die. The ministry did not intervene. This time the social workers, supervisor, and regional manger were suspended, pending inquiry, and they were later disciplined. This was the first formal use of discipline for failure to fulfill a statutory responsibility in at least ten years (B. Plecas, interview, 2005). On 6 November 1996, Les Leyne, the legislative reporter for the *Victoria Times Colonist,* wrote an article entitled "Ministry staff get first class in Accountability 101."

This effectively ended the intense press coverage that had tracked the Matthew Vaudreuil "story" from its beginning. The public coverage, rightly or wrongly, had a character of its own, which included an "innocent" victim (Matthew), an irresponsible and wicked mother (Verna), and a cast of inept, unaccountable social workers, prone to wishful thinking, who failed to provide Matthew with the protection to which he was entitled (Callahan and Callahan, 1997). With Verna in jail and the superintendent (Joyce Rigaux) dismissed,[1] and with the added assurance that social workers were now being fired,[2] the press could rest its case.

The Gove Report's Impact on Child Welfare Policy

When Judge Gove's recommendations were received, it was thought that they had a substantial effect on the direction of child welfare policy (Armitage, 1998). However, a decade after the inquiry, their significance appears more limited. Some of the recommendations were implemented and the changes remain in effect; some were implemented in rather different ways than Gove had proposed; others have not been implemented at all, and in a few cases changes were made that Gove clearly opposed.

Safety and the "Protection" of Children

The effect of Gove's recommendations is most marked in the subsequent establishment of the safety and well-being of the individual child as the paramount consideration in child protection investigations.

When the inquiry was initiated in 1994, the social services minister, Joy MacPhail, also tabled two new acts in the legislature: *The Child, Family and Community Service Act (CFCSA)* and the *Child, Youth and Family Advocacy Act*. These acts were the final products of an extended process of consultation that had begun in 1992 when MacPhail's predecessor, Joan Smallwood, appointed two community panels to review ministry legislation (see Chapter 6). Implementation of the new legislation was put on hold pending receipt of Gove's recommendations. To permit final debate of these statutes in the following (1995) legislative session, Gove delivered an interim report (Gove, 1995c) that proposed changes in the legislation which clarified that the safety and well-being of the child was paramount in the administration and interpretation of the act. These changes were adopted through an amendment to the legislation.

Additional evidence of Gove's influence on child protection issues can be found in recommendations that

- opposed the use of family group conferences in the child protection process (recommendation 1)
- recommended that child protection report intake procedures and policies be tightened (recommendations 6-8)
- advocated the use of "risk assessment" protocols and instruments in investigations (recommendations 9-15).

There were also legislative recommendations contained in the final report (recommendations 68-70) that emphasized the importance of child protection. In particular, the safety and well-being of a child was to be the paramount consideration for the *CFCSA*, and children were to be given the right to an early determination of decisions related to them.

Recommendations 77 and 78 dealt with issues related to Aboriginal children. These recommendations were intended to clarify the definitions of culture, heritage, and identity in the legislation, particularly within Aboriginal communities, but many people have interpreted them as *opposing* the inclusion of Aboriginal identity in a protection hearing. These policy recommendations had a marked effect on ministry intake and investigation procedures and led to the introduction of intake and assessment instruments developed in other jurisdictions. In the end the legislation includes both a provision for family group conferences and a statute that recognizes Aboriginal identity within the protection hearing – recommendations supported by the community panel report (Aboriginal Committee of the Community Panel on Family and Children's Services Legislation Review, 1992).

Quality Assurance
A second major theme of Judge Gove's policy recommendations concerned quality assurance and ministry review procedures. Here Gove recommended a complex and multi-layered set of structures and practices, including the following:

- The role of the Child, Youth and Family Advocate was to be strengthened with regard to the advocate's powers and jurisdiction (recommendations 36, 92-94).
- Internal ministry practice audits were to be performed systematically and frequently (recommendations 29-32).
- Complaint procedures were to be strengthened, and reviews were to be conducted by a statutory Child Welfare Review Board (recommendations 39-43).
- A separate Children's Commissioner would also have power to review all child deaths and serious injuries (recommendations 49-54).

These measures were in addition to the powers exercised by such established government agencies as the Ombudsman, Human Rights Commission, Coroner's Office, Comptroller General, Provincial Health Office, and Auditor General, each of which also had jurisdiction to make recommendations about aspects of ministry operations. In addition, Treasury Board had jurisdiction to set spending and request various actions be taken around policies and programs.

Gove's recommendations were initially adopted, and between 1996 and 1999 the Children's Commissioner reviewed the deaths of four hundred BC children, the vast majority not "known" to, nor in the care of, the ministry (Morton, 2002, p. 171). Most of the deaths were of medically fragile children or were the result of motor vehicle accidents – not the result of child neglect or abuse.

The effect of Gove's recommendations was to subject the then Ministry of Social Services to continuous and sometimes conflicting review processes from external agencies, which became a major drain on resources (B. Plecas, interview, 2005; C. Haynes, interview, 2004). When there was a change of government in 2001, the new Liberal government began a review of administrative justice measures across government, which resulted in the authority of the Child and Youth Advocate and the Children's Commissioner being combined in a single office that reported to the Attorney General. (Previously, the advocate had reported to the Legislature, whereas the commissioner had reported to the Attorney General, and was therefore subject to direction from the Attorney General.) The responsibility for reviewing child deaths was transferred to the Coroner's Office. An independent voice for children, and a sophisticated mechanism for reviewing child deaths, was lost in this amalgamation (Hughes, 2006; see also Chapter 9).

The Ministry for Children and Families

The establishment of the Ministry for Children and Families was a major result of Gove's work (recommendations 95-108). Initially, the government appeared hesitant about these recommendations, buying time by appointing Morton to study them. In the end, the period of study was ended more for administrative and political reasons than policy ones (Morton, 2002, p. 168), and the new ministry was created. It brought together child and family services from

- the former Ministry of Social Services (child protection, child and family support services, services to children with developmental delays)
- the Ministry of the Attorney General (youth corrections)
- the Ministry of Health (child mental health and substance misuse programs, services to children with disabilities, as well as financial responsibility – but not management responsibility – for child-related public health services)
- the Ministry of Education (school for the deaf and school-based social programs)
- the Ministry of Women's Equality (child care).

At the same time, the long-standing relationship between child welfare and income assistance services was severed, with income assistance services going to a new and separate Ministry of Human Resources.

This was a major government reorganization, and, understandably, the work of establishing the new organization became a preoccupation of senior administration (B. Plecas, interview, 2005). However, Gove had recommended not only an administrative reorganization, but also major changes in ministry philosophy and policy, including

- focusing on the welfare of all children, not just child protection (Gove, 1995b, pp. 243-49)
- introducing an infant support program similar to the Hawaii Healthy Start program (recommendation 96)

- establishing community-based children's centres as the primary means of providing services (recommendations 97-101)
- devolving responsibility for service management to the community level (recommendations 102-103)
- establishing twenty regional Child Welfare Boards composed of elected officials appointed to the boards (recommendations 104-105)
- focusing the ministry's provincial roles on policy development, service design, training, quality assurance, financial management, and board co-ordination rather than service delivery.

These recommendations were, in the main, not adopted. The new ministry was as focused on child protection as the old one had been and gave first priority to its child safety mandate. As the number of children coming into care increased substantially (see Chapter 2), resources were reallocated from preventive programs to cover the costs of children in care. The recommendations for a change in philosophy, the Healthy Start program, and community-based centres were not implemented. A measure of devolution was sought, and the ministry established regions with the same boundaries as health authorities, headed by regional operating officers, but it deferred implementing the regional boards, and service accountability remained centralized.

Aboriginal Child Welfare Policy

The significance of the Aboriginal community to child welfare policy in BC was downplayed in the findings and recommendations of the Gove Inquiry. At one level that was understandable, as neither Matthew nor his mother were from the Aboriginal community. However, the 1992 community panel reports, particularly the report of the Aboriginal committee, *Liberating our Children, Liberating our Nations* (Aboriginal Committee of the Community Panel, 1992), had clearly defined the differences in the Aboriginal experience of child protection and the need for policy built on the needs and knowledge of the Aboriginal community. Furthermore, at any time in the previous twenty-five years, between 30 and 40 percent of the children in care had been from the Aboriginal community (Foster and Wright, 2002, p. 114).

Gove's recommendations did not take these facts into account. Indeed, his recommendations on Aboriginal ancestry (recommendations 77-78) and family conferencing (recommendations 1-2), previously referred to, opposed measures that had been recommended on the basis of Aboriginal community suggestions. Gove also missed the extent to which mainstream inquiry and policy processes have, historically, been insensitive to Aboriginal issues (Schmidt, 1997, p. 75). Although Gove did commission two papers on First Nations family and child services by Herbert (Gove, 1995b, p. 327), they did not seem to influence his conclusions. However, the policy issues raised by the Aboriginal community were, in the end, too substantial to be ignored. Hence the ministry continued to set up separate delegated Aboriginal agencies, introduced family conferencing, and retained legislation that allowed Aboriginal identity to be recognized in protection hearings, all measures that appeared to be contrary to Gove's policy objectives.

Ministry Practice, Organization, and Structure

Judge Gove envisioned a new ministry that would integrate all services to children, youth, and families. Service delivery would be through community-based children's centres working under the auspices of regional boards. This vision was not put in place. Management responsibility for public health nursing services for families with children and youth remained with the Ministry of Health. Transition houses for women, and child care programs for young moms, remained with the Ministry of Women's Equality. Special needs educational services, and some child and youth care workers, remained in school districts funded by the Ministry of Education. Family court counsellors and related juvenile justice programs remained with the Ministry of Attorney General. In addition, all financial support services became part of the newly formed Ministry for Human Resources, so "some financial assistance for families in crises and for youth," which Gove recommended, did not become part of the new Ministry for Children and Families' service system. All were services that Gove had considered essential to the creation of a Ministry for Children and Families (Gove, 1995b, p. 107).

In establishing the new ministry, Bob Plecas and Penny Priddy first directed their attention to risk assessment. This resulted in the establishment of separate intake and investigation teams in all the newly established regions. The new Director of Child Protection, Ross Dawson, oversaw the creation of the positions of child protection consultant and child protection manager, and he personally provided leadership and case practice advice from Victoria. The effect of this emphasis on investigations with a clear focus on risk to the child was an increase in the numbers of children in care, from 7,600 children in September 1996 to about 9,800 by September 1998. This increase put massive pressure on all resources that were not required to service children once they were in care. One program that was sacrificed was the community development program that had been in effect since 1992 and that had been very positively evaluated for the contribution it was making to child welfare (Swets, Rutman, and Wharf, 1995).

In addition, the court system became overburdened. More and more children came into care through apprehension, often as a result of a crisis and investigation, rather than through the use of voluntary arrangements, which had been one of the intentions of the new *Child, Family and Community*

Service Act. It had been expected that children would be reunited with families after a few weeks or a few months, using a range of support options, but there were significant delays in processing and hearing the cases. Thus, children stayed in care as a result of case adjournments, made more complicated by parents contesting the apprehension. Social workers spent more and more time in court, which took them away from planning for a voluntary approach to servicing children.

Children's centres were a core element of the Gove vision, but the reality was far different. The intake teams focused on risk assessment, and the family service teams did not have sufficient alternative tools to manage families without apprehension. If financial services had been available, if preventive programs had been accessible, and if there had been a co-ordinated effort to create integrated services within a community context for child protection, this might have become a different story.

At the same time as this huge intake of children in care was occurring, the newly created external review body recommended by Gove further complicated the process of implementing his vision. Both the Children's Commissioner (recommended by Gove) and the Child, Youth and Family Advocate (recommended by the Making Changes Community Panel) were positions created to oversee the work of the ministry and report on it to the Attorney General and the cabinet, respectively. These oversight roles were new for the ministry, and they required the ministry to establish a corresponding internal system in order to communicate effectively with these agencies. Thus, regional quality-assurance offices, established throughout the regions, were linked with the provincial quality-assurance office under the jurisdiction of the Director of Child Protection.

With the addition of the new review bodies, there were up to eight external agencies that had some type of review or monitoring role over the work that was being performed, and resources used, by the ministry's child welfare services. Besides the two mentioned above, there were the Ombudsman's Office; the Coroner's Office; the Public Trustee's Office; the Auditor General; the provincial courts for all apprehensions; and the Internal Audit, located in the Office of the Comptroller General, which examined contracting practices with community agencies and service providers. Treasury Board oversaw spending and staff complements. In addition, the ministry had its own review procedures in order to ensure that it obtained as good a report as possible from the external agencies. As a result, social workers spent considerable time meeting review demands.

The requirement that the office of the Children's Commissioner review all plans of care for every child in care every nine months was even more onerous. This requirement alone created a procedural nightmare for the ministry to manage. With more than ten thousand children in care, there were ten thousand reports to be sent in; many were returned, often for what ministry staff felt were minor reasons. Just keeping track of the reports, regionally and provincially, became a huge task, which was being done only so that the ministry could say that it had met the expectations of the commissioner's office. Little of this work was perceived by social workers in the field as useful to their primary task of helping children and families.

The mandate of the Child, Youth and Family Advocate's office was less problematic to the ministry. Its primary role was to ensure that youth had more voice, while reporting on systemic issues to the legislature. This was done without requiring procedures that were onerous to the field workers, as decision making and accountability stayed with the ministry.

On a positive note, some integration did occur in various locations throughout the province. Many family service offices (as opposed to child protection intake and investigation offices) placed family service and youth social workers in the same location as mental health workers, probation officers, and youth alcohol and drug counsellors. They began to implement integrated case-practice concepts and to adopt the concept of having one case manager who did not have to be a social worker. As a result of this integration and collaboration, far fewer youth were sent to custody centres. Planning and services were provided to youth in conflict with the law through this integrated system, which allowed judges to support alternative sentencing options other than custody (T. Gove, interview, 2004). In time it became possible to close down several custody centres, reducing costs.

In addition, the total number of social workers practising in the province was increased by over three hundred positions, and caseloads per worker became lower than they had ever been.

The Ministry and the Contracted Services Sector

In seeking to establish a new child welfare system, Judge Gove made the case for an integrated and co-ordinated system of child and family services. However, in order to create such a system, the new ministry needed to establish clear roles and responsibilities for the contracted services sector. This sector had grown phenomenally since 1984, when, following the Social Credit government's 1983 restraint program, growth had been directed to it rather than to ministry offices. As a result, after two decades of change, the ministry's direct services budget had become small when compared to the cost of the services that were contracted to community agencies. At the community level, many agencies, both for profit and not for profit, were developed without the benefit of a policy or accountability framework that could rationalize, co-ordinate, and integrate the range of preventive and residential services for families, youth, and children (Korbin, 1993).

The problem this posed for the service reorganization was not formally addressed in any recommendation made by Gove. However, it was a major theme in the chapter on contracted social services contained in the report of the Commission of Inquiry into the Public Service and Public Sector (ibid.), and it was recognized by the newly formed Ministry for Children and Families in the ministry's contract and program restructuring initiative that began in 1997. This was a major attempt to create the conditions in each of the ministry's twenty regions that would see the effective integration and co-ordination of services for children, youth, and families within its jurisdiction. The initiative was also required to gain efficiencies necessary to live within the ministry's reduced budget for the 1997-98 fiscal year.

Throughout the province, community meetings were held, steering committees were established, and processes were put in place, both formal and collaborative, to achieve a vision of service integration and ensure that an equitable range of all services were available in each community. Agencies were asked to consider creating partnerships and/or consolidating their services. Intake and assessment processes were to be co-ordinated and rationalized, simplifying life for clients. Ministry staff were to work collaboratively at common tables to ensure effective and meaningful information was exchanged with contracted services staff. Case management was to be done by those staff who worked "hands on" with children and families, not just by ministry workers. Together, these changes would have gone a long way toward creating the community-based approach to the provision of children's services that Gove had advocated.

Timing, however, was not on the side of the ministry, as both Deputy Minister Plecas and Minister Priddy left in March 1998 before the necessary changes had been made. The first decision of the new minister, Lois Boone, and her deputy minister, Mike Corbeil, was to review the contract and program restructuring initiative (Allen, 1998) and then to abandon it in response to union opposition to change. Had Plecas and Priddy stayed, they might have been able to provide the leadership necessary to accomplish the much-needed restructuring of the community sector.

Qualifications and Training

The Gove Report had a major impact on university education and on ministry training programs. Until the Gove Report, the Ministry of Social Services' policy on the qualifications required for working in child protection was to give preference to applicants who had a Bachelor (or Master) of Social Work (BSW or MSW), but to accept candidates with Bachelor of Art degrees. Accepted candidates would then be prepared for child protection practice through a core training program consisting of one week of district office orientation, two weeks of training at the ministry training centre, and six weeks of self-study, on-the-job training under supervision (Gove, 1995b). Professional registration as a registered social worker was on a voluntary basis, and, in practice, few child protection workers took this step.

Gove considered these arrangements and the lack of commitment to professional qualifications totally inadequate and a major cause of the failures in case practice that had contributed to Matthew's death. In place of these arrangements, Gove made the following recommendations:

- The BSW (or MSW) degree should become the required qualification for child protection social work (recommendations 55-56).
- The schools of social work should review their curricula to ensure that there was adequate preparation for child welfare practice (recommendation 57).
- The ministry should introduce a new, competency-based, twenty-week training program for all child protection social workers (recommendation 59).
- Provisions should be made for effective professional development (recommendations 64-67).
- All social workers should be brought under the regulatory authority of their professional body (recommendations 44-47).

Immediately after the report was released, the ministry adopted the BSW (or MSW) degree as the required qualification for all social work positions. Subsequently, and after intensive lobbying, the Bachelor of Arts in Child and Youth Care (BA[CYC]) and the Masters in Educational Psychology degrees were also accepted as offering the university education required for child protection social work positions. In response to this commitment, the schools of social work and the schools of child and youth care throughout the province began comprehensive reviews of their curricula and reached agreement on the changes that would be made. The result was the development of specialized child welfare and protection programs within the BSW and BA(CYC) degrees that provided the consistency and depth of attention to child welfare work that Gove had recommended (Armitage, Callahan, and Lewis, 2001). Hiring additional faculty, making these changes in curriculum, and then teaching the required content took time, and the first graduates with a specialization in child welfare completed their programs in 2001.

Gove's proposal for a twenty-week training program was also adopted. Initially the training was offered by the MSS training division, but after the Ministry for Children and Families was established, training was contracted out through a call for proposals. The successful proposal was presented by the Educational Alliance, a consortium of BC educational institutions that was led by the Justice Institute and included the university schools of social work and child and youth care, together with college-level partners. The Educational Alliance also became the major supplier of professional development courses for child welfare workers, although this function was not developed with the consistency that Gove had recommended.

Gove's recommendations for professional regulation were not adopted. There were many obstacles to bringing all child protection workers under the regulation of the social work profession:

- Many long-time child protection workers had entered practice without social work degrees and so could not be registered.
- BA(CYC) degrees could not be brought under social work regulation.
- The ministry needed to retain direct accountability for the performance of child protection and hesitated to involve an independent professional body in making judgments about child protection practice.

A working group was set up in May 1999 to study the regulation of human and social services professions and try to overcome some of these obstacles. The working group had "overwhelming consensus ... that regulation of human and social professionals is essential" (Ministry for Children and Families, 1999, p. 6). Like many other government reports, however, this one has not yet resulted in professional regulation, although work has continued on the concept from time to time.

Nevertheless, the effect of Gove's recommendations on qualifications and training was enormous. The university programs of social work and child and youth care were brought into a much closer working relationship with the ministry and made long-term commitments to give students the education and training that he had recommended.

The Gove Report as Politics

It is said that "timing in life is everything." In 1992, the new minister of social services, Joan Smallwood, had appointed a new Superintendent of Child Welfare, Joyce Rigaux, to change the ministry's approach to child welfare. At that time, the death or serious injury of any child in care was routinely reviewed by the audit and review division. Even though few social workers had ever been disciplined as a result of a review, there was a belief, which gained currency with the new NDP government, that the low morale of MSS social workers was caused by a culture of blame.

When Rigaux took office, it was her intent to create a different culture within the ministry by developing a different approach to child welfare, an approach that would support ministry social workers and implement new preventive procedures in managing child welfare situations. When Matthew died, Rigaux ordered a review of the case that not only looked at the practice of individual social workers, but also reviewed the systemic issues that created this situation. What this audit found was not worker wrongdoing, but a series of failures of the child welfare system itself. Rigaux's report concluded that the system failed this child, who should have been removed from his mother's care. Through this report she called upon the government to increase its commitment to child protection and recommended changes that could be made to improve the child welfare system (J. Rigaux, interview, 2004).

While Rigaux's review was underway, the minister and deputy minister were replaced. Joy MacPhail was appointed minister, and Dr. Sheila Wynn was appointed deputy minister. In an interview, MacPhail said that Rigaux's review and its conclusions were totally unacceptable to her. MacPhail believed that if what had happened to Matthew was acceptable social work practice, then many other children were also at risk. Her reasoning was that if the ministry was prepared to condone this level of poor practice, then her confidence that the system could protect children was seriously impaired. As a result, MacPhail established a commission of inquiry and appointed Judge Gove to provide an independent review of the case and make recommendations to ensure these problems would not happen again (J. MacPhail, interview, 2004).

Gove had begun his career as legal counsel for the Superintendent of Child Welfare in the 1970s, and he had a great deal of knowledge about, and passion for, the rights of children and youth. He took up the task with energy and zeal. Furthermore, he wanted to ensure that the government would act on whatever recommendations he submitted. To this end, Gove chose to follow a formal public inquiry process. This ensured that the media would be able to attend the inquiry and listen to the witnesses (mainly ministry staff) called to give evidence and be cross-examined. This served to keep the story of Matthew in the public eye (T. Gove, interview, 2004), putting pressure on the government to accept and act on his recommendations.

The process of review selected meant that individual workers were named throughout the report in conjunction with the activities they apparently did or did not do. This naming of individuals ended with a judicial review in the Supreme Court of BC when the former superintendent, Joyce Rigaux, challenged Gove's written conclusions about her behaviour. The Supreme Court review, conducted by Madame Justice Marion Allan, ruled that an entire chapter should be removed from the final report that had been submitted to government. Never before in BC had a commission of inquiry's findings been challenged, and having a section ordered removed may well be a first in the British Commonwealth (Foster and Wright, 2002).

Judge Gove's strategy of keeping the media involved in the life of Matthew Vaudreuil was only partially successful. A new ministry was created that brought together some (but not all) of the programs recommended in the report. However, the funding that was needed to implement the vision was never found. Within six months of being formed, the new ministry's budget was reduced, and it was soon in a deficit budget position. Funding commitments that had been made to Bob Plecas when he accepted the appointment as deputy minister were not fulfilled (B. Plecas, interview, 2004). Under the new Director of Child Protection, Ross Dawson, administrative rigour and accountability were brought to child protection in the form of a risk-assessment tool and through the creation of specialized investigation teams. As a result, many more children were brought into care. The funds needed to pay for their care were taken from the preventive programs that were to have been the core functions of the new ministry and its regional boards. Perhaps if Penny Priddy and Bob Plecas had had six more months they would have accomplished much of the restructuring that Gove recommended. However, between September 1992 and March 1998 the ministry had five ministers and five deputies (see Appendix 2), along with corresponding changes to the executive structure, and the impetus for change that Gove had created was waning.

In the end, the Gove Inquiry was a solution to a "political" issue created by the death of Matthew Vaudreuil. However, the solution to the "political" problem came before the complex changes identified by Gove could actually be carried out. A new ministry was created to implement the vision and many of the specific recommendations, but the budget did not match the new ministry's mandate. The political resolve and stable leadership (not to mention the appropriate budget) needed to achieve integrated, co-ordinated service delivery, locally accountable to its community, had been lost, and many of the changes recommended by Gove became a list of "might have beens."

In this way the Gove Report followed the same path as the 1992 community panel report *Making Changes: A Place to Start*. It too had recommended an integrated, co-ordinated set of services accountable to community. Ironically, the Gove Inquiry slowed the momentum this report had built throughout the province for a fundamental change to child welfare services (J. Berland, interview, 2004).

Conclusions

The Gove Inquiry was a death review, and death reviews had a major impact on child protection practice and policy making in many jurisdictions during the 1990s (Reder, Duncan, and Gray, 1993). Like other death reviews (and despite its own attempts to defy the trend), it led to a reassertion of the traditional "child saving" role at the expense of other broader and more structural family and child service objectives.

The report of the Gove Inquiry led observers to think that the abuse and neglect problems faced by the child protection system could be solved by improvements in legislation, organization, management, and professional services. Such a view encouraged the idea that if the right children were taken away from their parents, the problems of neglect and abuse could be solved. Perversely, government's attempt to "protect children" used many of the resources that might have been made available to support them, as minimal funding for services was provided to change the system.

Even more perversely, the report's recommendations led to more children being placed in care, making them vulnerable to the same cycle of placement instability and deprivation that Verna Vaudreuil had experienced during her time in care.

In the end, there was a concern that the effect of increased child protection activity was not to "drain the swamp" but to make it bigger. Like other death reviews, the Gove Inquiry led to what Chris Haynes referred to as "little understanding of the child welfare enterprise as a whole" (C. Haynes, interview, 2004).

It is unfortunate that Judge Gove was unable to move beyond the scope of a "death review" and, instead, draw media and public attention to poverty's impact on the cycle of child abuse and neglect, or to the critical state of many Aboriginal children, families, and communities, from which many children come into care. Perhaps if he had been able to draw attention to these areas, the child welfare system would have been given tools that would allow it to ensure the safety of the child and work toward community-based solutions for families (particularly lone-mother families) that would stop the cycle of abuse and neglect. A community development approach and a co-ordinated strategy to offset poverty have still not been implemented as central features of a co-ordinated approach to dealing with the underlying causes of abuse and neglect. Indeed, the overall impact of the Gove Inquiry was to make the adoption of such a strategy even more distant.

Notes

1 Joyce Rigaux had been dismissed for an unrelated expense account concern, not for any failure in her duty as superintendent. Rigaux rejected this cause for dismissal and was successful in an action against the government for damages.
2 Many ministry staff regarded the suspensions and disciplinary actions in the Baker case as unwarranted and unfair, with the social workers being "singled out" in order to convey a political message of "toughness."

Persons interviewed

Jeremy Berland. Director of Family and Child Service Division, MSS, MCF, 1995-97; director of special projects, MCF, 1997-2000; executive director of Aboriginal services, MCF, MCFD, 2000-03; MCFD assistant deputy minister, 2003-present. Interviewed 2004.

Justice Thomas Gove. Commissioner of public inquiry into child protection in BC, 1994-95. Interviewed 2004.

Chris Haynes. MSS assistant deputy minister, 1990-96; MCFD deputy minister, 2001-04. Interviewed 2004.

Joy MacPhail. Minister of social services, 1993-96. Interviewed 2004.

Bob Plecas. Deputy minister of the Ministry for Children and Families, 1996-98. Interviewed 2005.

Joyce Preston. Child and Youth Advocate, 1994-2000. Interviewed 2004.
Joyce Rigaux. Superintendent of Family and Child Services, 1992-94. Interviewed 2004.

References

Aboriginal Committee of the Community Panel on Family and Children's Services Legislation Review. (1992). *Liberating our children, liberating our nations.* Victoria: Ministry of Social Services.

Allen, D. (1998). *Contract and program restructuring review: Report to the Honourable Lois Boone.* Victoria: Ministry for Children and Families.

Armitage, A. (1998, Summer). Lost vision: Children and the Ministry for Children and Families. *BC Studies, 118,* 93-108.

Armitage, A., Callahan, M., and Lewis, C. (2001). Social work education and child protection: The BC experience. *Canadian Social Work Review, 18*(1), 9-24.

Bala, N., Zapf, K.M., Williams, R.J., Vogle, R., and Hornick, J.P. (2004). *Canadian child welfare law* (2nd ed.). Toronto: Thompson Educational Publishing.

Callahan, M., and Callahan, K. (1997). Victims and villains: Scandals, the press and policy making in child welfare. In J. Pulkingham and G. Ternowetsky (Eds.), *Child and family policies: Struggles, strategies and options* (pp. 40-57). Halifax: Fernwood.

Community Panel on Family and Children's Services Legislation Review. (1992). *Making changes: A place to start.* Victoria: Ministry of Social Services.

Durie, H., and Armitage, A. (1995). *Legislative change: The development of BC's Child, Family and Community Service Act and Child and Family Community Advocacy Act.* Victoria: University of Victoria, School of Social Work, Child, Family and Community Research Program.

Foster, L.T., and Wright, M. (2002). Patterns and trends in children in the care of the province of British Columbia: Ecological, policy and cultural perspectives. In M.V. Hayes and L.T. Foster (Eds.), *Too small to see, too big to ignore: Child health and well-being in British Columbia* (pp. 103-40). Canadian Western Geographical Series, Vol. 35. Victoria: Western Geographical Press.

Gove, T. (1995a). *Report of the Gove Inquiry into Child Protection in BC. Vol. 1. Matthew's story.* Victoria: Ministry of Attorney General.

–. (1995b). *Report of the Gove Inquiry into Child Protection in BC. Vol. 2. Matthew's legacy.* Victoria: Ministry of Attorney General.

–. (1995c, 31 March). *Interim report: Letter to the Lieutenant-Governor in Council.* Victoria: Ministry of Attorney General.

Hughes, E.N. (2006). *BC children and youth review: An independent review of BC's child protection system.* Victoria: Ministry of Children and Family Development.

Korbin, J. (1993). *Commission of inquiry into the public service and public sector.* Victoria: Ministry of Attorney General.

Ministry for Children and Families. (1999, November). *Report of the working group on regulation of social service professions.* Victoria: Author.

Morton, C. (1996). *Morton report: British Columbia's child, youth and family serving system – Recommendations for change.* Victoria: Transition Commissioner for Child and Youth Services.

–. (2002). Learning from the past: Improving child-serving systems. In M.V. Hayes and L.T. Foster (Eds.), *Too small to see, too big to ignore: Child health and well-being in British Columbia* (pp. 161-92). Canadian Western Geographical Series, Vol. 35. Victoria: Western Geographical Press.

Reder, P., Duncan, S., and Gray, M. (1993). *Beyond blame: Child abuse tragedies revisited.* London: Routledge.

Schmidt, G. (1997). The Gove Report and First Nations child welfare. In J. Pulkingham and G. Ternowetsky (Eds.), *Child and family policies: Struggles, strategies and options* (pp. 75-84). Halifax: Fernwood.

Swets, R., Rutman, D., and Wharf, B. (1995). The community development initiative of the Ministry of Social Services. Victoria: University of Victoria, School of Social Work, Child, Family and Community Research Program.

8

Great Expectations and Unintended Consequences: Risk Assessment in Child Welfare in British Columbia

Marilyn Callahan and Karen Swift

For over fifty years, since its inception at the turn of the twentieth century, public child welfare in British Columbia has been largely governed by a professional-managerial alliance. Early reformers in child welfare in British Columbia forged a strong partnership with government managers as they fought for legislation and public funding for what were mostly voluntary efforts. (Unfortunately, Aboriginal leaders have consistently been left out of this partnership.) In time, managers in child welfare, including those in government and the large children's aid societies, were almost always experienced social work practitioners, a criterion for obtaining their positions. Supervision focused on improving the quality of practice as well as ensuring the implementation of policy.

Since the early 1980s, however, particularly as governments began contracting out many services to non-government providers (Callahan and McNiven, 1988), there has been a gradual shift from this professional-managerial partnership of governance to a system almost solely controlled by managerial approaches. (Note that some individuals occupying mid-level and senior management positions may have social work training or field experience, but the emphasis is on managerial approaches.) This has limited the influence and scope of social work and continued the virtual absence of Aboriginal perspectives in shaping overall policy. This trend is not confined to BC, but is evident broadly as neo-liberal thinking has gained prominence (Ife, 2001). The professional bureaucracy has been transformed into one modelled on the business world (Parada, 2002) but with little input from its customers.

Ironically, many of the seeds for this shift to managerial approaches are contained in the professional discourses of social work itself, as well as in the managerial discourses intent on transforming welfare systems in a post-welfare world. The intent of this chapter is to examine the development of risk assessment in BC over the decade and a half between 1990 and 2005 and to demonstrate how it has continued the process of transforming social work into a set of management activities. The chapter will also explore some of the consequences of these shifts for social work practice (see also Anglin, 2002; Armitage, 1998).

Data for this study were collected through a series of interviews with five key informants who were involved in the development of risk assessment in BC, ten social workers throughout the province who use it in their daily practice, and twelve parents who have been through the risk-assessment process. We also held a focus group for workers in contract agencies involved in creating risk-reduction plans with parents, and we examined the many documents related to risk assessment. Practitioners and parents helped us understand how these documents are put into action in the risk-assessment process.

Theoretical Perspectives on Risk and Risk Assessment

Globalizing tendencies toward economic growth and exploitation of new global markets are closely tied to the restructuring of "liberal welfare governments" (Kelly, 2001), including Canada's. Neo-liberalism is the political approach taken to support this direction. Neo-liberal governments concern themselves with facilitating the global movement of capital and producing wealth, at least for some. These goals are given priority over support and assistance to people "in need" and, in fact, require that these individuals decrease their demands on the state and simultaneously increase their activities as producers and consumers in service to economic growth.

Rose (1996) has theorized "risk" as one of the organizing concepts of this shift in governing. Neo-liberals contend that welfare states shared substantially in the costs of meeting needs during previous decades and thus created budget deficits and unacceptably high taxes by the turn of the century. Neo-liberal regimes typically focus on reducing taxes and shifting away from notions of present need and social problems. Instead, they use the organizing concept of risk, focusing on possible future harms that individuals themselves must address, while the new task of governments is to create smaller "risk classes" requiring state support (Rosanvallon, 2000).

Strategies for accomplishing the shift from the welfare state to the neo-liberal agenda are often referred to as the new managerialism, which brings management practices from business into public services, including social welfare. Social and economic issues are viewed as problems to be addressed by management practices. Tsui and Cheung (2004) list eight features of new managerial strategies, including a strong focus on the market rather than society or community; efficiency rather than effectiveness as the main criterion of success; money and contracts rather than care and concern as the "foundation" of relationships; and standardization as the measure of quality in service provision. In this scenario, professional knowledge is subordinate to managerial knowledge, and professionals themselves are less important, since managers can carry out required tasks through delegation and standardized controls.

Together, the shift in focus from need to risk and the strategy of managerialism have produced the administrative tools for "risk assessment," which are widely used in human services. These tools are supposed to predict difficulties and dangers in advance so that administrative steps can be taken to manage problems and reduce, deflect, or obviate the need for actual services.

Castel (1991), tracing how this transformation has occurred in psychiatry and mental health over time, contends that professionals have participated in the makeover of their discipline, at least initially. Risk thinking fits with professional concerns about preventing problems before they occur or become unmanageable. However, Castel concludes that the promise of risk assessment has been unfulfilled. He states that professionals are increasingly expected to use their expertise in classification using progressively more technical tools instead of working with clients. Some of this same transformation has occurred in child welfare, as this chapter will illustrate.

Child welfare has always concerned itself with assessing the safety of children within their families, but formal risk-assessment instruments and procedures, introduced in the last decade in several jurisdictions, add other dimensions to investigations. Although risk assessment includes an initial assessment of immediate safety concerns, it is first and foremost "a process of *predicting* whether or not a child will be maltreated at some future point in time" (Jones, 1994, p. 1037) and is based on identifying particular characteristics shared by specific groups (Silver and Miller, 2002). Two types of risk-assessment items are used in child welfare: actuarial (based on research similar to that used for car insurance) and consensus (based on professionals' views about which are the most important items). Previously, child welfare investigations were mostly limited to assessing the present safety of children. They did so by examining the particular features of an individual case. Now, regardless of the method used, risk-assessment items are expected to predict future harm to children.

Although risk-assessment instruments vary in their length and rating criteria, they typically require workers to gather information and score parents and children on a number of dimensions, adding considerably to the factors for which parents are held accountable. Most of the twenty-three items in the New York risk assessment model, used in BC and Ontario, focus on child-specific factors (such as the age of the child and the number of children in the home) and caretaker factors (such as the caretaker's abilities, age, and previous history). Other factors include family characteristics (marital status, family coping abilities), environmental factors (home living conditions, community supports), and service-related factors (co-operation with agency). Risk assessment places emphasis on gathering evidence from various sources upon which scores are determined. Workers score parents on each variable according to a four-point scale, with descriptors provided for each level.

Risk assessment is not just a set of instruments but also a work process that moves through a series of stages from evaluating the initial complaint to making an immediate safety assessment and then creating a risk assessment and risk-reduction plan. The activities of each stage are outlined in detail through practice standards and agency policy. In most large child welfare agencies, including many district offices in BC, different social workers are assigned responsibility for different stages. The "case" moves from one worker at screening and intake to a second worker for investigation, a third worker for developing and monitoring the risk-reduction plan, and a fourth worker, often an employee of an agency contracted by government, to work with the family to implement the plan. The "file," with its standardized format, becomes the key to connecting the activities of these workers.

Setting the Stage for Risk Assessment in British Columbia

By 1985, risk assessment was emerging in the United States and United Kingdom as one response to a number of highly publicized child welfare "scandals" in which social workers had removed children, seemingly precipitously, from their parents or left them in dangerous situations (Parton, Thorpe, and Wattam, 1997; Schene and Bond, 1989). At the same time, the rising number of reports to child welfare organizations about child abuse and neglect situations, in part a result of these "scandals," led to the system becoming overburdened with work and chronically underfunded. In BC, the number of children in the care of government, which had fallen steadily over the previous two and a half decades, began to rise in 1994 (Trocme and Siddiqi, 2002; see also Chapter 2).

The first formal consideration of risk assessment in BC occurred in 1990. Two independent experts from Manitoba, Eric Sigurdson and Grant Reid made a two-day presentation to the Superintendent of Child Welfare and other key policy makers in the Ministry of Child and Family Development (MCFD)[1] on the development and use of risk-assessment instruments (see Reid, Sigurdson, Wright, and Christianson-Wood, 1996). In an interview for this chapter, one participant clearly recalled his impressions of those meetings:

> The more they talked, the more skeptical I became about what they were saying. The results seemed very questionable, you know, about what it was that we were preventing and how perfected it was ... And by the end of it, by about noon on the second day, most of the people, the ministry people that were there, ... [it] just didn't seem to make any sense to us, that the process would get you to a different result than a good social work interview

with a family, do a family history, you know, find out details and make direct observations of what was going on at home ... And we didn't go any further with it ... You know, we really, it had seemed interesting and very appealing because, you know, you can come to some clear conclusions and do all this stuff and there would be no doubt it would be, that kind of thing would be helpful. But ... there were too many questions about the research and too many questions about the usefulness beyond the obvious. And who needs a risk-assessment tool for the obvious? ... It's in difficult cases that you need some help ... We didn't have another discussion about risk assessment again for a couple of years. (Key informant, May 2003)

During the next two years, several events occurred that placed risk assessment more firmly on the child welfare agenda in BC. The provincial government changed from a Social Credit to a New Democratic Party (NDP) administration, a shift that, given the stated policies of the NDP, invigorated calls for reform in child welfare. The government appointed two panels to investigate the state of Aboriginal and non-Aboriginal child welfare and to make recommendations for changes in legislation and policy directions. (The Aboriginal panel was not appointed initially but was convened after protests from Aboriginal peoples about their interests being combined with those of mainstream child welfare.) The panels presented their findings in two reports, *Liberating our Children, Liberating our Nations* and *Making Changes* (Aboriginal Committee of the Community Panel, 1992; Community Panel, 1992). Both documents debated ideology and goals for child welfare without paying much attention to the particulars of legislation and policy. Neither report advocated for risk assessment in any formal sense, but both reinforced the need for change, with *Making Changes* arguing for preventive intervention and resources, and *Liberating Our Children* affirming the crucial need for a shift in values (see Chapter 6). Subsequent legislation, the *Child, Family and Community Service Act (CFCSA)* and the *Child, Youth and Family Advocacy Act*, reflected some but by no means all of the aspirations contained in these reports, dealing most meagrely with those recommendations from the Aboriginal panel (Armitage, 1998; Wharf, 1993).

Yet the legislation was a major shift from the previous act, expanding the definition of child welfare from a narrow focus on child protection to include also the provision of family supports and family involvement in child welfare processes. Most importantly for this discussion, it also contained authority for the development of risk assessment by expanding the definition of children in need of protection. Previous legislation focused only on children who were harmed at present or in the past, but Section 13(1) a, b, c, and d of the *CFCSA* included the phrase "has been or is likely to be" when defining child maltreatment, introducing the notion of future harm and the necessity of being able to predict it. Among other features of the legislation were alternatives to investigating every complaint in an attempt to manage the burgeoning number of investigations facing child welfare workers (Section 16 of *CFCSA*).

Responding to Crisis: The Gove Inquiry and the Necessity of Risk Assessment

The NDP government was in the midst of introducing this legislation in the BC legislature in June 1994, when it was shaken by a series of media stories focusing on the death of Matthew Vaudreuil, a five-year-old child who died in 1992, and on the government's apparent inability to prevent the death and deal with it afterwards (see Chapter 7). The NDP minister of social services, Joy MacPhail, agreed to commission a judicial inquiry into the death and appointed Thomas Gove, a provincial court judge, to lead the investigation. In his first interim report in March 1995, Justice Gove recommended that the aims of the new legislation be modified to make the safety of the individual child the paramount concern of child welfare, a recommendation that was quickly implemented. Gove's final report, issued in November 1995, continued this stated emphasis on safety and the accompanying administrative systems that were supposed to ensure it. In its haste to put the matter behind it, the beleaguered government promised to implement all the final report's recommendations (Gove, 1995).

Two specific recommendations dealt with risk assessment. Recommendation 15 stated that "child protection social workers must complete a comprehensive risk assessment when investigating a child protection report. The risk assessment should include corroboration from collaterals of explanations for injuries or neglect which the parent may give about the child. The assessment should not give 'strengths' of the parent disproportionate weight" (ibid., Vol. 2, p. 75). Recommendation 9 emphasized that "child protection investigations should be done by qualified and experienced social workers who have been specifically trained in investigation and risk assessment" (ibid., p. 69). (In preparing the inquiry report, Gove commissioned a number of background papers. None of these focused on risk assessment, and the concept is mentioned only briefly in two of them. We do not know how Judge Gove conceived of risk assessment or what material he used to make these recommendations.)

In citing his rationale for these recommendations, Justice Gove claimed that risk assessment and its numerical scoring could improve empirical accuracy of decision making and make for more standardized assessments across the province. Yet he also cautioned that "the danger with standardized forms is that they may come to be seen as a replacement for professional skill and judgment. No formal risk assessment system can replace social worker judgment and the ability of the social workers to complete a thorough assessment of the child and family" (ibid., p. 74).

In September 1995, two months before Gove's final recommendations were made public, the ministry set up a planning group to develop approaches to improve child protection work. The planning group, composed of some ministry staff and outside professional experts, conducted a survey of key people in the community and ministry to identify the most urgent needs for child protection. Risk assessment emerged as the top priority, which was not surprising given the attention that the Gove Inquiry had focused on social workers' seeming inability to protect a young child. The team consulted with Ross Dawson, former director of the Institute for the Prevention of Child Abuse in Ontario. Dawson had experience in risk assessment and subsequently became a member of the planning group. It also held meetings with Diane English, an American scholar who has written extensively on risk assessment.

Afterward, team members examined various risk-assessment instruments already in existence and settled on the New York model. Team members thought that this particular model was less prescriptive and offered more room for professional judgment than others under consideration. They also talked about the research base underpinning the model. In many ways, it is not surprising that the New York model was selected. Many of the same criteria for assessing whether children were in need of protection were already in use in BC, including such factors as

- the age and vulnerability of the child, including the child's ability to protect himself
- the extent and severity of injuries/neglect, including previous reports of unexplained injuries or chronic, severe neglect
- the ability of the non-abusing parent to protect the child, including the location and access of offender to child
- the parent's mental or emotional condition, including the impact of parental behaviour on child
- the availability of family support, including the home environment and family dynamics
- the parental ability to admit responsibility and use supports and services
- the availability of community support
- the reliability of the information of reporters or collaterals.

However, social workers in BC were also required to consider strengths of the parent, a very limited feature of the New York model. In this respect, the model also fit nicely with Gove's recommendation, cited earlier, that strengths of the parent were to be given no special weight. Although there was some talk among team members and social workers about modifications that were necessary to fit the circumstances of BC (Sullivan, 1997, p. 1), few if any alterations actually occurred.

The team held high hopes that risk assessment would advance professional social work practice in child welfare. One team member mentioned that if individual risks could be documented through a "scientific" instrument such as risk assessment, then workers and their clients and even the courts would have a stronger case to insist that services required by families to reduce risk should be provided (Key informant, October 2003). Another team member commented that risk assessment, buttressed by a centralized resource team, was viewed as a way to provide a standardized approach to practice throughout the province, adding that "Gove pointed that out very clearly, that there wasn't a standardized approach. There wasn't a framework. So social workers that were doing good child protection practice were doing it because they had the background and the supervision. But unfortunately that wasn't the case for many" (Key informant, September 2003). A third team member mentioned that risk assessment had the potential to organize workers' testimony in court, giving it more force and making it easier for provincial court judges to reach their decisions (Key informant, September 2003).

Implementing Risk Assessment: The Best-Laid Schemes ...

The planning group also recommended a lengthy and comprehensive implementation process, reckoning that harried workers would resist the imposition of the model, and that graduated implementation involving the sixteen child abuse consultants throughout the province would yield better co-operation. The government had appointed Ross Dawson as Director of Child Protection. Dawson was well-known for his commitment to a professional role for social workers in child welfare, a role that emphasized social workers' clinical expertise in making assessments and developing service plans for individuals and families. He also identified strongly with the dangers that children might find themselves in because of their parents' circumstances and behaviour. His particular view of social work as primarily a clinical activity was shared by members of the planning group.

While the group was carrying out its work, further difficulties beset the ministry. The government urged that the timetable for implementation of Gove's recommendations be speeded up substantially, largely because the premier apparently wanted to fast-track the whole implementation process in the context of fresh cases reported in the legislature and media about child protection problems and the apparent foot-dragging within the bureaucracy (Morton, 2002; Petch and Scarth, 1997). Pressures mounted on child welfare officials to implement risk assessment quickly.

Assigned to guide this task and to manage the most comprehensive of Gove's recommendations – the unification of all government services for children in one ministry – was a new deputy minister, Robert Plecas, who had a reputation as a formidable manager under the previous Social Credit government (see Chapter 7). That the NDP would have appointed him was a surprise because of his past and close association with previous Social Credit administrations, but it was perhaps a measure of the daunting organizational tasks to be undertaken quickly. One of our informants recalled Plecas's views on child protection: "It was basically whatever could be expedited, and Bob Plecas, I remember him saying this at a team meeting, that anybody can do this work. You don't have to be a social worker to do this. Anybody can do it. That kind of jaded perspective. There were a lot of things that were hard to swallow, let me tell you" (Key informant, May 2003).

At the same time, planning group members felt that they had lost the support of influential champions for risk assessment as a professional practice tool when Chris Haynes and Joy MacPhail left the ministry. Haynes, a longstanding experienced practitioner and assistant deputy minister, who had authorized the formation of the planning group, left for another post in government. MacPhail, who had been minister of social services and who was a powerhouse in cabinet, also transferred to another ministry. The leadership of the ministry continued to change until the defeat of the NDP government, with six ministers and five deputy ministers responsible for child protection between 1996 and 2000, continuing the trend of rapid turnovers that began in the late 1980s (Foster and Wright, 2002; see also Appendix 2).

Early in 1997, members of the planning group were advised that all workers had to be trained in the risk-assessment model by the end of March, with no room to implement the developmental aspects of the model, which included learning from experience and modifying the instrument on the basis of that experience (Sullivan, 1997). The sixteen child abuse consultants, who were decentralized throughout the province and who reported to the leader of the planning group, were gradually reassigned to their regional managers. Risk-assessment training was hurriedly put into place, but little time was spent developing and training for the risk-reduction aspect of the policy. By the end of April 1997, 1,526 staff, including 258 supervisors, had completed the training (ibid.). Personnel changes occurred during this time. Early retirement packages had been offered to experienced workers, presumably as a cost-saving measure, and 180 of the social workers assigned to implement the *CFCSA* were relatively new to the job. A staff member at headquarters described how, under the pressures of publicity, time, inexperience, and workload, the developmental process was transformed into a prescriptive one:

At some point, I think in 1997, child protection standards were developed that replaced the complex policy associated with the new act. The standards, instead of being enabling, tended to be prescriptive and were designed with the risk assessment in mind. So we got a group of staff together, Ross [Dawson] included. We took the policy manual, and what we did was, we developed a set of standards, well, what became a set of standards. And now we have risk assessment, which is just about ready. Risk assessment became absolutely integral in those standards. It became a central part to the way the standards document developed ... And we didn't really eliminate any policy, but it was redrafted into a set of must-do's, must-do statements. And so now you have a standard that says you must do a risk assessment. So instead of saying ... take a look at section 16 (of the legislation) and do what section 16 says, you get the information and then you decide what you're going to do. We moved directly into the lock-step approach that we were trying to get away from, which was you must do risk assessment ...

The people were so overwhelmed with work. The numbers [of intakes] weren't going down. They stood, the total number of intakes has actually not changed very much for quite a long time. It hovers, I think we hit our peak around 32,000, but it hovers up to, between 30,000 and 32,000. (Key informant, May 2003)

Part of the job of reorganizing the ministry into a super-ministry charged with all programs related to children and families involved developing compatible computer systems for new divisions and transforming paper documents, such as files and policies, into computer documents. Risk assessment became part of these computer records. Completing risk assessments became a demanding computer job that occupied a great deal of time and actually could perpetuate misinformation. One informant explained that

if you do not fill out every [computer] screen on the assessment, then you can't move to the next screen. So, if you don't have adequate information, you enter a score of 9 in order to move to the next screen. When staff are clearing up old files or incomplete risk assessments, they may see a lot of 9s and should go and gather more information. But busy staff don't have time. So when they do the next risk assessment, they may or may not find information to improve the last one or may perpetuate the errors of the previous one by continuing to use 9s. Thus it might look like two or three risk assessments have been done, but in fact these are largely incomplete. (Key informant, May 2003)

Planning group members felt that one of the casualties of this hurried implementation was the whole issue of risk reduction. They had envisioned a process in which, after risks were identified, there would be space for identifying family strengths, making a thorough assessment of the family, and designing with them a plan to reduce risks. There were still opportunities to take these steps, and they were included in the documents, but they came after all the negative features of the family had been featured, and they occupied a much smaller and less well-defined part of the work process. Social workers mentioned how these steps can be rushed or overlooked in practice. It is not clear why implementation of risk assessment was hurried while other Gove recommendations were tackled on a leisurely basis or abandoned over time. However, risk assessment looked like the answer to many of the problems with social work decision making that had been raised by the media, and it was already a feature of child welfare systems in other jurisdictions.

The NDP government was defeated in 2001, after the risk-assessment process had been entrenched in child welfare practice. The new Liberal government found no reason to tamper with it until it became apparent that it might be contributing to the increasing number of children in care. With a promise to reduce these numbers, the government began to consider some alternatives to risk assessment, an issue discussed in the final section of this chapter. Regardless of their differing ideological stances, risk assessment as a management practice appealed to both political parties.

The Compatibility of Professional Thinking and Managerial Practices

The central point in this narrative is that rather than advancing professional practice in child welfare, as those in the planning group envisioned, risk assessment has contributed to the erosion of professional practice and has strengthened managerialism's hold on child welfare. The people we interviewed for this chapter confirmed this impression, with some qualifications, giving mixed reviews of risk assessment eight years after its introduction.

The planning group members made a persuasive case that it was the hurried introduction of risk assessment, amid enormous staff changes and at a time of reduced federal transfers for social spending (Sullivan, 1998), that led to its use as a managerial tool. Sullivan states that risk assessment was supposed to be an *aide-mémoire* for practitioners that would provide "a framework for clinical judgment in the social worker's assessment of the factors in individual and family life central to safe outcomes in child welfare" (ibid., p. 1). Thus, this story could be told as one in which professional dreams were dashed because of political expediency and managerial imperatives. This may be largely true, but it is not as simple as that.

From the beginning, social workers, politicians, and managers were on the same page – how could they prevent child maltreatment scandals that harm children and tarnish the reputation of government and the social work profession?[2] Risk assessment seemed like the answer. Although there was some skepticism that risk assessment could deliver on this central promise, there was little professional debate about it in the ministry, the professional social work community, or the child welfare literature (some exceptions include Swift, 2001; Wald and Woolverton, 1990). The context of the times, with the daily and unremitting public criticism of social work practice and government ineptness in child protection, quelled debate to some extent. However, it is important to examine critically some of the assumptions and features of risk assessment. It can be like the proverbial Trojan Horse, spiriting managerial assumptions into professional practices. Ross Dawson (Callahan and Dawson, 2001), in defending risk assessment as a professional tool, succinctly outlines three particular elements of risk assessment that seem to bring together managerial and professional discourses and thus push forward the risk-assessment agenda.

The Importance of Prediction

Both government policy makers and social workers in the planning group hoped that risk assessment would make it possible to identify which parents were most likely to abuse or neglect their children in future. For professionals, this ability to predict meant that they would then be able to develop appropriate responses for those particular parents and prevent future maltreatment of children, a long-sought professional goal. Moreover, as more than one key informant told us, risk assessment could help garner resources because after the risk assessment of an individual family was completed, it would be politically dangerous to ignore its findings. Badly needed resources would be found. Further, social workers anticipated that reducing risk would involve working with families on jointly developed plans emerging from their professional assessments.

What professionals did not foresee was that the prediction of who was "at risk" could be used as a management tool to limit the development of resources. Risk assessment claims to offer a means to restrict the number of people in the "risk" class, and these people will be required to reduce their own risk variables. The tools can be administered so that only those who score at a particular level can be admitted to the class, and these scores can vary according to resources. It is significant that most risk-assessment models were introduced in response to the overwhelming number of complaints and were seen as a way to narrow the focus of child welfare (English and Pecora, 1994). Thus, for management, predicting who might maltreat their children in future becomes an efficient and defensible means of triaging resources, not expanding them.

Throughout the development of risk assessment in BC, few voices questioned the capacity of risk assessment to actually predict who might or might not maltreat their children. Repeatedly, written documents (Callahan and Dawson, 2001; Sullivan, 1997) and verbal accounts from key informants and social workers that we interviewed for this study referred to the grounding of risk assessment in research. *The Risk Assessment Model for Child Protection in British Columbia* states that it is a "well researched instrument designed to predict future harm to children" (Ministry for Children and Families, 1996, p. 3). Although it is true that there is some agreement in research about which factors professionals *think* are associated with child maltreatment, there is little research confirming that these factors *are actually predictors* of future maltreatment of children. Even Diane English, one of the key consultants to the planning group, was writing at the time about the uncertainty of the research in terms of risk assessment's capacity to predict. She and co-author Peter Pecora, reviewing the results of research in risk assessment and remarking favourably on the prospect of continuing research, nonetheless agreed with the statement that "much of the literature criticizes efforts to develop predictive models for abuse because of a lack of clarity in definitions of risk factors and outcomes, methodological problems with previous research, and poor specificity and sensitivity of models that have been developed" (English and Pecora, 1994, p. 458).

Research almost a decade later revealed many of the same problems. In the most wide-ranging review of the literature, sponsored by the North American Resource Centre on Child Welfare, the authors examine the issues of predictability in risk assessment and state that "the preponderance of research literature continues to raise serious questions about the reliability and validity of most of the risk assessment models and instruments currently used by child welfare agencies. In practice, many child welfare professionals are making decisions about children and families with little more accuracy than flipping a coin, while believing they are using technologies that reduce subjectivity and bias, and that increase the quality of their decisions" (Rycus and Hughes, 2003, p. 23).

Because risk assessment promised both professionals and managers in BC a way to predict, neither dug beneath its promises to see if they were substantive.

Standardization as Quality
One of the promises of risk assessment is that it will provide a standard format for carrying out investigations and undertaking work with families. The same variables will be considered in each case, and workers will judge these variables using the same scales. The step-by-step process for making decisions about children's safety will be laid out for each worker to follow. Indeed the risk-assessment instruments and work process introduced into BC were touted for their ability to harmonize the actions of social workers throughout the province in the face of complex and unique family, cultural, and community circumstances, as well as different levels of training and experience for social workers (Callahan and Dawson, 2001). One of the first evaluations of the implementation of the risk-assessment model focused on

ascertaining whether social workers, when given similar case vignettes, would score them similarly using the risk-assessment instrument.

For social workers, it is desirable to think that a high standard of practice exists when different workers nonetheless assess problems in a similar fashion and recommend similar remedies. It suggests that there is a "science" to the work and not merely a personal response. Social workers believe that achieving this kind of standardization will occur primarily through increased training and practice experience, and that the use of tools such as risk assessments provide a framework for thinking rather than a recipe for action. Social workers also believe that when clients receive similar levels of service from different workers, it means that clients will not be disadvantaged wherever they go for assistance. Social workers in child protection, where families are often in crisis and children in danger, mention the importance of standardization for ensuring that their work is measured favourably should something go wrong. As long as social workers have completed all the steps and documents in the standardized fashion, then their work will be assessed as meeting the standard for child protection, a connection with accountability that will be discussed later in this chapter.

For managers, standardization has a somewhat different meaning and purpose. They also aim to ensure that service is the same wherever it is delivered, but they place additional emphasis on the use of standardization to ensure that the activities of social workers and parents can be itemized, monitored, and ultimately controlled and measured. In Ontario, the risk-assessment model has been used in precisely this fashion, facilitating government allocations to individual children's aid societies. Workers' activities are identified, the time needed to complete these activities is estimated, and funding formulas are developed on the basis of these measures (Parada, 2002; Swift and Parada, 2004). Such precision has not occurred in child welfare investigations in BC, where government funds all services directly. But risk assessment has brought new levels of specificity to contracts between workers and parents or between government and community-based agencies that undertake risk reduction. For instance, informants showed us contracts that require parents to be able to name three age-appropriate behaviours for their particular children or four approaches to dealing with misbehaviour. This may have benefits, as it gives clients, workers, and contract agencies clear expectations and may be used to measure outcomes. It can also transform "good parenting" into a list of specific behaviours that may be difficult for the most marginalized parents to achieve and that may not actually result in improved conditions for children.

Documentation as Accountability

At the heart of the critique of child welfare played out in the media and in judicial inquiries is the idea that it is an unaccountable system in which social workers apparently "get away with" inappropriate actions that harm children and parents do not get caught. The first stated objective of the BC risk-assessment model is to "reduce the likelihood of further incidents of abuse" and to "improve documentation of major risk decisions" (Ministry for Children and Families, 1996, p. 1). Thus, accountability to children appears to be at the core of the aims of risk assessment.

Social workers agree to some extent with the value of risk assessments in making clear their decision-making process, apparently bringing a previously murky process into the open. No longer must clients puzzle about why the worker decided to remove their children, for instance, because workers can show them the risk assessment and their scores. Ross Dawson makes this plain when he writes that "a visible, articulated risk assessment model can also be a tool through which families can seek to hold child protective services accountable for their actions. By knowing how child protection decisions are made, families can seek to change assessments and decisions by providing additional information, correcting errors, and challenging interpretations and conclusions. This level of openness and accountability is not possible when risk assessment is an informal process undertaken differently by each individual practitioner" (Callahan and Dawson, 2001, p. 153).

Many of the social workers we interviewed showed the risk document to at least some of their clients and discussed the evidence and scores with them as part of the investigation process, although nowhere in the policy manual does it state that this is a requirement. Workers also said that the documents are useful for gaining the attention of recalcitrant parents. One worker described these benefits clearly:

> It brings it on the table and I really think it offers the opportunity for the client to put down in the record what they think. [They'll say,] "Oh, you know, I don't agree with that. You've rated me a four. Forget it. I'm definitely not a four." [I say,] "Well, how come? What makes you think that you are not a four?" ... They'll go off on a tangent and I'll say, "Yeah, but I have this information here" or "You're right. I can live with that. And you're right, you're right, I probably rated that too high. I must have had something going on. You're right I don't have that correct information. I don't mind dropping that down a notch." Sometimes I get caught on the threes, fours, and I say, "It doesn't really matter, they are pretty close, both high risk." (Key informant, April 2004)

Some parents brought their risk assessments with them to our interviews and seemed knowledgeable about the basis of different scores, although they may disagree with them. Similarly, in court proceedings, social workers stated that they are able to produce much clearer evidence using the risk-assessment documents than they could do previously. All decried the time that was required to complete the risk-assessment documentation, time that they wished could be spent in face-to-face work with families and children.

However, some social workers also stated that although risk assessments appear to document their decisions and make plain the evidence they used to make such decisions, they actually obfuscate the values and assumptions that come into play as they think about evidence and scoring. These decisions are not value free. What evidence is collected and evaluated depends on theoretical and ideological positions. Some workers believed that it made their knowledge even more powerful than the views of their clients. It also narrowed the range of issues to consider to the items on the safety and risk-assessment instruments.

For managers, the documentary features of risk assessment have considerable value as well. It gives them written records of the activities of workers, which they can use to explain the outcomes for any particular case. The tasks of supervisors and managers are also clarified through the risk-assessment process, in which their roles are specifically identified. According to one of our key informants, audit teams can make thorough assessments of compliance with standards and procedures and can rate offices based on the percentage of cases that have been appropriately documented.

Some Outcomes of Prediction, Standardization, and Documentation

It is clear that social workers and managers shared some common beliefs about what risk assessment could offer them in dealing with the difficult challenges of child protection. Although their understanding of each issue differed, they agreed that risk assessment could help them predict which parents might harm their children in future, could offer a standardized service, and could allow them to document work so that accountability would be clear. However, in practice, these three issues have played out in unexpected ways for both managers and social workers.

Ironically, neither social workers nor managers realized what they thought would be the benefits of prediction in risk assessment. More parents did not get the help they needed to prevent further child maltreatment, which was what the social workers hoped for, and the caseload in child protection was not reduced, as the managers had hoped. After the introduction of risk assessment in 1997, child protection activities increased markedly, as Table 8.1 illustrates.

What is important about this increased activity is that requests for voluntary service – where parents themselves usually called for assistance – was the only category where the workload decreased; the numbers of protection reports, investigations, children under supervision, and children in care

Table 8.1

Child protection activities in British Columbia, 1993-2000

Multiple measures	1993-94	1994-95	1995-96	1996-97	1997-98	1998-99	1999-2000
Voluntary request for service							
Family support	15,143	16,324	16,535	14,785	14,616	12,539	10,183
Youth	6,630	6,695	9,803	5,884	5,062	5,124	4,350
Protection reports	27,415	28,981	30,253	29,304	31,378	33,036	34,700
Investigations completed during year	18,460	20,260	21,497	20,431	23,425	24,136	24,321
Children under supervision	239	340	523	627	975	1,355	1,632
Children under supervision by delegated agencies	0	0	0	4	13	43	42
Children in care*	6,200	6,723	7,278	8,232	9,366	9,813	9,523
CICs delegated to Aboriginal agencies*	0	0	0	101	119	346	464

* March year-end.

Source: Ministry for Children and Families, Annual Report 1999-2000, p. 24.

increased markedly. These figures cannot be explained by increases in the child population overall (Foster and Wright, 2002; see also Chapter 2).

Although other policies and events – including changes to income support policies and the ongoing reports of child protection problems in the media – can account for some of this increased activity, risk assessment undoubtedly contributed. Whether more "risk" was discovered is questionable. More likely the risk-assessment instrument simply documented the factors – such as "low-income, single-parent households" or "parents suffered abuse and neglect themselves" – common to families that are reported to child welfare. Social workers reported that the increase in investigatory activity did not lead to parents obtaining help to reduce risk. Risk reduction, a key feature of risk assessment, was given short shrift in BC. Risk-reduction plans for "changeable risk factors" (the only factors to be addressed in these plans) usually involved sending parents to parenting and substance abuse programs, with social workers monitoring their progress. As these resources were frequently unavailable or seen to be "too little too late," the children were removed from their parents. With the "risks" clearly documented, workers had little choice, as the figures in Table 8.1 attest.

This increase in caseload was also not expected by managers. Instead of limiting the "risk class," risk assessment expanded it. More families were under surveillance by child welfare authorities. Expenditures in child welfare also increased. However, these expenditures went toward investigating families and maintaining children in care, not to programs that would assist the parents. Resources for these latter programs continued to dry up as they were transferred to cover the costs of children in care, increasing the likelihood of even more children coming into care. Of course, an overcrowded care system led to increasing risks for children and further scandals (Petch and Scarth, 1997).

Did risk assessment achieve standardization of practice, as intended by social workers and managers, and did that standardization lead to services that were equitable for clients? Our interviewees reported mixed findings. Clearly social workers felt that the risk-assessment instrument and work process guided how they did their work and how they reported it. For some it was a straitjacket; others welcomed the order that was brought to their work. All developed their own style of doing the work within the risk-assessment framework and took pride in their ability to manipulate it to suit their style and, occasionally, the circumstances facing clients.

However, there were questions about whether standardization necessarily led to better service. One of the most trenchant critiques of standardization was the simple observation that "the same" does not always mean high quality. Hamburgers, for example, can be the same at any branch of a franchise, but they may all be equally fatty and tasteless. And while customers can choose another restaurant, families in the child welfare system are not there voluntarily and have little or no choice concerning services. Racial and cultural groups have raised questions about the use of standardization to impose foreign values that damage or decimate their own (Aboriginal Committee of the Community Panel, 1992; Herbert and McDonald, 1995). Chapters 1 and 5 in this volume report the harm that was inflicted on Aboriginal communities during the 1960s when a Euro-Canadian child welfare system was imposed on them without undergoing fundamental adjustments that would support Aboriginal values. The middle-class Euro-Canadian assumptions underlying risk-assessment instruments and work processes stand in contrast to the traditional thinking of Aboriginal peoples and other groups. Moreover, risk assessment does not take into account the economic circumstances and history affecting Aboriginal peoples, and it could, if applied to some reserves, result in a large-scale removal of children without addressing conditions there.

Yet Aboriginal people are required to take on at least some aspects of risk assessment in order to assume control of their own child welfare system, and they are required to participate in the existing risk-assessment process when they live off-reserve. As one worker noted,

> I think sometimes, I have the general feeling that for Aboriginal people it's a white instrument. It can look like, "Oh my God, the whities have got me again, I don't know what the hell this is. It's a risk assessment. It looks like a big clump to me. I don't understand it." Because culturally they don't appreciate the way we work bureaucratically with people so it doesn't make sense to them, whereas a white person knows you're being an intrusive government bureaucrat and you're going to tick him off on the box scale and he culturally has a sense of how we operate. (Key informant, May 2005)

After the introduction of risk assessment, and in spite of government policies promoting the idea of Aboriginal communities caring for their own children, the number of Aboriginal children in care, already very high at 31 to 33 percent of all children in care, jumped to 37 percent between 1998 and 2000 and stands at nearly 50 percent in May 2006 (Foster and Wright, 2002, p. 124; see also Chapter 2).

For managers, standardized instruments and work processes enable the hiring of novice workers who can be quickly trained in risk-assessment processes and thinking. Although Judge Gove had hoped that risk assessment would be used as a professional tool and recommended that only professionally prepared social workers be hired for child protection, this recommendation was altered to include other related professions. Training to prepare new staff to understand risk assessment and child protection practice, which formerly took twenty weeks, has been replaced by a few days of preparation. It appears that standardization has been used to guide novice workers in terms of the nature of the tasks undertaken, the skills required to perform these tasks, the competencies necessary to perform the skills, and the evidence needed to show that the work was completed as required.

Both social workers and managers argued that risk assessment and its attendant demands for documentation helped to improve accountability. For both, the process meant the work of identifying and dealing with the "risks" to children could be made visible to workers, managers, clients, and the public. However there was an undercurrent of doubt about this argument among our informants. They wondered whether there was improved accountability to clients and children or to themselves, their organization, and politicians. They questioned whether following all the steps in the process and completing the documentation actually minimized risk for children or if it simply increased the surveillance of families without offering them service and protected workers from disciplinary measures, echoing similar questions in research (Rycus and Hughes, 2003). At the heart of their concern was a question: Does risk assessment promise too much by guaranteeing that it is possible to prevent calamities from happening to children by using the right instrument, following the identified procedures, and documenting the process throughout (Parton, 1998)? (This question is the focus of a current study in the Ministry of Children and Family Development that examines whether risk assessment actually results in safer conditions for children [R. Sullivan, personal communication, 2005]). In spite of early claims by the Children's Commissioner (Morton, 2002), the introduction of risk assessment has not resulted in fewer deaths of children involved with or in the care of government. A review of child deaths in these categories (www.mcf.gov.bc.ca/child_protection/index.html) from 1996 to 2004 reveals no consistent changes either way, and the numbers are too small to make any assumptions about them.

Conclusions

This chapter opened with the statement that child welfare in BC and other jurisdictions had long been governed by people with an appreciation of both professional and management orientations, and although it was not perfect, it provided room for a more complete understanding of complex child welfare matters. The subsequent narrative demonstrated that in recent decades this balance has become out of kilter. Managerial practices that have been penetrating child welfare and other human services for several decades have gained ground, using risk as the governing concept and risk assessment as a central tool of practice.

Instead of critiquing these developments, professionals have often embraced them, providing them with increased purchase. Management thinking has become ubiquitous. Recently, a graduate of a school of social work and senior member of a child welfare agency approached one of the authors and stated that she should be teaching management language and practices to students wishing to enter child welfare. We dispute this advice. Given the analysis in this chapter, we think that a central challenge for child welfare is to consider the benefits of professional, management, and consumer perspectives and find avenues to redress the present imbalance. Carl Bernstein, writing in Bob Woodward's book *The Secret Man* (2005), makes the case for a partnership between investigative reporters and their managers, arguing that "the reporter has to set his or her own course, to push against editors at times, to roam and be free to explore, to defy the conventional wisdom if necessary. And to find the sources to help him get to the bottom of things and to protect those sources. At the same time, as Woodward and I had learned, reporters need good editors and courageous publishers and brave broadcast executives. In the end, this collaboration is what anchors the credibility of the press" (p. 231).

The loss of a professional-management partnership is an important topic to address. In a spirited examination of the social work shortage in the United Kingdom, Harlow (2004) argues that the incursion of managerialism into social work practice is a significant force driving social workers, predominately women, out of the field and preventing others from entering. She argues that what attracts people to social work are relationships with others and the opportunities to make change, features of the work that are sharply curtailed under managerial regimes. In response, government is recruiting social workers from other countries and offering bursaries to UK students to pursue social work studies. It is interesting to consider whether a similar exodus from social work might occur in Canada. If it does, will it represent a logical outcome of managerialism in which employers will be free to hire untrained staff? Or will it force some examination of the principles of managerialism that work against social work aims and ideals?

We suggest a few ideas for re-establishing this partnership and, in fact, expanding it to include Aboriginal people and those most affected by child welfare policies – namely parents, mainly women and young people. One clear lesson from this narrative is not new. Child welfare is filled with contradictions and challenges. Failures are obvious while success often goes unnoticed. It is tempting for social workers and managers to embrace policy ideas that promise a quick fix, and child welfare history is littered with the remains of "the latest idea." These new ideas are often promulgated by consultants who have much to gain by promoting the next solution. We suggest that managers and social workers critically examine these policy ideas in partnership with those who will be most affected by them. This is a difficult proposition, perhaps, but it is one that, if ignored, can lead to enormous public expenditures and dubious practices. We need to redefine debate and the airing of differences as elements of good policy making and not as attacks on one group or another.

The opportunity for such examination is at hand. As we write this chapter, risk assessment is firmly entrenched in child welfare practice in BC, but it seems to have lost some of its lustre. The sharp rise in the number of children removed from their families did not sit well with the Liberal government elected in 2001. It planned to reduce these numbers through the introduction of new policies, including two – differential response and kinship care – that address some of the problems of risk assessment.

Under differential response, only some cases merit investigation with risk-assessment tools, which limits the numbers of assessments required and the number of children taken into care. For example, the use of risk assessments for situations based primarily on neglect, where parents simply do not have the resources to care for their children, is questionable (Weller and Wharf, 2002). These cases usually represent about half of the complaints coming to child welfare. In many situations, risk assessment is scarcely necessary as it is obvious that continued deprivation will be harmful to children. A more useful response would be to help parents acquire needed resources. Others also wonder about the usefulness of risk assessment in obvious and egregious cases of abuse, where the outcomes are clear and children require alternative caregivers. The use of kinship care, including family group conferencing, in which children are placed with members of their extended family rather than coming into government care, would also limit the incidence of risk assessment as children and their extended family members would be removed from the formal process requiring ongoing assessments. Yet these policies are not without problems that should be addressed openly. Differential response returns to social workers some opportunities for judgment, but it leaves intact many of the problems with risk assessment discussed previously. Kinship care offers potential for children and their families, but it cannot be simply a measure to cut costs and offload care onto family members (Callahan, Brown, MacKenzie, and Whittington, 2005). One of the controversies raging in BC during 2005 and 2006 involved the death of a young child who was in a "kith and kin" agreement (see Chapter 9).

This narrative suggests that managerialism and its recent expression, risk assessment, represent a powerful ideology that supersedes political ideologies and professional orientations. Managerial discourses have framed the agenda, and to be opposed to their key components – prediction, standardization, and accountability – appears irresponsible. Yet it is clear that there are ways to achieve these goals while retaining the essence of human services: relationships built on mutual respect with attention to needs and self-determination. For instance, a practical idea is to open up a debate on the issue of prediction. Should we remove from child welfare legislation the clauses that authorize the use of risk assessment? In BC, this would mean removing or rewriting phrases that refer to a child who "has been or is likely to be" in need of protection for whatever reason. Professionals believed that such clauses could prevent harm to children, but have they done so? Or is the science of prediction simply too weak and likely to remain so? Should we emphasize the child welfare mandate, examining the present safety of children and planning to ensure that safety on an ongoing basis, without pretending that we are predicting the future?

Another issue for debate is the argument that risk assessment as a standardized instrument and work process is essential because of the difficulty attracting and keeping experienced social workers in the job of child protection, which means there is a need for mechanisms to monitor novices. Yet an obvious alternative is to raise the prestige and salary of child protection work and to find and reward the most experienced practitioners (R. Sullivan, personal communication, 2005). Maintaining the balance between standardized approaches and discretionary practices in the rough-and-tumble world of child protection is a task for the most skilled and highly trained workers.

At the heart of the critique of risk assessment, managerialism, and child welfare is the concern about defining accountability as the completion of specific tasks with measurable outcomes defined by managers for workers and by workers for parents. In this framework there is little room for subjectivity, relativity, and reflexivity (Houston and Griffiths, 2000), and it endangers a fundamental talent of social workers: the ability to uncover the meaning of experience for others and to explain how that meaning shapes their behaviour. Building upon this idea, Krane and Davies (2000) suggest that we return to investigations that focus on parents', children's, friends', and families' narratives about what is happening and build bridges between these stories and our own understanding of the situation. The challenges facing parents, children, and social workers are often deeply confounding and contradictory, and they change at a rapid pace. They cannot be captured in the precise and stationary instrument of risk assessment (even if it is repeated on several occasions). It is essential that approaches to accountability take into consideration social workers' views about parents' and children's circumstances and what makes a difference to their lives (Weller and Wharf, 2002). Risk assessment offers very little room for their narratives and action on their solutions, nor for documenting their strengths. These are not pie-in-the-sky suggestions. Groups fighting violence against women have used such methods as a staple approach, and police involved in family violence units are trained in dispute resolution based on these principles. Indeed, family group conferencing offers an opportunity to return these approaches to child welfare.

Advocates also suggest that accountability in child welfare continues to focus on improving the behaviour of individual parents, the key objective in risk assessment, without attending to the large issues that define the parents' circumstances, such as poverty, housing, child care, and employment. In fact, a recent study of the risk-assessment work process demonstrates how it is extremely effective in translating large social issues, such as inadequate housing, into the personal problems of individual parents, usually mothers (Swift, Parada, and Callahan, 2005). Social workers must stand up for group and community approaches in child welfare, particularly as Aboriginal peoples take over their own child welfare matters (Brown, Haddock, and Kovacs, 2002).

As this cautionary tale illustrates, social workers should be reluctant to disregard their professional wisdom and to adopt solutions that have not been critically appraised nor shared with those who will be most affected by them.

Acknowledgements

This paper arises from a study of risk assessment in child welfare that aims to examine the work processes of risk assessment in two provinces, British Columbia and Ontario, and to investigate how these processes affect the organization of social work and other human service professions in the social and economic conditions produced by globalization. See Swift and Parada (2004) for a comparative analysis of the introduction of risk assessment in Ontario. The study is funded by the Social Science and Humanities Research Council of Canada.

Notes

1 The name of the government ministry in charge of child welfare has changed frequently (see Appendix 2). In this chapter we refer to it using its current title.
2 Throughout this discussion we use the term "social workers" to identify with a professional orientation and "management" to identify with a managerial one. In fact, this distinction is not always true, but we use it as a shorthand way of comparing the orientations.

References

Aboriginal Committee of the Community Panel on Family and Children's Services Legislation Review. (1992). *Liberating our children, liberating our nations.* Victoria: Ministry of Social Services.

Anglin, J. (2002). Risk, well-being and paramountcy in child protection: The need for transformation. *Child and Youth Care Forum, 31*(4), 233-55.

Armitage, A. (1998, Summer). Lost vision: Children and the Ministry for Children and Families. *BC Studies, 118,* 93-122.

Brown, L., Haddock, L., and Kovacs, M. (2002). Watching over families and children: The Lalum'utul' Smuneem child and family services in B.C. In B. Wharf (Ed.), *Community work approaches to child welfare* (pp. 131-51). Peterborough, ON: Broadview Press.

Callahan, M., Brown, L., MacKenzie, P., and Whittington, B. (2005, Fall/Winter). Catch as catch can: Grandmothers raising their grandchildren and kinship care policy. *Canadian Review of Social Policy, 54,* 58-78.

Callahan, M., and Dawson, R. (2001). Debate: Risk assessment in child protection services: Yes or no? *Canadian Social Work Review, 18*(1), 155-64.

Callahan, M., and McNiven, C. (1988). Privatization and social services in B.C. In J. Ismael and Y. Vaillancourt (Eds.), *Privatization and provincial social services in Canada: Policy, administration and delivery* (pp. 13-40). Edmonton: University of Alberta Press.

Castel, R. (1991). From dangerousness to risk. In G. Burchill, C. Gordon, and P. Miller (Eds.), *The Foucault effect: Studies in governmentality* (pp. 281-98). Chicago: University of Chicago Press.

Community Panel on Family and Children's Services Legislation Review. (1992). *Making Changes: A Place to Start.* Victoria: Ministry of Social Services.

English, D., and Pecora, P. (1994, Sept.-Oct.). Risk assessment as a practice method in child protective services. *Child Welfare, 73*(5), 451-73.

Foster, L.T., and Wright, M. (2002). Patterns and trends in children in the care of the province of British Columbia: Ecological, policy and cultural perspectives. In M.V. Hayes and L.T. Foster (Eds.), *Too small to see, too big to ignore: Child health and well-being in British Columbia* (pp. 103-40). Canadian Western Geographical Series, Vol. 35. Victoria: Western Geographical Press.

Gove, T. (1995). *Inquiry into child protection: Report on the Gove Inquiry into Child Protection* (2 vols.). Victoria: Ministry of Attorney General.

Harlow, E. (2004). Why don't·women want to be social workers any more? New managerialism, post-feminisim and the shortage of social workers in social service departments in England and Wales. *European Journal of Social Work, 7*(2), 167-79.

Herbert, E., and McDonald, K. (1995). An overview and analysis of First Nations child and family services in BC, prepared for the Gove Inquiry into Child Protection in British Columbia. Unpublished paper.

Houston, S., and Griffiths, H. (2000). Reflections on risk in child protection: Is it time for a shift in paradigms? *Child and Family Social Work, 5*(1), 1-10.

Ife, J. (2001). *Human rights and social work: Towards rights-based practice.* New York: Cambridge University Press.

Jones, D.P. (1994). Assessing and taking risks in child protection work. *Child Abuse and Neglect, 18,* 1037-38.

Kelly, P. (2001). The post welfare state and the government of youth at-risk. *Social Justice, 28*(4), 96-113.

Krane, J., and Davies, L. (2000). Mothering and child protection practice: Re-thinking risk assessment. *Child and Family Social Work, 5,* 35-45.

Ministry for Children and Families. (1996). *The risk assessment model for child protection in B.C.* Victoria: Author.

Morton, C. (2002). Learning from the past: Improving child-serving systems. In M.V. Hayes and L.T. Foster (Eds.), *Too small to see, too big to ignore: Child health and well-being in British Columbia* (pp. 161-92). Canadian Western Geographical Series, Vol. 35. Victoria: Western Geographical Press.

Parada, H. (2002). *The restructuring of the child welfare system in Ontario: A study in the social organization of knowledge.* Unpublished thesis. Ontario Institute for Studies in Education of the University of Toronto, Toronto.

Parton, N. (1998). Risk, advanced liberalism and child welfare: The need to rediscover uncertainty and ambiguity. *British Journal of Social Work, 28,* 5-27.

Parton, N., Thorpe, D., and Wattam, C. (1997). *Child protection, risk and the moral order.* Basingstoke, UK: Macmillan.

Petch, H., and Scarth, S. (1997). *Report of the Task Force on Safeguards for Children and Youth in Foster or Group Home Care.* Victoria: Ministry for Children and Families.

Reid, G., Sigurdson, E., Wright, A., and Christianson-Wood, J. (1996). Risk assessment: Some Canadian findings. *Protecting children, 12*(2), 24-31.

Rosanvallon, P. (2000). *The new social question: Rethinking the welfare state.* Princeton, NJ: Princeton University Press.

Rose, N. (1996). Psychiatry as a political science: Advanced liberalism and the administration of risk. *History of the Human Sciences, 9*(2), 1-23.

Rycus, J.S., and Hughes, R.C. (2003). *Issues in risk assessment in child protective services.* Columbus, OH: North American Resource Center for Child Welfare, Centre for Child Welfare Policy.

Schene, P., and Bond, K. (1989). *Research issues in risk assessment for child protection.* Denver, CO: American Humane Association.

Silver, E., and Miller, L. (2002, January). A cautionary note on the use of actuarial risk assessment tools for social control. *Crime and Delinquency, 43*(1), 138-61.

Sullivan, R. (1997). *Evaluating the risk assessment model, part one.* Victoria, Ministry for Children and Families.

–. (1998, Spring). Implementing the B.C. risk assessment model. *Social Workers' Perspectives, 20*(2), pp. 1 and 21.

Swift, K. (2001, Spring). The case for opposition: An examination of contemporary child welfare policy direction. *Canadian Review of Social Policy, 47,* 59-76.

Swift, K., and Parada, H. (2004, Fall). Child welfare reform: Protecting children or policing the poor? *Journal of Law and Social Policy, 19,* 1-17.

Swift, K., Parada, H., and Callahan, M. (2005, June). *Transforming problems into mothers' responsibilities: Risk assessment and the new managerialism in child welfare.* Paper presented at the Canadian Social Policy Conference, *Forging Social Futures,* Fredericton, NB.

Trocme, N., and Siddiqi, J. (2002, September). Child maltreatment investigations in Canada: Judicial implications. Paper presented at the National Judicial Institute's Child Protection and the Law Seminar, Ottawa. Available on the Centre of Excellence for Child Welfare website (www.cecw-cepb.ca/Pubs/Pubs.html/).

Tsui, M., and Cheung, F. (2004). Gone with the wind: The impacts of managerialism on human services. *British Journal of Social Work, 34*(3), 437-42.

Wald, M., and Woolverton, M. (1990). Risk assessment: The emperor's new clothes? *Child Welfare, 69*(6), 483-511.

Weller, F., and Wharf, B. (2002). Contradictions in child welfare. In M.V. Hayes and L.T. Foster (Eds.), *Too small to see, too big to ignore: Child health and well-being in British Columbia* (pp. 141-60). Canadian Western Geographical Series, Vol. 35. Victoria: Western Geographical Press.

Wharf, B. (1993, September). *A comparative analysis of three policy documents – Making changes: A place to start, Liberating our children, liberating our nations, and Making changes: Next steps.* Unpublished article. Victoria: University of Victoria, Faculty of Human and Social Development.

Woodward, B. (2005). *The secret man: The story of Watergate's Deep Throat.* New York: Simon and Schuster.

9
Back to the Future:
Toward Community Governance
Leslie T. Foster

After ten years in power, the New Democratic Party (NDP) was almost anni-hilated in the May 2001 election by Gordon Campbell's Liberals, winning only two of seventy-nine seats. Making things even worse for the NDP was the fact that the Speaker of the legislature declined to recognize the party as the official opposition (as was his right, given the low number of seats held by the NDP), denying it additional resources to support its activities as the opposition. This gave the incoming Liberals pretty much free rein to imple-ment their agenda as they saw fit. They set out with gusto to achieve, in a very short time frame (ninety days), major changes that they had promised in their "New Era" election campaign document.

The Liberal government's first move was to implement across-the-board income and corporate tax cuts worth about $2.1 billion annually, while strengthening legislation that required the government to balance the budget. These actions were taken before the Liberals had undertaken a thorough review of the province's fiscal position and its future commitments related to labour contract increases. The NDP had introduced a balanced budget before the election, but once the Liberals completed their review, taking into account the tax cuts they had promised, it was clear that it would be necessary to make major reductions in programs, especially social programs, given that health and education were to be protected from cuts. The pro-gram reductions have been described as "the largest budget and public sec-tor cuts in Canadian history" (Caledon Institute of Social Policy, 2002).

This was the backdrop to much of what has happened in child welfare during the Liberal's regime. This chapter describes and analyzes the events in child welfare during the five-year period from May 2001 to June 2006. It looks at the vision for child welfare developed by the new minister, Gordon Hogg, including the initial push toward community governance; the effects of a severe budget reduction for child welfare services; the focus on an Aboriginal governance model for child welfare; and the impact of the death of a young Aboriginal child who was in a "kith and kin" agreement arranged by a delegated Aboriginal agency.

The Vision for Child Welfare

In the weeks after it was elected, the Liberal government created a new Ministry of Children and Family Development (MCFD). Gordon Hogg was sworn in as minister, and Linda Reid was named minister of state for early childhood development, the first such position in Canada. There was a wholesale change at the executive level of the ministry, with a new deputy minister, Chris Haynes (a long-time public servant in the area of social services, who was, in the mid-1990s, Director of Child Protection), and the replacement of three assistant deputy ministers. In addition, Ross Dawson, who had been Director of Child Protection for the last four years of the NDP administration, left for a post in Washington State, creating a major vacancy in the ministry. These changes, along with the natural concern caused by a change in political administration, had an initial destabilizing affect on the new ministry. Staff felt beleaguered as major programs such as child and family services, public health, family support, child and youth mental health, youth addictions and youth justice services were slated to be moved to other ministries. In the end, only public health and addictions programs moved, thus leaving key programs in the ministry.

Early in the mandate of the new government, each ministry was asked to undertake a "core review" of its existing programs to ensure consistency with the New Era election promises and to assess whether current programs, which had developed over many years, were still necessary. The new MCFD had several issues to address:

- *The ministry had to stop the endless bureaucratic restructuring that had drained resources from children and family services.* This was in response to concerns expressed about constant changes of responsibility and organization in the ministry, which resulted in the major focus being on change rather than service delivery.
- *It had to focus on early intervention with at-risk children and measures aimed at preventing crisis situations before they arose.* This was in response to concerns about the amount of resources being drained from family support to pay for the costs of the increasing number of children being taken into care.
- *It had to work with foster parents to help them improve care and placements of foster children.* This was in response to major concerns expressed by the various foster parents associations around the province about inadequate supports for looking after the children in their care, as well as concerns about deteriorating relationships between the ministry and foster parents.

- *With the Ministry of Public Safety and the Solicitor General, the MCFD had to fight child prostitution and youth crime with specific legislation aimed at providing greater protection for children at risk and greater parental responsibility for children who commit crimes.* This was in relation to concerns about safety and about children and youth entering the sex trade.
- *It had to increase emphasis on early childhood intervention programs for families with special needs children.* The community-living services sector had undertaken a major lobbying effort after it suffered a cutback of 1.5 percent in contract amounts under the previous administration. Further, increased resources were flowing to the province from the federal government to support early childhood development.

Based on these directions arising from the core review, the ministry developed six strategic shifts to help guide it through the coming years (MCFD, 2002b). By achieving these shifts, the MCFD would

- establish open, accountable, and transparent relationships
- enable communities to develop and deliver services within a consolidated, coherent, community-based service delivery system
- make strategic investments in capacity and resilience building and would provide funding for programs and services known to work
- promote family and community capacity to protect children and support child and family development
- develop a community-based service delivery system that would promote choice, innovation, and shared responsibility
- build capacity within Aboriginal communities to deliver a full range of services, with an emphasis on early child and family development.

As a result of its work on the core review, the ministry also articulated the following vision, mission, principles, role, and mandate that would guide its work (ibid.).

Vision
The Ministry of Children and Family Development envisions a province of healthy children and responsible families living in safe, caring, and inclusive communities.

Mission
Our mission is to promote and develop the capacity of families and communities to

- care for and protect vulnerable children and youth
- support adults with developmental disabilities.

Principles

The following principles guide the ministry in its work:

- We believe in the right and primary responsibility of families to protect and support the growth and development of children and youth.
- We believe that government must acknowledge and reinforce the capacity of communities to support and enhance the resilience of children and families.
- We believe that this ministry should provide the minimal intervention necessary to ensure the safety and well-being of our most vulnerable community members.

Ministry Role and Mandate

The ministry's role and mandate are to

- advance the safety and well-being of vulnerable children, youth, and adults
- advance early childhood development through strategic investments
- advance and support a community-based system of family services that promotes innovation, equity, and accountability.

This vision was clearly driven by the new minister, Gordon Hogg. Before being elected to the provincial legislature in the mid-1990s, Hogg had been a long-time municipal politician and the mayor of White Rock and had served as a board member on numerous community non-profit human services agencies. He had also worked in the public service in youth probation and youth custody and had been a foster parent. Furthermore, he had been a local representative on one of the community resource boards (CRB) established by the NDP in the early 1970s. At the time of his appointment to the CRB, Hogg was a White Rock civic councillor and still in his twenties. Given this background, it was not surprising to see a major focus on "community" in the strategic shifts.

Philosophically, Hogg was a strong supporter of increased community participation in human service delivery. He had been influenced by his own experiences and by his graduate studies, in which he had looked at system-wide approaches to service delivery. In an interview for this chapter, Hogg expressed his belief that human services delivery did not respond well to a highly centralized, power/hierarchical perspective of the kind that was then in place in the province for delivering child welfare services. He also indicated that he had been impressed by the works of J.L. McKnight (1995) related to community development and of R.D. Putnam (2000) with respect to the concept of social capital development (G. Hogg, interview, 2005).

Perhaps the most important idea that came out of the core review was the decision to move the governance of the child welfare system to five regional authorities, geographically similar to the five health authorities in the health care system. British Columbia had the biggest single child welfare system in the country and one of the largest on the North American continent; other provinces had either smaller centralized systems or regional authorities in place and/or used children's aid societies to deliver services. Hogg stressed the importance of having an engagement process much closer to communities than had heretofore been the case. He felt this would achieve the needed cross-sectoral approach to child welfare and be more reflective of what was happening in society overall. Hogg wanted to establish a community-oriented approach to child welfare and hoped to depoliticize child welfare in the province following the raucous years during and after the Gove Inquiry (Gove, 1995).

The Budget Reality

While the core review process was underway, the ministry was going through a separate budget-development process. After reviewing the province's commitments in terms of tax cuts and promised wage increases, each ministry was asked to develop three-year budget planning scenarios based on reductions of 20 percent, 35 percent, and 50 percent from the current year's budget, which had been developed by the NDP government but ratified by the new government. The MCFD faced substantially higher reduction targets, given that it had to deal with sizeable wage increases negotiated by the previous administration. It also had to develop the five regional governance authorities for children and family development services that had been approved under the core review process. And it had less than two weeks to develop its budget plan based on the various scenarios.

After numerous trips to Treasury Board and individual meetings with the chair of Treasury Board, the net outcome for the ministry was a budget reduction over the next three years of 23 percent overall and 30 percent for children and family programming. This was despite Hogg's intense eleventh-hour lobbying for a smaller reduction. Other social services ministries, including the new Ministry of Community, Aboriginal and Women Services and the Ministry of Human Resources, were also hit with major reductions to safety nets and long-standing preventive programs (Hayes, 2002). Only the health- and education-related ministries received no reduction, but they had to absorb certain cost pressures.

Many commentators expressed concern about this reduction in funding and the effects it would have on children at risk, especially given the reductions being made to other ministries that had traditionally provided support programs to children and families at risk. For example, the outgoing Children's Commissioner and Child, Youth and Family Advocate, both of whom were losing their jobs as part of government restructuring, were skeptical about the ministry's ability to meet its budget target (Pallan, 2002; MacFadden, 2002). Others were even more critical, especially the schools of social work in the province. Most people in the ministry also had doubts about their ability to implement the changes needed in the time available to meet the budget targets, despite an increase in resources in 2002-3 to help deal with the massive one-time restructure that would be required to achieve the final budget target.

The ministry determined that the main way to reduce budget requirements for child welfare was to reduce the rate of children in care from eleven children per thousand to the national average of about nine per thousand (see Table 9.1) and to reduce the average costs of those children in care.

Table 9.1

Rates of children in care (CIC) by province (per thousand children)

Age group	Province	CIC	Population[a]	CIC rate
Under 16[b]	Ontario	14,098	2,426,362	5.81
	Newfoundland	700	101,871	6.88
	New Brunswick	1,104	146,522	7.53
	British Columbia[e]	7,963	789,436	10.09
	Nova Scotia	2,019	184,298	10.96
	Saskatchewan	2,839	236,744	11.99
	Northwest Territories[c]	408	23,210	17.58
Under 18[d]	Prince Edward Island	207	33,787	6.13
	Alberta	7,948	760,077	10.46
	British Columbia[e]	9,692	897,764	10.80
	Manitoba	5,440	289,854	18.77
	Yukon	189	8,086	23.37
Under 19	British Columbia[e]	10,454	952,323	10.98
Composite[f]	Canada	47,357	5,163,044	9.17

Notes: Data for Manitoba and the Northwest Territories are from 31 March 2000; data for Newfoundland are from 31 March 1999; Ontario data are from 1 January 2001. CIC numbers are not available for 31 March 2001, from Newfoundland or Northwest Territories. Other figures are for 31 March 2001. Because of differing policies and practices between provinces and territories, comparison of CIC rates serves only as a rough guide to relative CIC rates.

a Population estimates as of 1 July 2000.

b Services are provided to children in Saskatchewan, Newfoundland, Nova Scotia, New Brunswick, Ontario, and the Northwest Territories under the age of sixteen.

c Northwest Territories and Nunavut population and CIC caseload amalgamated.

d Services are provided to children in Prince Edward Island, Manitoba, Alberta, and Yukon under the age of eighteen.

e Services are provided to children in British Columbia under the age of nineteen. British Columbia CIC caseload excludes migrants and includes children in the care of delegated Aboriginal agencies.

f Canada's population is an aggregation of the relevant provincial populations (data for Quebec are unavailable and are not included in the Canada series). Canada's CIC caseload is an aggregation of the provincial CIC numbers. As a result, Canada's CIC rate is a composite rate over a range of age groups.

These reductions were to be accomplished through a variety of measures, including the use of "kith and kin" agreements, in which children would not be taken into care but placed with extended family; doubling the number of children adopted each year from about 150 to 300; increasing the percentage of children in family foster care rather than in the more expensive group home system; increasing the number of youth agreements to about two hundred per year; investing heavily in early childhood development programs; and, finally, moving to a community-based governance model that promoted choice, innovation, and shared family and community responsibility for children (MCFD, 2002b).

Minister Hogg had made it clear publicly that if more resources were needed, he would go back to Treasury Board to request them. It was also his hope, given that the reductions were heavily loaded toward the end of the three-year period, that the economy would improve, government revenues would increase, and the full reductions would not be necessary.

Over the following year (2002) the ministry made major strides toward its targets. To the surprise of many observers, given reductions in support programs offered by other social service ministries, the number and rate of children in care came down from its historic high of 10,775 in June 2001 to 9,603 by March 2003. This drop was assisted by a reduction in the number of protection reports received by the ministry, part of a longer-term trend.

There are several explanations for this downward trend, as noted in Chapter 2. First, children brought into care during, and following, the Gove Inquiry were now aging out of the system at the rate of about seven hundred per year. Second, youth agreements, kith and kin agreements, and adoptions were all increasing in numbers, thus reducing the number of new children coming into care and reducing the length of time they stayed in care. Furthermore, the average cost of a child in care was reduced as many of the expensive group homes had been shut down in favour of the less expensive and more appropriate family foster care residential model. During and immediately following the Gove Inquiry, the system was overwhelmed with children coming into care as social workers became more risk-averse. There was not enough time to develop new foster care homes, so the ministry was forced to go to the private sector to provide group home accommodation for these additional children entering care. As the children-in-care (CIC) caseload increased until mid-2001, there was little choice but to keep these more costly homes open and operating.

As BC reduced its CIC rate in 2002, other provinces were going in the opposite direction, especially Alberta and Ontario (see Figure 9.1). By 2003, BC had a lower-than-national-average CIC rate for non-Aboriginal children, but a higher rate for Aboriginal children (see Table 9.2).

Despite this progress, Treasury Board was concerned that the ministry might not meet its third-year budget target, given the backend loading of

Figure 9.1

Trends in the rates of children in care per thousand children in population

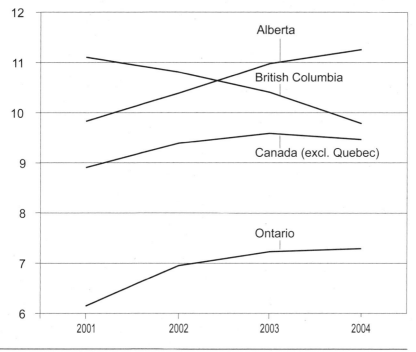

Note: These should be viewed as approximate rates only, given various assumptions in their calculations. See notes to Table 9.1 for details.

budget reductions and its focus on establishing regional authorities. The board ordered the ministry to undertake what became known as the "mid-term review." Before the results of the review were announced, documents leaked to the media indicated the "draconian" measures necessary to achieve the original three-year budget goal, causing a public furor and distrust of ministry management.

After more discussions, Hogg announced at a televised cabinet meeting that the ministry could not make the original budget and keep clients safe; the original assumptions were incorrect, and in order to be able to keep clients safe, the reductions required would have to be modified. This "humiliation" was the price Hogg had to pay to get more money for his ministry. More than $120 million was reinstated to the ministry's budget, modifying the original 30 percent reduction to child welfare services to about 11 percent. This "add back" was not without its fallout, and for the second time in two years there was a major change at the executive level, with three assistant deputy ministers and an executive director being replaced.

Table 9.2

Rates of Aboriginal and non-Aboriginal children in care (per thousand children)

Age group	Province	Total	CIC rate Aboriginal	CIC rate Non-Aboriginal
Under 16	Newfoundland	5.7	N/A	N/A
	Ontario	6.9	24.4	6.5
	New Brunswick	9.6	5.9	9.8
	British Columbia	9.7	64.3	5.4
	Nova Scotia	10.1	44.4	9.0
	Saskatchewan	11.3	33.9	4.0
	Northwest Territories	34.9	55.6	4.2
Under 18	Prince Edward Island	7.5	42.3	6.9
	British Columbia	10.3	65.9	6.0
	Alberta	11.1	71.2	5.6
	Manitoba	19.3	70.8	4.7
	Yukon	33.4	59.9	19.3
Under 19	British Columbia	10.5	66.3	6.2
	Nunavut	21.5	24.6	N/A
Composite	Canada	9.4	52.5	6.3

Notes: Data for 31 March 2003. These should be viewed as approximate rates only, given various assumptions in their calculations. See notes to Table 9.1 for details.

The Push for Regional Governance

As noted earlier, the ministry's plan was to move to regional governance. Ministry staff and various communities devoted much effort to this initiative. There were extensive consultations, directed by Hogg, who was following his vision for community governance and wanted to ensure community input and buy-in for this move. One reason Treasury Board believed the ministry might not achieve its budget plan was that the effort being made to develop a new governance system was detracting from the focus on achieving budget targets. Initially, five regional planning committees were established, but after the government signed the Tsawwassen Accord (Union of BC Indian Chiefs, 2002), which made it clear that separate Aboriginal authorities would be required for Aboriginal child and family development services, a further five committees were established so there were five Aboriginal and five non-Aboriginal planning groups.

Hogg chose members of the non-Aboriginal planning groups from community leadership in the various regions. For the Aboriginal groups, Aboriginal communities put forward names for Hogg to approve. Each committee was supported by funding from the ministry, and the ministry was reorganized into five regions, each headed by an interim chief executive officer. In addition, the role of Director of Child Welfare was delegated down to the regional level. A total of $20 million in one-time strategic investment funding was provided to the five Aboriginal and five non-Aboriginal regional planning groups to develop capacity building and to support initiatives that would facilitate devolution and reduce the number of children in care. The money was managed not by the province, but by the planning committees and sub-groups themselves, within specific agreed-to guidelines. The organization and funding decisions showed that the minister was committed to the principle of involving the communities in planning for and controlling the new governance system.

What impressed Hogg deeply was the community members' enthusiasm for, and commitment to, the governance initiative. Even though many of them were concerned about the budget reductions, they made it clear to Hogg that they wished to be involved in the decisions about where to make the cuts. This did not, however, lessen the concern about the ministry's attempt to reduce the budget at the same time as it was developing and introducing new governance structures. Critics noted the incompatibility of doing both at the same time (G. Hogg, interview, 2005).

The plan was to have the new governance structure in place by fiscal year 2004-5, and specific funds were earmarked both within the ministry's budget and within the Ministry of Finance's budget for restructuring initiatives (MCFD, 2002b). Legislation was also passed to allow the establishment of interim authorities as a first step toward establishing permanent regional authorities. As interim authorities reached the stage where they were ready to take on the work of permanent governance, full authority and budget could be transferred from the province. The ministry felt that, realistically, each authority would be ready at a different time, so there would be a phased transfer of services. As the complexity of adding five separate Aboriginal authorities to the mix was recognized, the timelines were pushed back by a year, setting fiscal 2005-6 for Aboriginal authorities to be developed (MCFD, 2003).

The 2003-4 fiscal year proved to be a watershed for the ministry in its plans for regional governance. Due to the emphasis on the mid-term review, noted earlier, implementing community governance took on a secondary, though still important, role in the ministry. The first priority was clearly to convince Treasury Board that the ministry could manage within its new (although still reduced) budget. Unfortunately for the ministry, the one-time restructuring funds available centrally and held by the Ministry of Finance would no longer be available after the end of the 2003-4 fiscal year. In addition, a review requested by the premier's office suggested that regional governance should not occur before budget goals had been met and budget stabilization had been achieved (Sage Group, 2003). The report suggested that the need for separate Aboriginal and non-Aboriginal interim authorities was ill-advised, and recommended that a single provincial interim authority be created for both Aboriginal and non-Aboriginal services. After further consultation with Aboriginal leaders, Hogg rejected the recommendation for a single interim authority and directed that there would be separate authorities for Aboriginal and non-Aboriginal services.

In early 2004, Hogg resigned from the cabinet after he was made aware of contracting irregularities in the MCFD. He forwarded material to his executive financial officer for review; this material was provided, in turn, to the comptroller general, Arn van Iersel, for independent review. Hogg indicated that his resignation was to ensure that his presence would not interfere with the review. Hogg was replaced by Christy Clark, who had held the education portfolio and was also deputy premier. In a letter dated 20 March 2004 she informed the chairs of the regional planning committees that the non-Aboriginal planning committees were being disbanded and that the funding for Aboriginal planning committees was being reduced. This put into question not only the timing of the shift to regional governance, but also the commitment of the government to the process. Further development of separate interim authorities was put on hold. As noted in the ministry's 2004-5 service plan, "the move to the new community-based governance model has been reviewed and extended ... Regional authorities will be created incrementally ... based on their readiness" (MCFD, 2004, p. 41). The 2005-6 service plan, overseen by Minister Stan Hagen, who replaced Clark when she resigned in September 2004 after only eight months as minister, still envisaged five Aboriginal regional authorities in place by 2006-7, to be followed by the creation of five non-Aboriginal authorities in 2007-8 (MCFD, 2005), though this was a far cry from the original intention to have authorities in place by 2004-5.

The Aboriginal Governance Agenda

One of Hogg's first actions as minister was to meet with Grand Chief Ed John, his NDP predecessor in what was then the Ministry for Children and Families. Given the large number of Aboriginal children in the child welfare system, Hogg realized that he not only needed to learn from his predecessor but also needed to gain the trust of the Aboriginal communities. He recognized the importance of developing relationships if he was to make a difference in this human services portfolio (G. Hogg, interview, 2005).

Hogg had one of his executive staff, Jeremy Berland, travel throughout the province to consult with, and hold community meetings with, Aboriginal groups concerning Aboriginal child welfare governance. Given the large number of bands (nearly two hundred) and their great diversity (more than a dozen different cultural groups within the Aboriginal communities), and given that many Aboriginal people now lived off-reserve, in urban areas, there was a diverse response in terms of a preferred governance model for child welfare. There was unanimity, however, on the need for Aboriginal people to control Aboriginal child welfare, echoing the voices from previous reports and organizations on this point dating back several decades (see Chapters 2 and 5). The Aboriginal communities wanted nothing less than what the non-Aboriginal child welfare governance system would get.

This unanimity was made clear at a July 2002 meeting of Aboriginal groups and selected ministry executive staff. This was when the so-called Tsawwassen Accord (Union of BC Indian Chiefs, 2002) was developed, primarily by Stewart Phillip of the Union of BC Indian Chiefs, and agreed to by all the Aboriginal leaders in attendance. Many groups were most distressed that Minister Hogg was not attending the meeting (he was attending a cabinet meeting elsewhere), but he was kept up-to-date on discussions through several telephone conversations with Grand Chief Ed John.

Following the Tsawwassen meeting, Hogg requested Semiahmoo Grand Chief Bernard Charles, a long-time family friend, to host a feast for ministry executive staff and key Aboriginal leaders later in the summer. This was Hogg's way of embracing the Aboriginal approach to discussing the business of Aboriginal child welfare. Much of the feast was devoted to traditional Aboriginal games and the exchanging of gifts between Aboriginal people and ministry staff, but Hogg also took time to meet with the key Aboriginal leaders. The formal meeting was very short, and attendees agreed to embrace Grand Chief Ed John's proposal to develop a memorandum of understanding (MOU) on child welfare. This MOU between Aboriginal peoples and the province was signed in September 2002 by three members of the province's executive council, including the premier, and fifteen key Aboriginal political and service delivery figures representing thirteen Aboriginal agencies. There had never been such a consensus among Aboriginal people on one topic before. Curiously, however, the existing delegated child welfare agencies, which were largely funded by the federal government did not sign the MOU, nor was there any representative of the federal government (MCFD, 2002a).

The MOU created the Joint Aboriginal Management Committee (JAMC) to oversee the implementation of Aboriginal governance of child welfare. Although it was co-chaired by Hogg as minister and supported financially by the ministry, the JAMC was primarily run by the Aboriginal community. This was Hogg's method of respecting the intent of Aboriginal people and ensuring that the community led the way to the extent possible.

The Aboriginal conception of children and family services was much more holistic than the existing system. The Aboriginal approach was to have all services related to children and families integrated under regional governance authorities. Not all Aboriginal and First Nations groups could agree on the accountability mechanism that should be put in place, but generally they envisioned a system that would be moving to prevention and healing, driven by the community, and clearly focused on family and community, factors that were very much supported by Hogg. Whatever model of governance was to be developed, it was clear that additional resources would be required and that it would be necessary to develop capacity in order to institute a successful and safe governance model.

Based on this requirement, Hogg, along with executive staff person Jeremy Berland and Aboriginal leader Debbie Abbott, travelled to Ottawa to meet with several federal cabinet ministers, including the minister of Indian and northern affairs, Robert Nault; the minister of human resources development, Jane Stewart; the secretary of state for Indian and northern affairs, Stephen Owen, who was also a British Columbia MP; and the federal interlocutor for Métis and non-Status Indians, Ralph Goodale, who had previously been responsible for the Office of Indian Residential Schools. There was even a phone discussion with Paul Martin, the finance minister at the time. Hogg discussed with his federal counterparts the idea of having Aboriginal authorities develop a long-term social development plan and administer both federally and provincially funded social development programs for Aboriginal people. Accountability would be achieved by holding authorities to their long-term plans.

When federal, provincial, and territorial social services ministers met in Yellowknife later that year, they invited key Aboriginal leaders, including Grand Chief Ed John of the BC First Nations Summit and Phil Fontaine, the national chief of the Assembly of First Nations, to attend, a unique event in itself. Both spoke glowingly of the route that BC was taking to establish independent Aboriginal authorities that would take responsibility for their own child welfare and family and related services. Hogg was hoping to keep the momentum flowing and to get the federal government onside with the proposal for Aboriginal authorities.

Despite all of this progress, when Hogg resigned in late January 2004, community and Aboriginal governance lost much of its impetus (see also Chapter 2). It was challenged even further when, as mentioned previously, Hogg's replacement, Christy Clark, reduced funding for Aboriginal planning committees. Furthermore, Aboriginal representatives began to see that taking over the governance of child welfare would be a complicated task, especially given government expectations about accountability. For example, it was estimated that new authorities would have to abide by no fewer than twenty different pieces of provincial legislation and their regulations, as well as potentially many more federal statutes, to fulfill "normal" accountability requirements.

Nevertheless, in early June 2004, the JAMC was mandated to develop a joint multi-year plan outlining the elements, related activities, and timelines that would be necessary to establish the five Aboriginal governance authorities by 2007. In February 2005 a draft plan was developed. Progress was slow, however, because of several factors. First, it was still not clear that there was any consensus about what a governance authority might look like. Some viewed it as merely an "interim measure" on the road to treaty settlement; for others it was about getting control of services without a clear understanding of what they would be controlling and what that control would entail; for still others it was about redress for historical unequal relations between Aboriginal groups and government. As a result, achieving "consensus" with one group might mean another would disagree. And apparent consensus achieved one day might disappear the next. Within this mix were Aboriginal service providers who had contracts with both the federal and provincial governments. This further complicated governance issues because these providers reported to three sets of government: federal, provincial, and Aboriginal bands (see Chapter 5). Finally, just as there had been changes within the MCFD, there were changes in the leadership of some of the Aboriginal political groups that signed the MOU in 2002, particularly the United Native Nations and the Métis Provincial Council of British Columbia. With these changes in leadership came differing perspectives on governance, which also served to slow progress.

The run-up to a provincial election in 2005 – subsequently won by the governing Liberals, although with a much reduced majority – diverted attention from preparing governance plans. Further, it seemed that the attention of some of the First Nations signatories to the 2002 MOU had shifted to other issues, particularly work on the "New Relationship," a government-First Nations accord to improve economic, social, and cultural opportunities for Aboriginal people. Although this accord was partially focused on the need to improve the health and well-being of First Nations people so that they could contribute fully to life and development in BC, it has, to date, primarily related to land and resource-based issues (Ministry of Aboriginal Relations and Reconciliation, 2005). In the document outlining the vision for the New Relationship there was no mention of Aboriginal peoples who are not First Nations, which could potentially cause a split among Aboriginal communities, including the Métis Nation of BC, which had agreed in 2002 to co-operate for the purposes of improving the welfare of their children.

The Best of Intentions

Gordon Hogg was minister of children and family development for less than three years, but his influence was widely felt. He entered the child welfare portfolio with a clear vision, and he was willing to modify his expectations as the results of community consultations became evident.

Throughout, however, he never wavered from his vision of community-based governance, despite several setbacks, particularly on the budget front. With respect to budget cuts to child welfare, he essentially lost the fight with Gary Collins, who was minister of finance from 2001 until late 2004. Although the mid-term review saw some funding restored to the ministry budget for child welfare, Hogg was forced to admit at an open cabinet meeting that some of his and his staff's assumptions when making the original cuts were faulty.

Hogg was able to make substantial progress in persuading diverse Aboriginal organizations to rally around child welfare governance, at least for a time. The MOU on Aboriginal child welfare was a historic document, and Hogg certainly went a long way to helping Aboriginal groups feel respected, listened to, and included in government policy-making.

Reflecting on developments during his tenure as minister, Hogg was still strongly committed to regional governance, seeing it as the right thing to do. His major regret was that he maybe had not managed expectations as well as he could. He should have recognized the large amount of work and consistent effort and leadership required to move the governance agenda forward (G. Hogg, interview, 2005). The plans for community-based governance developed much more slowly than originally anticipated, but they remained a mainstay of the ministry's service plans even after Hogg was succeeded as minister by Christy Clark and then Stan Hagen. Had Hogg remained as minister, it is likely that regional governance would be much further advanced than it currently is, even given the politics of governance and the additional costs involved. Certainly progress was made in the community-living services sector through the establishment of Community Living BC, which moved the provision of services to a governance structure outside the ministry. The plan also called for Community Living BC to take over certain child welfare functions related to some special needs children. This innovative approach may hold the key for child welfare governance structures.

As minister, Hogg was able to make some headway in his attempt to depoliticize child welfare in the province. He was known to support front-line workers and would often phone individuals who were dealing with difficult cases to let them know he realized they had a tough job to do and to provide them with moral support while not interfering with their professional judgments. He also made it clear publicly that mistakes will be made. No child welfare system is impervious to such mistakes, as decisions involve making judgments when not all the information may be available. Hogg pushed the idea that the ministry and child welfare workers needed to learn from the mistakes. He also suggested to his cabinet colleagues that child welfare should perhaps report to an all-party committee through an officer of the legislature, rather than through a politician, in order to depoliticize this service area.

The More Things Change, the More They Stay the Same

In 2005, two events combined to bring child welfare concerns back into the public spotlight. First, a letter that three prominent child welfare advocates had sent to the premier in June 2004 was released to the media a couple of months before the May 2005 election. The three advocates – former ombudsman Dulcie McCallum; former Child, Youth and Family Advocate Joyce Preston; and former Children's Commissioner Cindy Morton – had expressed their concerns about the impact of budget cuts on children's services. When they did not receive a reply from the premier, they felt compelled to express their concern more publicly. A second event, following the re-election of the Liberals, involved the release of a report (with much of the information blacked out, or severed, under privacy provisions) on the death of Sherry Charlie, a young Aboriginal girl who had been in the care of her aunt under a kith and kin agreement. The aunt's husband was charged and found guilty of the death of the child.

Together, these two events left the public with a sense that the child welfare system was again in crisis. This impression was reinforced when the new legislative session opened and the recently re-elected Liberal government found itself at the centre of a raging controversy as a result of consistent, penetrating questions from the NDP during daily Question Period in the Legislature. By November 2005 there were no fewer than ten separate reviews/inquiries, either completed or underway, stemming from this one death. The reviews went far beyond the original issue of the death to examine other factors related to government cutbacks and restructuring in ministries other than MCFD.

The severed report had been completed by an outside consultant for the Director of Child Welfare (such a review of a critical incident such as the death of a child under ministry support is referred to as a "Director's Review"). The consultant was now an NDP MLA. The Child and Youth Officer had no less than three individual reviews, one requested by the Attorney General. The coroner had two – an inquest as well as a formal child death review. There were two separate court cases to be heard. The acting ombudsman initially indicated that his office was doing a separate review, but he backed off, awaiting the outcome of the other reviews. Finally, a special "Blue Ribbon Panel" was appointed to make recommendations with respect to how children's deaths in the province should be reviewed. This panel was originally headed by Judge Thomas Gove, but he was removed by the chief justice because the latter had not been consulted prior to Gove's appointment, and there was concern about a judge being involved in a "political" process. There was also concern about the existing workload Gove needed to carry on the bench.

Subsequently, Ted Hughes, the former provincial Conflict Commissioner, was appointed to head the panel, which included Jane Morley, the Child and Youth Officer; Terry Smith, the coroner; Joyce Preston, the former Child, Youth and Family Advocate for the province; Maureen Nicholls, a former deputy minister and previous head of the Workers Compensation Board; and Grand Chief Ed John, the former minister for children and families. Before the group had a chance to meet, it was reduced to a one-person panel, with Ted Hughes as its sole member. This was because Hughes (and others) had been worried about potential conflicts, given that Morley and Smith were doing their own reports. (Morley had also recommended the disbandment of the Children's Commission, which had previously been responsible for child death reviews.) All former members, including Gove, were made "advisors" to Hughes, and Nicholls provided ongoing support.

Three separate ministers became involved in the issue of child deaths – the minister of children and family development; the Attorney General, who had responsibility for the Child and Youth Officer; and the Solicitor General, who had responsibility for the coroner's service – and each was grilled both inside and outside the legislative chambers. In addition, the premier accepted some of the responsibility for the situation related to the failure to continue child death reviews.

What had started as a concern about one death mushroomed into concerns about all children's deaths – particularly after the Solicitor General revealed that over seven hundred child deaths had not been reviewed during the transition period when responsibility for child death reviews moved from the Children's Commission to the Coroner's Office – and public confidence in the child welfare system was again severely undermined. These issues dominated the front and editorial pages of the media for several weeks. There were accusations and counter-accusations and confusion about the number of death reviews not completed or "abandoned." One prominent journalist, Vaughn Palmer, in his *Vancouver Sun* column of 10 November 2005, referred to it as a "jurisdictional morass" (p. A03). Others suggested that this was "payback" by the NDP for the way they were grilled about child welfare issues when the Liberals were in opposition (see Morton, 2002). This emphasis on child deaths is rather ironic given that, when the Liberals came to power in 2001, the provincial health officer presented them with a report on child deaths that provided important evidence to help depoliticize such deaths in the child welfare system (Kendall, 2001a, 2001b). When they began their second term in office in mid-2005, the Liberals faced major embarrassments over their apparent failure to keep track of child deaths and to make reviews both transparently independent and public. This also shifted attention away from the governance agenda.

Coroner's Inquest

The inquest into the death of Sherry Charlie was conducted in February 2006, three and a half years after her death. Sherry Charlie was murdered by her aunt's husband while she was in their care under a kith and kin agreement negotiated by Usma, an Aboriginal delegated agency. It appeared at first that no inquest was to take place, but the politics around the death gave the coroner no choice but to hold an inquest. As a result of the inquest, the coroner made nineteen recommendations to individuals including the director of the *Child, Family and Community Service Act*; the director of the Delegated Aboriginal Child Welfare Agency and the Nuu-chah-nulth Tribal Council; the fire chief, Port Alberni Fire Department; the BC Ambulance Service; the RCMP; the medical director, West Coast General Hospital; the chief coroner; and Premier Gordon Campbell. In summary, the recommendations called for more and improved training; reminded professionals of their duty to report suspected child abuse; reminded health staff that external signs of injury must be reported; and called for more sharing of information between professionals. Finally, the premier was asked to reinstate the Children's Commission, the organization that had undertaken a review of all child deaths in the province before it was disbanded (Coroner's Court of British Columbia, 2006).

Children and Youth Officer's Review

The results of the review by Jane Morley, the children and youth officer, were released by the Attorney General in February 2006 (Morley, 2006). Morley was directed to investigate the director's case review into the death of Sherry Charlie. This report had been made public, but only after major deletion of information had occurred. Concerns were raised about the length of time it had taken to complete the review. Also, the terms of reference for the review were changed so that it focused solely on the Aboriginal child welfare agency (Usma) rather than the ministry and the agency. There were suggestions that the changes were made to "cover up" ministry mistakes, and delaying the release of the review until after the election was seen as a political decision. The key terms of Morley's inquiry were as follows:

1. The timelines involved in the writing, completion, and release of that Review;
2. Why the terms of reference for that Review were changed;
3. To review the policy concerning a Director's Case Review, including those where a Kith and Kin [Agreement] has been applied, and make any recommendations necessary as a result; and
4. Any other matters deemed relevant to a full consideration of the director's case review process in that case. (ibid., p. 2)

In establishing these terms there was much confusion in the Legislature about Morley's independence. The Attorney General, to whom Morley reported, indicated that she was an independent officer of the legislature, so her review would be objective. However, she was not actually an independent officer. The Attorney General had to admit his mistake about her status, but he stood by her objectivity. Such was the confusion that surrounded the Sherry Charlie case.

Morley conducted interviews under oath with eighteen individuals and looked at e-mail correspondence, notes of meetings, and relevant files. She found that it had taken almost three years and at least twenty-five drafts to complete the director's case review, and she concluded that "the story of this Director's case review is not a story of conspiracy and cover up, but rather one of organizational failure" (Morley, 2006, p. 3). This failure was brought on in part by the priorities driving the ministry between September 2002 and July 2005, which Morley summarized as a move to regional governance; transformation of the service delivery system; and implementation of a budget reduction imposed by Treasury Board. Each was a major initiative in itself and fully "engaged the attention and energy of the senior managers both at the provincial and regional levels of MCFD" (ibid., p. 4).

Morley made ten recommendations to help improve the clarity and the process of conducting director's case reviews. In the case of this particular review, she noted that "at the centre of that [organizational] failure was a lack of clarity about what the case review was about, its core principles and how [the] case review fit within MCFD's organizational objectives" (ibid., p. 72). Morley further noted that "the managers involved in this Director's case review were simultaneously engaged on moving forward with ... transformative change. They were doing so in a context of budget cuts that were seeing their numbers significantly reduced. A case review process that may have worked well in the past did not keep pace with the changes that MCFD was undergoing" (ibid.). Budget cuts may not have contributed directly to the death of Sherry Charlie, but Morley's review implied that there were some indirect effects in the form of reduced ministry staffing and the time given to other ministry priorities.

2006 Budget
When Finance Minister Carole Taylor introduced the provincial budget in the legislature on 21 February 2006, the headline for the budget presentation materials was "Budget 2006 Concentrates on B.C.'s Children," and the budget showed an increase of $421 million for children's services over three years (Ministry of Finance, 2006). Her speech indicated that

the largest portion of this new funding – $173 million – will be used to enhance services for children, including:

- more social workers and other front-line staff to stay in closer contact with families at risk;

- more counselling, treatment and support to help prevent problems such as child abuse, neglect and family breakdown;
- more culturally-appropriate services for Aboriginal children and families; and
- increased support for extended family members caring for children under kinship agreements – and for foster parents, without whom we could not provide safe, loving homes for children and youth unable to live with their families. (Taylor, 2006)

A further $100 million was set aside to improve child protection, primarily to respond to the expected recommendations from the Hughes Report, which was due in early April 2006. These funds were frozen by Treasury Board pending the development of an approved spending plan. By the end of June 2006, this plan had still not been developed to the point where it had received Cabinet or Treasury Board approval.

The new budget plan, however, increased the funding available for children and family development services within MCFD to $627.3 million in 2006-7 and up to $687.1 million by 2008-9. These figures did not include any wage increases negotiated for 2006-7 and beyond. The equivalent budget in 2001-2, the first budget approved by the Liberals (although it had been set by the outgoing NDP government), was $664.1 million. By 2005-6 it had dropped to $569.8 million (see Figure 9.2), but even with the lift in budget for 2006-7, there were still fewer resources for child welfare than were contained in the budget provided to the Liberals when they took power in 2001-2. One of the strongest criticisms of the current Liberal regime has been in response to its reduction of funding for children and families (Hayes, 2002). It took a major controversy about a child death, and a fortuitous increase in government revenues related, in part, to increases in commodity prices and real estate taxes, to return funding to the levels it reached at the turn of the century. Whether the funding makes a difference remains to be seen.

The Hughes Report

The most significant event affecting child welfare in BC in the first six months of 2006 was the release of the Hughes Report on 7 April. This report, which was subtitled "An Independent Review of BC's Child Protection System," contained recommendations that, if adopted, should lead to improvements in the delivery of child welfare. Hughes recognized that child welfare was a complicated business that, in BC, had been beset by numerous changes, not only in practices and regional/central administration, but also in leadership at both the political level and the senior levels of the public service. Hughes noted that these recent changes had occurred as funding was being reduced (as shown in Figure 9.2), "even though it is commonly understood that organizational change costs money" (Hughes, 2006, p. 3). He further

Figure 9.2

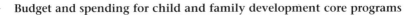

Budget and spending for child and family development core programs

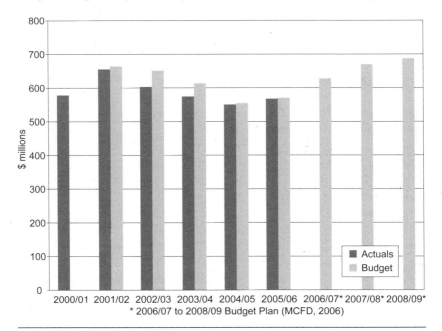

Source: Ministry of Children and Family Development, Financial Services Branch

noted that all the changes had essentially pushed the ministry to what could only be described as a breaking point, and it needed to regain equilibrium and stability.

As mentioned earlier in this volume (Chapter 4), Hughes had been chosen to undertake a review of child welfare back in the days of Social Credit in 1991, but the election of the NDP late that year changed those plans. Hughes had impeccable credentials both in the legal world and in other areas. He had been BC's deputy attorney general and later the province's Conflict Commissioner when a report on the premier of the day, Bill Vander Zalm, led to the premier's resignation. He had overseen a contentious federal inquiry into RCMP actions at an international summit meeting, and he was currently working for the federal government to adjudicate compensation payments for those who had suffered abuse in the Indian residential school system. This gave him a good knowledge of Aboriginal issues, which was necessary given the high numbers of Aboriginal children in the child welfare system.

In conducting his review, Hughes received nearly three hundred submissions from groups, organizations, and individuals involved with the child welfare system. In addition, he interviewed numerous individuals (though they were not under oath) and reviewed numerous files. His report resulted in sixty-two recommendations overall (see the appendix at the end of this chapter).

The first series of recommendations advocated the development of a new independent body to oversee the province's child welfare system. It would be headed by the Representative for Children and Youth, who would be an officer of the legislature, reporting to a standing committee, and there would be two deputy representatives. At least one of these three positions was to be filled by an Aboriginal person. The role of the representative was to "push for improvements to the child welfare system; it will support individual children and families who need help resolving conflicts with the Ministry; and it will monitor and report on government's services to children and families and on the Ministry's responses to child deaths and critical injuries" (ibid., p. 14). One of the last things the government did before it recessed in May 2006 was to pass new legislation to set up the representative position and function. Furthermore, an all-party committee, headed by Gordon Hogg, was appointed to provide some oversight to the representative and his or her work.

The second series of recommendations dealt with issues related to Aboriginal children. Hughes expressed deep concern about the increasing numbers of Aboriginal children being taken into state care. He noted succinctly that "there may be no quick solutions, but immediate measures can be taken to begin consulting in a meaningful way with Aboriginal communities so that the Ministry policy and procedures can better meet their needs; to attract and keep Aboriginal people in leadership and frontline child welfare positions; and to better support the 23 Aboriginal agencies now providing child welfare services to their communities" (ibid., p. 16). Hughes added that "the child welfare system alone cannot address the poverty, substance abuse, limited economic opportunities, substandard housing and other challenges facing Aboriginal families. The roots of these problems run deep in our history and they will not be overcome without the best efforts and full cooperation of Aboriginal leaders and federal and provincial governments" (ibid.). Hughes went on to note the devastating impact of the residential school program and its intergenerational effects, adding that the program was largely responsible for the high numbers of Aboriginal families involved with the child welfare system (ibid., p. 50).

The third set of recommendations considered the decentralization of services to the regions and to Aboriginal authorities, a move that Hughes supported. He felt that four things were necessary to avoid the stop/start approach to decentralization and regional governance that had characterized the ministry's recent history:

- The political leadership had to demonstrate a clear and continuing commitment to decentralization.
- There had to be a dedicated team, stable resources, and time for consultation.
- Decentralization had to be undertaken as a partnership between the ministry and communities.
- The government should transfer responsibility for governance to the regions only when they had demonstrated an ability to carry them out (ibid., p. 70).

Hughes noted the need for improved accountability, especially in a regionalized authority model. He also supported the continuation of policies to have fewer children in care through the use of such programs as kith and kin arrangements and youth agreements as long as they were supported with appropriate resources. He recommended support for required staffing and training, especially with respect to service transformation initiatives related to having fewer children in care.

The fourth set of recommendations dealt with the need to improve communications and information sharing, and suggested methods of overcoming some of the barriers to doing so. In particular, Hughes noted a need for enhanced statistical and public reporting of internal child death and injury reviews. Finally, he reviewed the government's failure to undertake satisfactory child death reviews following the closure of the Children's Commission. His conclusions were that there was no clear transition plan to move existing files to the Coroner's Office, which took over the job, and there were not enough resources made available to do a proper job anyway, despite statements by the premier to the contrary (Hughes, 2006). Throughout his report, and to his credit, Hughes refrained from blaming individuals, unlike similar reports, which commonly point fingers and lay blame. Only the premier and political leadership were subject to real criticism.

Recent Changes in the Ministry of Children and Family Development
As the various reviews were being prepared for release, the government was also preparing its response. On 9 February 2006, an announcement from the premier's office indicated that MCFD deputy minister Alison MacPhail was moving to a new assignment in another ministry. She was replaced by Arn van Iersel, associate deputy minister, on an acting basis, and Beth James was made acting associate deputy minister (Appendix 2). At the same time it was announced that

the Premier's Office will retain the services of Lesley du Toit, the executive director of the Child and Youth Care Agency for Development in South Africa, to provide advice on transforming services for children and youth in British Columbia. Ms. du Toit's advice will focus on the regionalization of child and family services, including the development of new Aboriginal authorities. Government's objectives are to bring services closer to communities, making them more effective, and targeting them on early intervention to ensure children can remain within their families and communities, while ensuring their safety and well-being. In addition, Ms. du Toit will assist government in developing a response to the recommendations of the Child and Youth Review Panel, headed by Ted Hughes, Q.C. (Government of British Columbia, 2006)

A week later, Jeremy Berland was relieved of his duties as Director of Child Welfare and took a secondment to the University of Victoria for a two-year period. Mark Sieben took over his position, again on an acting basis. Thus, all the key positions related to child welfare in the ministry were now held by individuals on a temporary basis, setting the scene for what was to be the third major wholesale change at the executive level of MCFD since July 2001.

Lesley du Toit's appointment was a surprise to many people, but she had been part of an international blue ribbon panel that operated from 2002 to 2005 out of the International Institute for Child Rights and Development at the University of Victoria. Gordon Hogg established the panel in order to get independent advice on the changes that were being made while he was minister. Ms. du Toit had visited BC on several occasions and provided her assessment of the changes being made. In two reports to Hogg, she had expressed concern, as had others before her, about the wisdom of reducing funding while making wholesale changes to service delivery. What many failed to realize was that du Toit, coming from outside BC and Canada, had very little "baggage," especially with respect to Aboriginal communities in BC. One reason for caution was her surprise that Aboriginal groups supported separate governance bodies for Aboriginal and non-Aboriginal children and family services, which she felt smacked of apartheid, a policy she had worked against in her native South Africa. This led some observers to question whether separate Aboriginal governance authorities would remain a priority. Subsequent events, however, have indicated that du Toit has moderated her view of this issue.

Soon after the release of the Hughes Report, du Toit was made deputy minister, and in the ensuing few weeks the executive committee was completely changed. Three assistant deputy ministers left: one was demoted, one was let go, and one transferred to another agency. Debbie Foxcroft, an advocate for Aboriginal child welfare, was appointed as a new assistant deputy minister. The associate deputy minister, Arn van Iersel, left to become acting Auditor General; Beth James, who had been acting associate deputy minister for a few months, also left; and one of the five regional executive directors left as well. So, yet again, government used the strategy of restructuring the bureaucracy to try to move the child welfare agenda onto a stable footing.

Only time will tell if this will work, but strong foundations have been laid to help make it a success. For one, Hughes suggested that people filling the executive positions should do so for at least four years, preferably five, to create some stability. Government has given du Toit a long-term contract (four years). In addition, there will be an infusion of resources that will bring the child welfare budget back to a level close to what it was when the Liberals came to power in 2001.

Immediately after the release of the Hughes Report, the media were fairly gentle on MCFD. Perhaps this was a case of MCFD fatigue, or perhaps there was a belief that all would now be well given a budget increase, the recommendations from Hughes, and the government's agreement to implement the recommendations. As this chapter was being written, however, the media jumped back into the fray following the TV broadcast of images from a dishevelled foster home. The minister asked his new deputy minister to provide him with a report as soon as possible, so the honeymoon with the media has been very short-lived.

Conclusion

The five years of Liberal administration have seen tremendous changes in the fortunes of child welfare. From an initial plan that would have seen funding reduced by 30 percent over three years has emerged a new plan that sees the funding reinstated over the next three fiscal years. But this came at quite a price. Child welfare has been perhaps the biggest social policy issue that the government has faced, and government has not looked good. MCFD resources were replenished only belatedly, after a major outcry over a child's death, media exposure, and subsequent reviews of the death.

While the response of government has been to change most of the executive for the third time in five years (so much for the New Era promise of stopping the endless bureaucratic restructuring), regionalization and separate Aboriginal governance still remain key parts of the government's agenda for child welfare. Resources have been set aside to help support these agenda items, and funding is being increased to support services.

The government can take away several lessons from this era of child welfare. First, major changes to complicated systems take time if they are to be implemented successfully. Second, such changes also require additional resources, not a reduction in resources, at least until the changes have been effected. Third, once government has set its direction, it should stay the course and not dither, as it did over the question of establishing regional authorities. Fourth, it needs consistent leadership to carry out major changes. This does not mean having three different ministers in less than one year and three wholesale changes in ministry executive members in less than five years. Finally, the government needs to ensure greater public understanding of the intent of the changes, and it needs to work continually to depoliticize child welfare in the province. In particular, although child welfare is not ever a vote-getter, it is important to ensure public understanding, and this will make it necessary to keep a relatively hostile media fully informed (Hardy, 2006). The appointment of an all-party committee to work with the new Representative for Children and Youth may help in the depoliticization process, and, we can hope, may result in a more sympathetic media. The fact that Gordon Hogg was asked oversee the work of this committee undoubtedly indicates the government's support for his original vision of delivering child welfare through regional authorities.

Appendix: Summary of Hughes Report Recommendations

A. External Oversight

1. A Representative for Children and Youth is to be appointed as an Officer of the Legislature for a five-year term, renewable to a maximum of ten years.
2. The legislature will strike a new Standing Committee on Children and Youth, and the representative and deputy representatives will report to this committee at least annually.
3. The Representative for Children and Youth will be mandated to support and advise children, youth, and families who need help in dealing with the child welfare system, and to advocate for change to the system itself.
4. The Representative for Children and Youth will be mandated to monitor, review, audit, and investigate the performance and accountability of the child welfare system, but this mandate will be reviewed in five years and revised as appropriate at that time.
5. The representative will be mandated to review certain child deaths and critical injuries. Reviews are to be limited to those children who were in care at the time, or who had been receiving ministry services during the preceding year. The deaths and injuries to be reviewed are those due to abuse or neglect; those due to an accident occurring in unusual or suspicious circumstances; or those due to self-inflicted injury or injury inflicted by another. They are to be reviewed only if the child welfare system might have contributed in some way to the death or injury. Critical injuries are those that are life-threatening or cause serious or long-term impairment.
6. Legislation will permit the Lieutenant-Governor in Council or the standing committee to refer a death to the representative, leaving it to the discretion of the representative to determine whether to undertake a review or not, and to report to cabinet.
7. The representative will have powers of a Commissioner of Inquiry under the *Inquiry Act*.

8. The representative will be mandated to report to the minister, the legislature, and the public through annual reports and special reports. This reporting will include reporting on compliance with recommendations by the ministry and other public bodies.
9. The coroner's child death investigation function, with funding as reflected in Budget 2006, will be continued.
10. The Child Death Review Unit within the Coroners Service is to continue.
11. The *Coroners Act* should be updated, in line with the coroner's role today, and expectations of the office should be clarified.

B. Keeping Aboriginal Children Safe and Well

12. Provincial and federal governments, in collaboration with Aboriginal communities, will begin work toward fulfillment of the commitments of the Kelowna Accord by assessing the health, economic, and social needs of Aboriginal communities, including urban, off-reserve populations.
13. The provincial government will actively collaborate with Aboriginal people to develop a common vision for governance of the Aboriginal child welfare system. Whatever Aboriginal child welfare model evolves from that process must be the subject of active and widespread community consultation before its enactment.
14. The provincial government will work with Canada to clarify their respective funding responsibilities, remove jurisdictional obstacles facing Aboriginal child welfare agencies, and replace Directive 20-1 with a new approach that is more supportive of measures that protect the integrity of the family.
15. Provincial and federal governments will provide Aboriginal agencies with:

    • modern information technology and help them acquire appropriate office management systems and skills
    • the same training opportunities as are offered to ministry staff, as well as specialized training directed at their particular needs, and
    • support during a crisis from an emergency response team.

16. At least one of the three senior positions at the new Representative for Children and Youth will be held at all times by an Aboriginal person; and the Representative will actively recruit some Aboriginal staff at all levels of the organization.
17. The Ministry of Children and Family Development is to find ways to recruit and retain more Aboriginal people for service in the ministry at all levels, but particularly among social workers who deal directly with children and families.

C. Ministry of Children and Family Development

18. The ministry and community representatives should jointly develop a plan for decentralization, beginning with a set of principles that will guide the process, a clear statement of expected results, and a course of action to achieve those results.

19. Government should commit itself to decentralization, which means supporting it with adequate resources, time, a dedicated team, and budget stability.

20. Responsibilities should be transferred to regions and to Aboriginal authorities once they have demonstrated their ability to meet key performance targets.

21. The ministry is to retain, at its headquarters, the authority it needs to set and ensure compliance with provincial standards and to meet its responsibility for public accountability.

22. The ministry should examine its management structure to find ways to realign roles and responsibilities in ways that will clarify lines of authority and facilitate collaboration across program areas and between regions and the central office.

23. The ministry should establish a comprehensive set of measures to determine the real and long-term impacts of its programs and services on children, youth, and their families and then monitor, track, and report on these measures for a period of time.

24. The ministry should continue its work with other BC ministries to establish common measures and linked data sets.

25. Once collected and analyzed, data must be used as a tool to support operational and management decision making, as well as program evaluation and policy development.

26. The ministry must devote sufficient resources to develop and maintain a strong central quality-assurance function at headquarters, in the regions, and in Aboriginal agencies. In consultation with the regions and Aboriginal agencies, headquarters must set provincial standards; provide training, support, and expertise; and monitor results.

27. The ministry needs to develop its capacity to do aggregate analysis of recommendations from case reviews and regional practice audits.

28. The ministry needs a regular, co-ordinated program of reporting on its activities and results achieved for children in care and children at risk.

29. The ministry must finalize, with a new sense of urgency, its complaint resolution process, ensuring that the process is timely, accessible, and simple; that it takes a problem-solving, rather than confrontational, approach; that it is respectful and responsive to the complainant; and that it involves the parties in resolving the issue.

30. The ministry is to develop processes for resolving complaints by Aboriginal children, youth, and families that incorporate and respect traditional cultural values and approaches to conflict resolution.
31. The ministry is to adopt a common review tool to guide the conduct of case reviews across all the program areas that are relevant to the life of a child who has died or been seriously injured.
32. The ministry is to adjust its timelines for internal reviews, ensuring timeliness, but taking account of current capacity. Once established, the timelines should be made public.
33. The ministry is to undertake reviews of critical injuries and deaths of children receiving services from any of its program areas.
34. The ministry is to rename its internal injury and death reviews and clarify the scope of each.
35. The death or critical injury of a child who is in care must always be subject to a review, regardless of the circumstances.
36. The ministry is to develop clear criteria to guide the decision as to whether to review the death or critical injury of children who are receiving or have received ministry services.
37. The ministry is to review injuries and deaths not only of children who were receiving ministry services at the time of the incident, but also of children who had received ministry services during the twelve months preceding and, in exceptional circumstances, going back even further.
38. The Regional Executive Director should be responsible for deciding whether a review should occur. He or she should record the reasons for that decision, establish the terms of reference for the review, decide who will do the review, and, finally, sign off on the recommendations that result.
39. The Provincial Director of Child Welfare is to retain the authority to conduct a review.
40. The ministry should provide required orientation, training, and mentoring for practice analysts who will conduct reviews. It should maintain a list of qualified reviewers.
41. The ministry is to make use of multidisciplinary teams in its child injury and death review process.
42. Government will provide sufficient funding, staffing, and training to support its newer approaches to child protection work.
43. External evaluation of all programs under the service transformation initiative, beginning with kith and kin agreements, will be undertaken both during the implementation phase and then later, on an ongoing basis.
44. Program evaluation is to become a routine part of the ministry's management role, to be carried out in consultation with the regions and with Aboriginal authorities once they are established.

45. Government is to provide training for current social workers and to recruit individuals with the necessary mediation and counselling skills to support the service transformation initiative.

46. The ministry is to reinvigorate its campaign to recruit foster and adoptive parents and to ensure that it is funded so that it can respond to public interest and participation.

D. Communication and Co-ordination

47. The ministry is to establish a forum or council, including the new Representative for Children and Youth, the Coroner's Service, the Ombudsman, and the Public Guardian and Trustee, that will meet regularly to review developments and issues of common concern.

48. The *Child, Family and Community Service Act,* which sets out powers and duties of the provincial Director of Child Welfare, should be amended to include the power to produce reports of internal child death reviews and to state that, although the main purpose of the report is learning, public accountability is also a purpose of these reports.

49. The *Child, Family and Community Service Act* should be amended to allow the provincial director to make information-sharing agreements with other agencies for the purpose of multidisciplinary child death reviews.

50. The *Child, Family and Community Service Act* should be amended to require the provincial director to give, on a confidential basis, a complete copy of the final child death review report to all agencies that participated in a multidisciplinary child death review team.

51. Annual reports of the Ministry of Children and Family Development should provide a statistical report of its reviews of deaths and critical incidents, as well as the recommendations that resulted from those reviews, and a progress report on their implementation.

52. Twice a year, the Ministry of Children and Family Development will publicly release a summary of each child death review it has completed during the previous six months. The summaries will contain no names, dates, or places.

53. If the death of a child who was in care or known to the ministry has already been disclosed by police, a court, or the coroner, the ministry will be permitted by the *Child, Family and Community Service Act* to disclose the child's name and relationship to the ministry and the contents of the ministry's case review, to the extent necessary for accountability but without unreasonable invasion of privacy.

54. The *Representative for Children and Youth Act* will contain an authority to collect information that is at least equivalent to section 11 of the *Office of Children and Youth Act*; provisions to ensure that the records it requests

are delivered promptly and without charge to the Representative; and provisions to permit public disclosure of personal information if it is in the public interest, necessary to support the findings and recommendations, and not an unreasonable invasion of privacy.

55. The *Representative for Children and Youth Act* will clearly provide for the creation, use, and disclosure of linked data sets for purposes specified in the act.

56. The Representative for Children and Youth, in collecting linked data from the Ministry of Children and Family Development and other public bodies for the purpose of fulfilling its monitoring role, will develop policies and practices to ensure that all identifying information is removed from public reports and that the highest privacy standards are met.

57. The Ministry of Children and Family Development, in collecting linked data from other public bodies for the purpose of decision making about individuals, will ensure that the absolute minimum information is collected, that each linking is necessary to enable the Director of Child Welfare to deliver mandated services, and that the highest privacy standards are met.

58. The *Representative for Children and Youth Act* should contain a provision similar to section 9 of the *Ombudsman Act* requiring that information collected by the representative be kept in confidence, with a limited right of disclosure.

59. The Ministry of Children and Family Development should not rely on research agreements to collect and link personal information from other ministries and public bodies. It has the authority under the *Child, Family and Community Service Act* section 96 to collect information and to use it to make decisions about individual children.

60. The Ministry of Children and Family Development should review the statutes that govern it to ensure that there are no statutory barriers to disclosure of information among program areas.

61. The Ministry of Children and Family Development should review its privacy policy documents to ensure that they are current, accurate, and easily useable by employees.

62. The *Freedom of Information and Protection of Privacy Act* should be amended to incorporate the "unreasonable invasion of privacy" test into section 33.2, which authorizes public disclosure of personal information under certain conditions.

Source: (Hughes, 2006)

Acknowledgments
Thanks are given to Gordon Hogg, MLA, for giving freely of his time to discuss this chapter. In addition, thanks are due to Jeremy Berland, who provided useful comments on an earlier version of this chapter. Useful comments and advice were also provided by Martin Wright of MCFD.

Persons Interviewed
Jeremy Berland. Executive director of Aboriginal services, director of child welfare (2003-6), and assistant deputy minister (2003-present) in the Ministry of Children and Family Development. Interviewed 2005.

Gordon Hogg. Former minister of Children and Family Development (2001-4). Interviewed 2005.

References
Caledon Institute of Social Policy. (2002). *A new era in British Columbia: A profile of budget cuts across social programs.* Ottawa: Caledon Institute. Retrieved 1 November 2005 from www.caledoninst.org/

Coroner's Court of British Columbia. (2006). Verdict at coroner's inquest: Sherry Laura Ann Charlie. Victoria: Ministry of Solicitor General.

Foster, L.T., and Wright, M. (2002). Patterns and trends in children in the care of the province of British Columbia: Ecological, policy and cultural perspectives. In M.V. Hayes and L.T. Foster (Eds.), *Too small to see, too big to ignore: Child health and well-being in British Columbia* (pp. 103-40). Canadian Western Geographical Series, Vol. 35. Victoria: Western Geographical Press.

Gove, T. (1995). *Report of the Gove Inquiry into Child Protection in BC. Vol. 2. Matthew's legacy.* Victoria: Ministry of the Attorney General.

Government of British Columbia. (2006). Government announces new appointments. Victoria: Office of the Premier.

Hardy, B.F. (2006). Exploring the process of change in British Columbia social services 1991-2001: The benefits of hindsight. PhD dissertation. University of Victoria, School of Child and Youth Care.

Hayes, M.V. (2002). Epilogue. In M.V. Hayes and L.T. Foster (Eds.), *Too small to see, too big to ignore: Child health and well-being in British Columbia* (pp. 273-76). Canadian Western Geographical Series, Vol. 35. Victoria: Western Geographical Press.

Hughes, E.N. (2006). *BC children and youth review: An independent review of BC's child protection system.* Victoria: Ministry of Children and Family Development. Retrieved 21 June 2006 from www.childyouthreview.ca/report.htm.

Kendall, P.R.W. (2001a). *Health status of children and youth in care in British Columbia: What do the mortality data show? Report of the Office of the Provincial Health Officer of British Columbia.* Victoria: Ministry of Health.

–. (2001b). *Children and youth in care: An epidemiological review of mortality, British Columbia, April 1974 to March 1999.* Victoria: Office of the Provincial Health Officer.

Laming, Lord. (2003). *The Victoria Climbié Inquiry: Report of an inquiry by Lord Laming.* London: Her Majesty's Stationery Office.

MacFadden, L. (2002). *Rethink the reductions: Children and youth need more; 2001 Annual Report.* Victoria: Office of the Child, Youth and Family Advocate.

McKnight, J.L. (1995). *The careless society.* New York: Basic Books.

Ministry of Aboriginal Relations and Reconciliation. (2005). *The new relationship.* Victoria: Author. Retrieved 21 August 2005 from www.gov.bc.ca/arr/popt/the_new_relationship.htm

Ministry of Children and Family Development. (2002a). *Memorandum of understanding for Aboriginal children.* Victoria: Author. Retrieved 21 August 2005 from www.mcf.gov.bc.ca/about_us/aboriginal/mou.htm

–. (2002b). *Service plan: 2002/2003 to 2004/2005. February.* Victoria: Author. Retrieved 1 November 2005 from www.bcbudget.gov.bc.ca

–. (2003). *Service plan: 2003/04 to 2005/06.* Victoria: Author. Retrieved 1 November 2005 from www.bcbudget.gov.bc.ca

–. (2004). *Service plan: 2004/05 to 2006/07.* Victoria: Author. Retrieved 1 November 2005 from www.bcbudget.gov.bc.ca

–. (2005). *Service plan: 2005/06 to 2007/08.* Victoria: Author. Retrieved 1 November 2005 from www.bcbudget.gov.bc.ca

–. (2006). *Service plan: 2006/07 to 2008/09.* Victoria: Author. Retrieved 21 June 2005 from www.bcbudget.gov.bc.ca

Ministry of Finance. (2006). *Balanced Budget 2006: Growing with confidence.* Victoria: Author. Retrieved 21 June 2006 from www.bcbudget.gov.bc.ca/2006/newsrelease/

Morley, J. (2006). *Report of the Attorney General of British Columbia under section 6 of the Office for Children and Youth Act on the director's case review relating to the Nuu-chah-nulth child who died in Port Alberni on September 4, 2002.* Victoria: Ministry of the Attorney General.

Morton, C. (2002) Learning from the past: Improving child-serving systems. In M.V. Hayes and L.T. Foster (Eds.), *Too small to see, too big to ignore: Child health and well-being in British Columbia* (pp. 161-92). Canadian Western Geographical Series, Vol. 35. Victoria: Western Geographical Press.

Pallan, P. (2002). *Looking back, looking ahead: B.C.'s child and youth services in transition; The Children's Commission annual report, 2001.* Victoria: Ministry of the Attorney General.

Putnam, R.D. (2000). *Bowling alone: The collapse and revival of American community.* New York: Simon and Schuster.

Reder, P., Duncan, S., and Gray, M. (1993). *Beyond blame: Child abuse tragedies revisited.* London: Routledge.

Sage Group. (2003, 24 September). *New governance – Some considerations.* Victoria: Sage Group Management Consultants.

Taylor, C. (2006). Budget speech 2006. Victoria: Ministry of Finance.

Union of BC Indian Chiefs. (2002). *Creating a vision for the future: A provincial conference on Aboriginal child and family services governance.* Retrieved 16 October 2005 from www.ubcic.bc.ca/News_Releases/2002.htm

10
Views from Other Provinces
Brad McKenzie, Sally Palmer, and Wanda Thomas Barnard

IN THIS CHAPTER we provide summaries of the views of colleagues in Manitoba (Brad McKenzie, professor in the Faculty of Social Work at the University of Manitoba), Ontario (Sally Palmer, professor emerita in the School of Social Work at McMaster University), and Nova Scotia (Wanda Thomas Barnard, professor and director of the School of Social Work at Dalhousie University). The editors of this volume asked these colleagues to read Chapter 11 and comment on the similarity, or otherwise, of the events and recommendations portrayed in this chapter to the situation in their own provinces. McKenzie, Palmer, and Barnard are well-known in their respective provinces and, indeed, across the country for their knowledge of, and commitment to, child welfare. Their responses vary in length, but all suggest that many of the same difficulties that plague the child welfare enterprise in BC are present in other provinces. Such difficulties include ignoring poverty as a primary cause of neglect and abuse, inattention to First Nations families, and a preoccupation with organizational reforms and intrusive investigations into complaints of child neglect and abuse. The chapter concludes with comments from a literature review of child welfare practice commissioned by the Canadian Association of Social Workers.

Manitoba
Historically, Manitoba has had a mixed organizational model for child welfare service delivery. Services to some parts of the province have been provided by government, while services to other parts have been the responsibility of voluntary non-profit organizations governed by community boards. This loosely coupled organizational structure has had a significant influence on policy development in the field of child welfare. For example, the non-government service delivery sector served as a model for the devolution of child welfare to First Nations, and by the late 1980s, all reserves in

the province were receiving a full range of child welfare services from delegated First Nations agencies governed by regional or community boards. This structure, however, has made it somewhat more difficult to roll out centrally designed organizational or policy changes. For example, efforts to integrate health and social service in a single-unit delivery system in the 1970s included child welfare, but only in areas where government was responsible for providing these services.

Although Manitoba's mixed organizational framework for delivering child welfare services has inhibited implementation of many centrally initiated strategies for change, it has not prevented the use of structural reorganization as a solution to identified problems in child welfare. The restructuring of services in the province has been driven by two general factors. First, it has been a response to perceived failures within the child welfare system. That is, restructuring has been seen as a means to improve service quality, efficiency, and accountability. Second, it has been a response to demands from Aboriginal communities for both an increased role in, and a new approach to, the delivery of child welfare services.

The single-unit delivery system of the 1970s was short-lived, and it gave way to two different developments in the 1980s. One was the delegation of child welfare services on reserves to First Nations agencies; the second was the adoption of a decentralized community-based system of service delivery in the city of Winnipeg. Within Winnipeg, six new agencies governed by community boards replaced a single agency that had adopted a highly centralized and specialized service model. Despite the many benefits associated with this community-based model (McKenzie, 1991), a more centralized administrative structure was established in 1991 when the provincial government disbanded the six regional agencies and reorganized services under a single agency with a government-appointed board. Nominally, this agency retained voluntary status, but ongoing budget and organizational problems led to its takeover by the province in 2001.

At about this time the province also embarked on a major restructuring of services in order to transfer responsibility for off-reserve Aboriginal child welfare services to three new Aboriginal authorities (Hudson and McKenzie, 2003). The three Aboriginal authorities are accountable to government but have major policy and administrative responsibility for the design and delivery of services to Métis and First Nations families throughout the province. There was a great deal of uncertainty for front-line staff, service users, and other community service providers in the early stages of implementation as new agencies were developed, staff changed, and cases were transferred from the old agency to the new one. However, it is still too early to assess the longer-term effects on families and social workers. Government has also introduced a new version of the 1970s approach to service integration, which involves the development of access centres. The initial strategy is to co-locate all services provided by the Department of Family Services and Housing within these centres. Although child welfare services are included, they are limited to those provided directly by the provincial government.

As in many other jurisdictions, child welfare workers in Manitoba have been bombarded with a number of new service models and different organizational structures over the past twenty-five years. There is also much more scrutiny of child welfare work. Although Manitoba has not adopted a rigid risk-assessment protocol, as some other provinces have done, there have been a number of child deaths within the child welfare service sector. It is common, in such circumstances, for the chief medical examiner or a judge to conduct an inquest. Two particularly controversial cases, both extensively covered by the media, have focused attention on the quality of service provided to parents and children. One involved the suicide of Lester Norman Desjarlais and the 1991 inquest into his death that uncovered the code of silence around abuse in one First Nations community (Teichroeb, 1997). In 1996, an inquest into the death of Sophie Schmidt identified errors in judgment and a lack of follow-up services by Winnipeg Child and Family Services when the agency returned the child, who was subsequently fatally injured, to her family (Teichroeb, 1996).

Although some form of practice oversight is important for identifying needed improvements, the costly, litigious nature of current inquest procedures, and the media focus on blaming individuals, is problematic. Another complication is the shifting focus of organizational restructuring. Although the current approach to restructuring favours a more community-based model, consistent with Aboriginal aspirations, there is no guarantee that future crises will not lead to calls for a more centrally controlled model of service delivery. One is left to ponder whether a more consistent commitment to community-based services and a focus on improving practice in response to identified problems might have produced greater benefits for both service users and social workers.

In summary, it is apparent that the child welfare scene in Manitoba bears many resemblances to that in BC. Manitoba has experienced its share of crises, and responses to crises have often taken the form of organizational restructuring. However, some of the restructuring has led to the formation of First Nations agencies, and in this respect, at least, Manitoba has grappled with one of the most serious issues in child welfare.

Ontario

In the 1990s, legislative changes expanded the definition of a child in need of protection, giving children's aid societies (CAS) and courts a greater mandate to intervene. Amendments to the *Child and Family Service Act* (1984) included neglect as grounds for protection and broadened the definition of "emotional abuse" to include, for example, exposure to domestic violence. Another legislative amendment required that children under the age of six years who had been in care for twelve months be made Crown (permanent) wards, and attempts were made to provide more permanency for this group of young children. A legislative change also strengthened the reporting requirements for professionals. Altogether, these changes have contributed to a substantial increase in children coming into CAS care.

First Nations

The increased rights given to First Nations in the *Child and Family Service Act* led to the formation of five First Nations (FN) agencies to take over mandatory child protection services in more remote parts of the province. It is difficult to evaluate the effectiveness of these agencies, but a video made by one of the first, in Sioux Lookout, Ontario, suggests that their practices are similar to those of traditional non-Native agencies. The video focused on placement and supervision in foster care, with no reference to strengthening children's families or their home communities.

In southern Ontario, communities with large FN populations, such as Toronto and the FN community at Ohsweken near Brantford (population over 10,000), have not opted to accept authority for child protection as allowed by the legislation. They have child and family agencies staffed by Aboriginal workers, but these agencies have not assumed the mandated function of taking children into care. The director of the Ohsweken agency told this author that her agency preferred the more limited role because she believed that the funds provided by the province for the child protection function would not be adequate to do effective work. She pointed to the high caseloads and high turnover of workers at Ontario's traditional child protection agencies, the children's aid societies (sometimes combined with family agencies).

Changes Introduced by the Political Right

Other government policies and actions that have affected child welfare in Ontario were introduced by the ultra-conservative government of Mike Harris, elected in 1995. In 1996, the provincial coroner's office launched a series of inquests into the deaths of children who had received child welfare services. These were followed in 1997 by a report from the provincial Child Mortality Task Force and in 1998 by a report from a panel of experts appointed by the minister of community and social services. Recommendations from these inquests and reviews touched on many aspects of child welfare service delivery and pointed to the need for an expansion of the legislation to include neglect and a broader definition of emotional maltreatment. At this point, the ministry decided to develop standardized investigation procedures in the hope of providing better protection for children. The result was a prescribed Ontario risk-assessment model (ORAM), similar to that adopted in BC in the mid to late 1990s.

The use of the ORAM tended to downgrade the assessment skills of graduate social workers by substituting a prescribed "tick-off" approach to measuring a child's need for protection. The model did not leave room for sound clinical judgment to inform the protection assessment. Combined with the stressful nature of the work, one effect of this compliance-based approach was to make child protection work less attractive to graduate social workers. In 2001, the Ontario Association of Children's Aid Societies (OACAS), which represents fifty CASs in Ontario, made a submission to the province's standing committee on finance and economic affairs. In the submission, OACAS stated that, despite government funding to hire new workers, "CAS's cannot find available workers for the eligible positions. Administrative requirements of front-line workers have increased because of amendments to legislation, new standards, the use of an automated recording package, and the implementation of the Ontario Risk Assessment Model" (OACAS, 2001a, p. 5).

In addition to the work generated by the government's administrative requirements, the new approach tended to diminish CAS workers' professional satisfaction by reducing their person-to-person work with families and children. A workload measurement study published in 2001 showed that front-line staff spent less than 30 percent of their time in face-to-face contact with clients. They spent most of their time doing government-mandated case documentation, and many worked significant amounts of overtime to complete the work expected of them (OACAS, 2001b).

Economic Cutbacks, 1995-2005

The increased number of children coming to CAS attention after 1995 is attributable to the reduced spending power of low-income families. The Conservative Harris government reduced provincial social assistance payments by over 21 percent in 1995, and except for a 3 percent cost-of-living raise by the Liberal government in 2004, these funds have never been replaced. Taking inflation into account, it is generally acknowledged that recipients of social assistance have 35 to 40 percent less spending power than they did before the Harris cutbacks.

The link between poverty and CAS involvement was shown by a London (Ontario) study. In 1995, 65 percent of families on the London CAS caseloads were on social assistance. In 2001, the figure was 64 percent (Leschied, Whitehead, Hurley, and Chiodo, 2003-4). The same study showed that the rate of children who were admitted to CAS care and whose families were on social assistance almost doubled, from 47 percent in 1995 to 80 percent in 2001.

At the provincial level, the number of child abuse and neglect investigations conducted in Ontario nearly tripled between 1993 and 2003, expanding from an estimated 45,000 investigations in 1993 to close to 130,000. The number of children in care has increased from 10,000 in the early 1990s to over 18,000. The province spends over $1.1 billion dollars a year on direct child welfare services, more than twice as much as it spent in the late 1990s. Part of this increase is attributable to changes in legislation that encourage CASs to intervene in a broader range of cases. In the early 1990s, many agencies kept their caseloads down by intervening only in cases of child abuse; now they are increasingly addressing more chronic and multi-layered problems associated with neglect, exposure to domestic violence, and socioeconomic disadvantage.

Child Welfare Evaluation, 2002-3

Following the reforms introduced by the Harris government, the ministry undertook a comprehensive evaluation of the child welfare system. The evaluation examined some of the unintended consequences of the earlier reforms and concluded that further changes were necessary. The increased workload, higher number of children in care, and associated expenses could not be sustained without modifications to the funding framework, to government policy, and to the CAS approaches to service delivery.

The program evaluation highlighted the need for a stronger emphasis on outcomes, an investment in research, and the development of a common information system. It encouraged implementation of an outcomes model of child assessment and a differential approach (rather than the ORAM) for responding to lower-risk cases. The evaluation also suggested the CASs should be using alternative dispute-resolution techniques to lessen their reliance on court-ordered interventions.

Promising Initiatives

Despite the continuing heavy workload and financial stress on CASs, some progressive moves have been made to prevent child abuse and neglect by strengthening families and communities. Building on the child welfare changes developed and implemented between 1998 and 2000, Ontario has embarked on a transformation agenda that has included moving child welfare services to the new Ministry of Children and Youth Services, completing a system-wide evaluation of child welfare programs, and establishing a Child Welfare Secretariat to address the findings and recommendations of the program evaluation (Ministry of Children and Youth Services, 2005).

Some of the positive initiatives aimed at families include:

- The "wraparound approach," in which family members, interested professionals, and friends come together to work on behalf of an individual child who needs extra support to continue living in the community, or on behalf of a family that requires support for its parenting capacity;

- Alternative dispute-resolution approaches, such as mediation, to help parents reach an agreement with a CAS about plans for a child, thus avoiding a prolonged court process;
- Family group conferencing, in which a range of interested family members are brought together to plan for children who seem to require care outside their immediate families;
- Kinship care, which involves placing children in the care of relatives who have the parenting capacity and are able to provide children with a permanent and secure family;
- Community capacity building, which improves child safety, well-being, and permanence;
- A "differential response" method of child welfare service delivery, which involves a system of alternatives/options determined by the type and severity of maltreatment.

One form of community development aimed at helping children before they are in need of protection was initiated by the Offord Centre for the Study of Children at Risk in Hamilton. The centre collaborated with schools in southern Ontario to develop recreation and skills development programs to enrich the lives of children from low-income, at-risk families.

Summary

Conditions for children at risk in Ontario seem to have worsened over the past decade, driven partly by the 1995 cutbacks to social assistance, combined with the escalating cost of living. Living at a subsistence level undermines the efforts of low-income parents to care for their children. Changes to legislation have resulted in many more children coming to the attention of CASs. The 2004 creation of a separate Ministry of Children and Youth Services may help to focus public attention and funding on the child welfare system, which is presently stretched beyond capacity. The ministry has developed a plan for reforming the system and has released funds to help CASs identify best practices.

Nova Scotia

In 1990, the provincial government enacted new provisions under the *Children and Family Services Act*. The new provisions were designed to focus attention on prevention in addition to the more narrow concern around the protection of children. However, this laudable intent did not materialize. A study conducted five years later concluded that "with poverty, unemployment, job insecurity, drug abuse and other health issues creating enormous stress for families, personal problems are becoming more serious and are manifesting at an earlier age. Agencies do not have sufficient resources to do preventive work as emphasized in the legislation and at the same time deal with the increasingly complex personal and family situations which demand their attention" (Gilroy, 2000, p. 26).

As a result, the only family situations that receive attention from child welfare agencies are those in which children are considered to be at risk. Agencies deal with these situations by conducting investigations to determine the safety of children, and a not-uncommon response is to recommend apprehension. Services are not provided to families if investigations have determined that the children are not at risk.

Child welfare practice in Nova Scotia has also become increasingly legalistic. Court and legalistic processes dominate practice: agencies hire lawyers to present cases in court, with the social worker being relegated to the role of witness. Court-ordered services, such as assessments of family situations, are contracted out to psychologists and social workers in private practice on the assumption that these individuals will be able to provide more objective assessments than child welfare workers can. In turn, the focus on investigations and on the documentation required for court has resulted in a vast increase in paperwork, leaving social workers little time for clients and social work practices. A major caseload review conducted in 2002 reported that "90% of social workers' time is spent entering notes in the computer system and workers have been told that not entering notes is a liability issue" (Nova Scotia Government Employees Union, 2002, p. 49).

Recent attention to child welfare has focused on the question of governance: Should child welfare services be provided by the province, by private agencies, or by a mixed model? The issue has not yet been resolved, but like other debates and reviews it has demanded the time and attention of child welfare workers, adding to their already overburdened work lives.

As noted above, many clients live in poverty, and many children come into care because their parents are poor. Children who come into care under voluntary care agreements tend to return to care. One obvious reason for this is that both children and parents agree that children are better in care than in their parental home. A reduction in poverty would eliminate the need for these voluntary (and many involuntary) care arrangements.

Finally, it should be noted that despite the over-representation of black and Aboriginal children in the care of child welfare agencies, there is an insufficient number of black and Aboriginal social workers in the province.

AS NOTED AT THE BEGINNING OF THE CHAPTER, we conclude with comments from a literature review of child welfare practice in Canada. The review came as a response to members of the Canadian Association of Social Workers who had voiced loud and continuing complaints about the ineffectiveness of child welfare policies and practices. The review sought to establish whether these complaints came from relatively few disenchanted social workers or whether they represented an accurate view of the state of the child welfare enterprise. The reviewer concluded that child welfare was indeed in need of substantial reform: "There is a plethora of evidence to suggest the current child protection system is not working. Despite a consensus on this, attempts to date have been concentrated on trying to 'fix' the system with rules, tools, techniques and conformity to procedures. There is an urgent need to challenge these iatrogenic attempts. Practice wisdom and research provide ample evidence to cease trying to reduce the complex, personal, professional and social issues associated with child protection work to problems of bureaucratic administration" (Barter, 2005a, p. 1).

Another comment from Barter provides an apt summary to this chapter: If we as a country had been asked to design child welfare services in such a way as to alienate clients, frustrate staff, and anger the public, we could not have done a better job than the present system (Barter, 2005b, paraphrased).

References

Barter, K. (2005a). Working conditions for social workers and linkages to client outcomes in child welfare: A literature review. Ottawa: Canadian Association of Social Workers.

–. (2005b). Re-conceptualizing services for the protection of children. In F.J. Turner and J.C. Turner (Eds.), *Canadian social welfare* (5th ed., pp. 316-32). Toronto: Pearson Education Canada.

Gilroy, J. (2000). The changing face of child welfare: Perspectives from the field. In M. Callahan, S. Hessle, and S. Strega (Eds.), *Valuing the field: Child welfare in an international context* (pp. 22-42). Aldershot, UK: Ashgate Press.

Hudson, P., and McKenzie, B. (2003). Extending Aboriginal control over child welfare services: The Manitoba Child Welfare Initiative. *Canadian Review of Social Policy, 51,* 49-66.

Leschied, A., Whitehead, P., Hurley, D., and Chiodo, D. (2003-4). Protecting children is everybody's business. *Journal of the Ontario Association of Children's Aid Societies, 47*(3), pp. 10-15.

McKenzie, B. (1991). Decentralization in Winnipeg: Assessing the effects of community controlled child welfare services. *Canadian Review of Social Policy, 27,* 57-66.

Ministry of Children and Youth Services. (2005, June). Child welfare transformation 2005: A strategic plan for a flexible, sustainable, and outcome oriented service delivery model. (Unpublished document circulated to Ontario CASs.)

Nova Scotia Government Employees Union. (2002). *Working group report.* Halifax: Author.

Ontario Association of Children's Aid Societies. (2001a). Submission to the Standing Committee on Finance and Economic Affairs. *Journal of the Ontario Association of Children's Aid Societies, 45*(1), pp. 2-6.

–. (2001b). Workload measurement project report: Executive summary. *Journal of the Ontario Association of Children's Aid Societies, 45*(1), pp. 2-6, 8-18.

Teichroeb, R. (1996, 1 November). CFS failed baby, report. *Winnipeg Free Press,* A1, A3.

–. (1997). *Flowers on my grave.* Toronto: Harper Collins.

11

The Case for a Comprehensive Vision for Child Welfare

Brian Wharf

The preceding chapters have chronicled numerous attempts to improve the child welfare enterprise. These attempts have taken different shapes, from inquiries and reviews designed to identify problems and propose solutions, to alterations in the responsibilities assigned to the ministry in charge of child welfare, to changes in the boundaries of regional and local offices, and finally to changes in the very name of the ministry. In this chapter we will examine the changes that have been made over the past thirty years and conclude with suggestions for a comprehensive reform of child welfare. The changes to the time of writing (June 2006) include the following:

- The proclamation of the *Community Resources Act,* based on a philosophical platform of community participation, integration, and decentralization of services. The act established locally-based resource boards and community health and human resource centres. This reform dissolved three children's aid societies and the social assistance programs previously provided by the cities of Victoria and Vancouver.
- The emergence of a different philosophy that sought to limit the responsibilities of the ministry in charge of child welfare and encouraged the voluntary and not-for-profit sectors to provide support services to families and children.
- A major reorganization of the ministry that was designed to increase its effectiveness by establishing three separate streams of services: income assistance, child welfare, and services for the developmentally delayed.
- The establishment of two community panels, including one specifically for Aboriginal peoples, to elicit the opinions of professionals, clients, and citizens about the ways in which child welfare services were being provided.
- The establishment of a community development program designed to connect local social services offices with their communities.

- The implementation of two of the key recommendations made by the Gove Inquiry: the transfer of juvenile justice programs and mental health services for children and youth to the Ministry for Children and Families, and the adoption of a risk-assessment instrument that would help practitioners be more rational and systematic when investigating child neglect and abuse.
- The delegation of authority to First Nations and Aboriginal child welfare agencies. This process began in 1987, and there are now twenty-four agreements in place. These agreements cover the residents of over a hundred bands, two urban areas, and Métis people in BC. Five more agreements in the planning/start-up phase will cover nearly fifty more bands and communities (see Appendix 3).
- An attempt to introduce a system of regional governance for child welfare. This plan has not yet been implemented, but, like all other changes, it has occupied the time of many ministry staff and diverted attention from the day-to-day responsibilities of serving clients. The latest review of BC's child protection has also recommended regional governance (Hughes, 2006). This time, however, $100 million has been made available over the next three years to implement the recommendations.

It is pertinent to include here a comment on the role of the media in child welfare. For the most part the media show little interest in the day-to-day activities of child welfare workers, but their attention reaches epic proportions in the event of an injury to, or death of, a child. This is by no means unique to BC or Canada (Ayre, 2001). Indeed, in many instances of government and ministry failures, media reports have revealed less than desired objectivity. Thus, in analyzing the *Vancouver Sun*'s coverage of the Vaudreuil case and the proceedings of the Gove Inquiry, Callahan and Callahan (1997) found that the newspaper had, from the outset, determined that Ms. Vaudreuil was an inadequate and uncaring mother and that the social workers involved were incompetent. All subsequent coverage was framed by these initial impressions.

The above list of major changes would be incomplete without noting the frequent alterations in the geographic boundaries of ministry regions and offices. For example, five regions were in place in 1947. Over time, the number increased to thirteen. By 1980 there were twenty regions, but the number decreased to nine in the early 1990s. With the creation of the Ministry for Children and Families in 1996, the number of regions expanded to twenty again, and three years later the number was reduced to eleven. Finally as part of Gordon Hogg's plan for regionalization, five regions were created – the same number that had existed in 1947. Following the Hughes Report, this number may change yet again (Hughes, 2006; see also Chapter 9).

And to the shifting sands created by the structural changes must be added the frequent changes of ministers and deputy ministers. From 1986 to 2004, fifteen ministers and no fewer than thirteen deputies served in these key positions, with some appointments lasting only a year or two. Indeed, between 1996 and 2006 there were three separate times (1996, 2000, and 2004) when three ministers were appointed in a single calendar year.

The Impact of Changes

The overall impact of the frequent changes in the ministry has been minimal. Some changes, such as the community resource board reform, had the potential to significantly improve the services provided by the ministry had they been allowed to continue. Some inquiries, like the community panel reports, contained positive recommendations for change that were never implemented. Changes in the geographic boundaries resulted in only minor alterations in the programs and services of the ministry. However, two changes in the day-to-day practice of child welfare work did represent substantial shifts in practice.

The first occurred during the long period (one is tempted to say "reign") during which John Noble was the deputy minister and for a time also the Superintendent of Child Welfare. As described in Chapter 4, Noble and his senior staff had a considerable impact on practice by gradually reducing the scope of the child welfare role to one that consisted mainly of investigating complaints of abuse and neglect. The objective was to focus on the set of skills required to investigate complaints and, where appropriate, to present information that a judge would accept as evidence that a child was being neglected or abused. The consequence of this change was to transform the role of social worker from helper to "social cop" – a label mentioned frequently by clients who voiced their opinions to the community panels (see Chapter 6).

In addition, during this period the ministry assumed responsibility for income assistance programs that had been formerly handled by municipalities. This move was welcomed by some, particularly municipal governments, but the increased responsibility involved protracted discussions and negotiations and added considerably to the size of the ministry. This change was designed to make the provision of income assistance consistent across the province, but it had the consequence of adding to the size and the complexity of local offices.

The second change that represented a major shift in practice was the adoption of a risk-assessment instrument. As noted in Chapter 8, this procedure was intended to assist experienced and well-trained practitioners. It would be a guide to practice. However, during the process of implementation, this intent was substantially altered. The instrument came to dictate the way in which practice was conducted: in effect, risk assessment reinforced the role of the "social cop" who conducted rigorous and impersonal investigations rather than providing assistance and support. Hence, risk assessment had a definite impact on practice, but it was not the kind of impact seen as desirable by the editors of this book. It must be mentioned, however, that some front-line staff, particularly those with little experience, adopted the instrument with enthusiasm because it spelled out the procedures to be followed in a very explicit fashion. Implementing these procedures meant that staff would be "protected" from management should a child be subsequently injured or neglected.

In our view, reform of the child welfare enterprise requires both a comprehensive view of, and a vision for, child welfare. To a certain extent the principles that drove the community resource board experiment – citizen participation, service integration, and decentralization of authority – met this criteria for change, but they ignored the contextual issues of poverty, culture, and, to some extent, intergenerational challenges. In the following discussion we set out what we see as the elements that must be addressed in a comprehensive vision: poverty, culture, organizational and governance issues, and the day-to-day practice of child welfare workers.

The Context of Child Welfare: Poverty

Any significant improvement in child welfare must begin by recognizing the context of the enterprise. It is a context dominated by poverty. As many others have done in the past, we contend that the single most powerful way to improve child welfare is to eliminate poverty among children and families (see, for example, Kitchen, Mitchell, Clutterbuck, and Novick, 1991; Kufeldt and Theriault, 1995; Prilleltensky, Nelson, and Peirson, 2001). The fact that poor families, particularly those led by single women, are substantially overrepresented in the child welfare enterprise has been documented in a series of studies dating back to reports by the National Council of Welfare in 1975 and 1979. Indeed the community panel report, referred to in Chapter 3, concluded that "poverty is a child welfare issue and when governments allow children to live in poverty they are in effect committing systemic child neglect" (Community Panel, 1992, p. 9).

Governments at many levels have acknowledged the existence of poverty among children and families. Indeed, in 1989 the federal government made a commitment to eliminate child poverty by the year 2000. However, despite this commitment, now embarrassingly long past its due date, there has been only the most marginal improvement in the rates of child poverty. One effort by the federal government – the introduction of a child benefit program – was offset by the action of some provincial governments, including that in BC, to reduce the benefits of those receiving social assistance by the amount made available through the federal program.

The impact of low rates of social assistance on child welfare is substantial. Thus, "in 2001, 65% of the children taken into the care of the Ministry came from families in receipt of social assistance" (Foster and Wright, 2002, p. 114). For Aboriginal children, the rates of poverty and the percentage of children taken into care are much higher. Like many other urban centres, Vancouver has a high number of First Nations and Aboriginal families; in 2001, "92.9 in every 1,000 aboriginal children were in care, a number 60% higher than the neighbouring community of Burnaby" (ibid., p. 126). By 2003 this figure had grown to 140 per 1,000 Aboriginal children (see the discussion in Chapter 2). The latest figures for BC show that 23.9 percent of the province's children live below the poverty line. This is the highest percentage of any of the provinces, and it compares to 17.6 percent for Canada as a whole (Campaign 2000, 2005; First Call, 2005).

We do not intend here to launch into a detailed discussion of the reasons for the existence of poverty and the suggested remedies (see Hunter, 2003, and Lightman, 2002, for extended reviews of these issues). But from a child welfare perspective, some points are worth noting. Poverty means that parents cannot afford adequate housing, skills upgrading, daycare, or a home in a safe neighourhood. It is not poverty alone that results in some parents neglecting or abusing their children, but if poverty is long-lasting, if it is intergenerational, if there is no light at the end of the tunnel and seemingly no end to a life of coping with the dilemma of choosing between "pay the rent or feed the kids" (Hurtig, 1999), then poverty is a substantial contributor to the neglect and abuse of children.

At first glance it seems curious that eliminating poverty is beyond our interest and capacity as a society, whereas tax breaks are routinely provided to corporations and to wealthy individuals. On closer analysis it is clear that the elected representatives of all political parties have profited extremely well from existing policies governing education, employment, and the accumulation of wealth. Hence, most are reluctant to alter the arrangements that have suited them and, indeed, seem convinced that those who live in poverty do so because of laziness or a moral failing. Even more damaging is the assumption that if they are incapable of earning a decent livelihood, they are also potential failures as parents. However, as one client in a child welfare study noted, these assumptions might change if there were a shift in circumstances: "I would love policy makers to live like we do – first of all let them find an apartment with the money that social services provide, let them try to find furniture, let them try to buy food, let them live like that for a year and they would soon change the system" (Weller and Wharf, 1996, p. 11).

The Context of Child Welfare: Cultural Issues

It is abundantly clear from Chapters 1 and 5 that the attempt of child welfare agencies to impose Euro-Canadian values and standards of practice on

First Nations families and children has been a dismal failure. Indeed, as noted earlier, the ministry has recognized this failure and the compelling need to transfer responsibility for services to First Nations agencies. The first transfer occurred in 1987, when authority was delegated to the Usma Nuu-chah-nulth Community and Human Service Agency, and the process of delegation has continued to this date. By May 2006, twenty-four agreements were in place with First Nations and Aboriginal agencies serving the residents of more than 100 bands, two urban areas, and Métis. Since there are approximately two hundred bands in BC, the agreements in place leave a large number of bands without control over child welfare, although close to fifty more bands are in the planning/start-up phase.

However, it is important to note that these agreements represent only a partial delegation of authority. Aboriginal child and family agencies that have day-to-day responsibility for providing services must do so under the jurisdiction of provincial legislation. Many of these agencies have developed their own distinctive approaches to providing services. For example, many First Nations agencies involve the entire community in making plans for services: What kind of services do we need? Can they be provided in an integrated fashion? Do we have the resources to develop these services? In addition, staff of First Nations agencies work in a respectful and collaborative way with their clients. Yet since many First Nations lack adequate resources, they are unable to adopt the position, recommended in the report of the Aboriginal Committee of the Community Panel (1992), that no child should be apprehended because of the lack of resources available to his or her parents.

The applicability of ministry standards to First Nations communities is contentious. Some First Nations leaders take the position that delegation of control should be complete and that ministry standards should not apply. Ministers and senior officials have generally taken an opposing view. Regardless of citizenship, the protection of children must conform to provincial legislation and standards. To date, the latter view prevails, but whether it will do so as the number of delegated agreements and the competence of First Nations and Aboriginal agencies increase is debateable.

The Context of Child Welfare: Organizational Issues

While changes, such as the shifting of organizational boundaries, have achieved little of substance, more attention should have been given to the long-standing and troublesome issue of the compatibility of the two functions of child welfare: the protection of children and the support of families. In Chapter 6, the authors state their view that "strong consideration should be given to separating and protecting the funding for these two essential, parallel, child welfare activities. This would go a long way to stabilizing unproductive swings in one direction or the other, when both activities are necessary for long-term progress to be made."

The case for splitting the two functions rests on several planks. First, resources for child welfare are never plentiful, and when cost-cutting measures are introduced, the resources assigned to the investigative function inevitably exceed those for family support measures. Second, it is difficult for many child welfare workers to balance investigation and support. Can one be a hard-headed inspector of family difficulties and, at the same time, a friendly counsellor and advocate? Third, if the family support function were assigned to voluntary, not-for-profit agencies like neighbourhood houses and family service agencies, it would be clear to families and other professionals where to go for help without fearing that a request or referral would result in an investigation.

A more radical argument, going beyond merely separating the functions, was advanced many years ago by Callahan (1993). In keeping with the conclusion of the Aboriginal Committee of the Community Panel (1992) that no child should be taken into care because of inadequate resources, Callahan called for the elimination of neglect as a cause for apprehension. She argued that child abuse is a crime, and like any other crime it should be dealt with by the criminal justice system, whereas neglect occurs largely because some parents lack sufficient resources to care for their children. Implementing these two reforms would allow the child welfare enterprise to concentrate most of its resources on supporting families and joining with voluntary agencies, such as neighbourhood houses and daycare centres, to plan for the community care of children.

Despite the considerable logic behind this argument, it has not been adopted in any province in Canada and, in our view, is not likely to be adopted in the near future. Removing the issue of neglect from child welfare legislation would require the elimination of poverty, and as we have noted above, this reform seems beyond not so much the capacity as the will of the nation. In addition, the justice system is unlikely to accept the troublesome responsibility of child abuse without a substantial increase in resources.

Other researchers in child welfare have pointed out that there is a strong argument against separation (see, for example, Cameron and Vanderwoerd, 1997). Putting aside her earlier argument due to the lack of attention to implementation, Callahan and her colleagues set out to determine the views of social workers and clients on the characteristics of best practice in child welfare (Callahan, Field, Hubberstey, and Wharf, 1998). Their study revealed that investigations have been, and should be, done in a manner that includes parents and children in assessing risk and in reviewing the adequacy of resources both in terms of material provisions and support from neighbours and family members. Just as counselling and other support measures can be provided respectfully and in a partnership fashion, so can investigations. In other words, best practice means that the two functions can be balanced. A previous study termed this respectful approach to investigation "family action planning" (Weller and Wharf, 1996).

Our thoughts on this issue were formed through the conceptualization of practice as community social work. We recognize that this conceptualization represents a marked departure from present practice, and as such it may not be adopted into mainstream practice. However, as argued in Chapter 3, community governance of child welfare would provide a hospitable environment for the practice of community social work. Given the extensive discussion of community governance in previous chapters, we will make only a brief comment on this issue in the final section of this chapter.

The Day-to-Day Practice of Social Workers in Child Welfare: Community Social Work

We want to emphasize at the outset that community social work cannot overcome the deleterious effects of public issues like poverty on the lives of clients. This approach does acknowledge the impact of public issues and helps clients recognize that they are not responsible for these conditions. By including public issues in individual and group discussions, community social work represents a considerable improvement over the current approach of casework.

Briefly, the current approach of social workers in child welfare has been dominated by a mode of practice that sees clients not as citizens or residents entitled to services, but as cases to be counted, inspected, and controlled. Casework involves individual social workers interviewing individual cases, preferably in the office. It is a practice modelled on the more prestigious professions of law and medicine, where home visits are a thing of the past.

However, office-based and individualistic practice renders invisible the home situations of the clients and the neighbourhoods in which they live. It denies social workers the opportunity to form close connections with schoolteachers, public health nurses, and the staff of neighbourhood houses. Casework transforms child welfare into an isolated venture in which only worker and case are present. Casework attends to private troubles and ignores public issues.

In addition, as noted in Chapter 8, the introduction of risk-assessment and case-management schemes into child welfare has made matters worse. Prior to this, caseworkers did strive to create positive relationships with clients, even though their efforts were hampered by being located in offices and by an unwarranted assumption that casework, as a professional activity, could resolve the problems faced by clients.

Contrast this approach to practice to that of community social work, where "workers no longer take responsibility for the problem at hand.

They recognize that most of the caring and monitoring is done informally in the family and neighbourhood and they work to build the caring capacity of the people and the networks involved. Using their time to build partnerships with families and their networks, with agencies, schools, churches and neighbourhood groups, they help interweave formal and informal caring. They spend less time doing to or for families and more time working with them, less time on crisis intervention and more on prevention and early identification" (Adams and Nelson, 1995, p. 103). As one client put it, community social workers initiate the relationship with an offer of help: "If a social worker had come to my door and rather than saying 'I'm here to check out a complaint' had said 'I'm here because I care about children and I want to help you to keep things together'" (Callahan, Hooper, and Wharf, 1998, p. 37).

The philosophical base of community social work is that those who come to the attention of child welfare are "harassed people doing their best to survive and care for their children in circumstances that would drive professionals to distraction" (Hern, quoted in Weller and Wharf, 1996, p. 31). "Clients" are seen as people with strengths, who are entitled to receive services and who should be involved in identifying problems, in working through these problems, and in contributing to the life of their neighbourhood. The relationship between worker and client becomes a partnership, with each bringing resources and ideas to the task of protecting children and supporting families.

Given the ministry's focus on investigating complaints of neglect and abuse and contracting with voluntary agencies for the provision of family support services, did this create an opportunity for the voluntary sector to engage in community social work and community organizing? Whether the sector possessed the interest and the capacity to adopt these modes of practice is not known. What is known is that the very precise expectations of the ministry virtually precluded engagement in these or other innovative approaches to practice. Rather, voluntary agencies were required to mount specific programs – such as budgeting, parent training, and anger management – and to provide evidence of client outcomes. Some clients undoubtedly benefited from these programs; others might have been assisted more by participating in groups and sharing both troubles and remedies to these troubles. In short, clients were expected to fit into programs rather than having access to programs developed to meet their particular needs.

Casework infiltrated by risk assessment dominates practice, but there are several examples of community social work in BC. Chapter 6 contains a description of the work of Peter Scott, a staff member of the short-lived community development program, as well as a mention of the "Empowering Women" project, an innovative partnership between the ministry and the School of Social Work at the University of Victoria that explored the viability of a community social work approach (Callahan, Hooper, and

Wharf, 1998; Callahan, Lumb, and Wharf, 1994). Following completion of the 1994 project, the minister at the time, Joy MacPhail, wrote to the directors of the project: "I am aware of the success of this project which was undertaken in two offices and assure you that the Ministry is committed to building on this success" (MacPhail, personal communication, 19 August 1994). The firing of Joyce Rigaux, the Superintendent of Child Welfare who had championed the project within the ministry, effectively spelled the end of ministry commitment.

There may well be other examples, but to this author's knowledge the longest-lasting example of community social work practice in the ministry occurred in the Hazelton office (Wharf, 2002). Two factors were instrumental in the office's decision to adopt a community approach. The first was the recognition that, like many other rural communities, Hazelton lacked the array of resources typically found in larger centres. The office did not have access to mental health services, it lacked residential treatment facilities, and foster homes were scarce. The second reason was the proximity to First Nations communities where a kitchen-table style of decision making involving all concerned in a particular issue had long been in effect.

These two factors pushed the staff of the office to recognize that the only way to provide effective child welfare services was to involve the community – schoolteachers, public health nurses, social workers from the First Nations bands, and foster parents. They copied the kitchen-table style when deciding what to do about complaints of child neglect and abuse. Their approach was so successful that although 125 children were taken into care over a five-year period (1998-2002), in only two instances did the parents contest the decision. In other words, parents recognized their inability to look after their children and agreed that care by the ministry was necessary. Typically, children are in care for a relatively short period of time, which gives their parents an opportunity to resolve personal issues or secure more adequate housing.

Because of the respect accorded to clients by community social work, this approach to practice is able to balance the two functions of protection and support. However, many factors, including the culture of the ministry and the propensity of many social workers to favour individualistic approaches, mean that only a few have chosen to practice community social work. Despite the fact that it represents a powerful way of working with clients, community social work has been a neglected approach within the ministry.

Day-to-Day Practice: Community Organizing in Child Welfare
As conceptualized by Adams and Nelson (1995), community social work represents a community-based and respectful approach to practice with children and families. It does not include working with clients and others to improve harmful environments, whereas community organizing is all

about changing environments. Community organizing is the only approach available to the staff of child welfare agencies that addresses public issues. Of course, it cannot change national social security policies, but it can draw attention to the impact of these policies and it can bring about modest environmental changes, such as establishing community gardens and kitchens or protesting against slum landlords.

Regrettably, there are few examples of community organizing by ministry staff in BC. Even the staff of the community development program noted in Chapter 6 concentrated its efforts on community social work such as organizing self-help groups and working on inter-agency co-operation.

There are few examples in other provinces, but two agencies with long-standing experience in community organizing are Toronto Children's Aid and the Winnipeg Family and Children's Service (Hudson, 1999; Lee and Richards, 2002). In these agencies, child welfare workers have been assigned to low-income neighbourhoods with the explicit objective of changing conditions that negatively affect families and children. Thus, staff have collaborated with residents and anti-poverty advocates to document the effects of poverty and inadequate housing and have presented reports on these matters to both municipal and provincial governments. Staff members have worked to improve recreational resources, to change dangerous traffic patterns, and to establish community kitchens. Although community organizing has remained on the periphery of practice, it has received plaudits from policy-makers who are aware of its contributions. Bruce Rivers, the executive director of the Toronto agency, has described it as "a remarkable program. Its staff have been able to mobilize communities to take responsible action for their children and to organize around critical social issues such as child poverty, a lack of affordable housing and inadequate child care resources" (quoted in Lee and Richards, 2002, p. 188).

Community organizing represents a more radical approach than community social work, given its commitment to addressing public issues. We would applaud a decision to resurrect the community development program in BC and to see staff of the ministry engage with residents in changing environments, although we realize this is not likely to occur in the near future. A first and most useful step would be the adoption of community social work.

Summing Up

The arguments presented in this and the preceding chapters make a compelling case that, as presently constituted, the child welfare enterprise is deeply flawed. It is an enterprise characterized by poor service to clients, a dispirited staff, and crises that inevitably provoke a cry for yet another inquiry. It is an enterprise viewed by First Nations families as the Wild Woman from whom children must be protected. In the same vein, many grandparents would rather care for grandchildren at considerable financial and emotional cost than have them placed in the care of the ministry (Callahan, Brown, MacKenzie, and Whittington, 2004).

Perhaps the most fundamental reason for the flawed nature of child welfare is that it lacks a comprehensive vision for the welfare of children and families. In our view, a comprehensive vision requires attention to the components that we have identified in this chapter: poverty, culture, the organization and governance of services, and the day-to-day practice of first-line workers. All previous efforts to improve child welfare have ignored poverty and, until very recently, culture; they scarcely took practice into account and have mistakenly assumed that tinkering with structures will suffice. Comprehensiveness means that all components must be addressed simultaneously and systematically.

BY LATE SUMMER 2006, the manuscript containing all of the preceding chapters had been submitted to UBC Press. However, in the fall of that year we received a commentary from England. We hasten to add that the delay cannot be attributed to the author of the commentary but rather to the tardiness of our request for it. Nevertheless, the commentary was of such significance that it prompted us to think again about our recommendations. The commentary and an alternative set of recommendations are presented in the following chapters.

References

Aboriginal Committee of the Community Panel on Family and Children's Services Legislation Review. (1992). *Liberating our children, liberating our nations*. Victoria: Ministry of Social Services.

Adams, P., and Nelson, K. (Eds). (1995). *Reinventing human services: Community and family centered practice*. New York: Aldine de Gruyter.

Ayre, P. (2001). Child protection and the media: Lessons from the last three decades. *British Journal of Social Work, 31*, 887-901.

Callahan, M. (1993). Feminist approaches: Women recreate child welfare. In B. Wharf (Ed.), *Rethinking child welfare* (pp. 172-209). Toronto: McClelland and Stewart.

Callahan, M., Brown, L., MacKenzie, P., and Whittington, B. (2004, Fall/Winter). Catch as catch can: Grandmothers raising their grandchildren and kinship care policy. *Canadian Review of Social Policy, 54*, 58-78.

Callahan, M., and Callahan, K. (1997). Victims and villains: Scandals, the press and policy making in child welfare. In J. Pulkingham and G. Ternowetsky (Eds.), *Child and family policies* (pp. 40-57). Halifax: Fernwood Publishing.

Callahan, M., Field, B., Hubberstey, C., and Wharf, B. (1998). *Best practice in child welfare*. Victoria: University of Victoria, School of Social Work, Child, Family and Community Research Program.

Callahan, M., Hooper, L., and Wharf, B. (1998). *Protecting children by empowering women*. Victoria: University of Victoria, School of Social Work, Child, Family and Community Research Program.

Callahan, M., Lumb, C., and Wharf, B. (1994). *Strengthening families by empowering women.* Victoria: University of Victoria, School of Social Work, Child, Family and Community Research Program.

Cameron, G., and Vanderwoerd, J. (1997). *Protecting children and supporting families: Promising programs and organizational realities.* New York: Aldine de Gruyter.

Campaign 2000. (2005). *Decision time for Canada: Let's make poverty history; 2005 report card on child poverty in Canada.* Toronto: Author. Retrieved 27 November 2005 from www.campaign2000.ca/rc/rc05/05NationalReportCard.pdf

Community Panel on Family and Children's Services Legislation Review. (1992). *Making changes: A place to start.* Victoria: Ministry of Social Services.

First Call. (2005, 24 November). *BC Campaign 2000: BC had the worst record.* Fact sheet #2. Vancouver: Author.

Foster, L.T, and Wright, M. (2002). Patterns and trends in children in the care of the province of British Columbia: Ecological, policy and cultural perspectives. In M.V. Hayes and L.T. Foster (Eds.), *Too small to see, too big to ignore: Child health and well-being in British Columbia* (pp. 103-40). Canadian Western Geographical Series, Vol. 35. Victoria: Western Geographical Press.

Hudson, P. (1999). Community development and child protection: A case for integration. *Community Development Journal, 34*(4), 346-54.

Hughes, E.N. (2006). *BC children and youth review: An independent review of BC's child protection system.* Victoria: Ministry of Children and Family Development.

Hunter, G. (2003). The problem of child poverty in Canada. In A. Westhues (Ed.), *Canadian social policy* (pp. 29-49). Waterloo, ON: Wilfrid Laurier University Press.

Hurtig, M. (1999). *Pay the rent or feed the kids.* Toronto: McClelland and Stewart.

Kitchen, B., Mitchell, A., Clutterbuck, P., and Novick, M. (1991). *Unequal futures: The legacy of child poverty in Canada.* Toronto; Child Poverty Action Group and the Social Planning Council of Metropolitan Toronto.

Kufeldt, K., and Theriault, E. (1995). Child welfare experiences and outcomes: Themes, policy implications and research agenda. In J. Hudson and B. Galaway (Eds.), *Child welfare in Canada* (pp. 358-67). Toronto: Thompson Educational Publishing.

Lee, B., and Richards, S. (2002). Child protection through strengthening communities. In B. Wharf (Ed.), *Community work approaches to child welfare* (pp. 92-115). Peterborough, ON: Broadview Press.

Lightman, E. (2002). *Social policy in Canada.* Toronto: Oxford University Press.

National Council of Welfare. (1975). *Poor kids: A report by the National Council of Welfare on children in poverty in Canada.* Ottawa: Author.

–. (1979). *In the best interests of the child: A report by the National Council of Welfare on the child welfare system in Canada.* Ottawa: Author.

Prilleltensky, I., Nelson, G., and Peirson, L. (Eds.). (2001). *Promoting family wellness and preventing child maltreatment.* Toronto: University of Toronto Press.

Weller, F., and Wharf, B. (1996). *From risk assessment to family action planning.* Victoria: University of Victoria, School of Social Work, Child, Family and Community Research Program.

Wharf, B. (2002). The neighborhood house project in Victoria and the Hazelton office of the Ministry for Children and Families. In B. Wharf (Ed.), *Community work approaches to child welfare* (pp. 47-62). Peterborough, ON: Broadview Press.

12

From Child Protection to Safeguarding: The English Context

Tony Morrison

This chapter provides an overview of the current framework for protecting or "safeguarding" children in England, set in the context of government policy developed since the election of New Labour in 1997. Note that the focus is England rather than the United Kingdom. This is due to the emergence of devolved government in Wales and Scotland. However, while devolution has led to some important differences in administrative arrangements for children's services, the broad thrust of policy with regard to children is shared across the United Kingdom.

In the description that follows, reference will be made to the "local authority," of which there are approximately 150 across England and Wales. These authorities are responsible for the delivery of children's social services, education, housing, and environmental health services and are funded mainly by central government grants supported by local taxation. Thus, where children's legislation refers to the local authority, this includes not only social services but also education and housing.

Emergence of the Child Protection System, 1974-89

In 1974, a young child named Maria Colwell was murdered by her stepfather, heralding the first in a succession of highly publicized inquiry reports that over the following thirty years played a substantial role in shaping the approach to child protection work in England. Many of the factors identified – such as failures of inter-agency collaboration, information exchange, assessment, planning, reviewing, supervision, and training – have been reiterated in the fifty or so major child death inquiries that have followed. In response, government has focused on three main areas: legislative change; "proceduralization" of professional practice; and the development of administrative arrangements designed to ensure inter-agency collaboration in child protection cases.

The message from these early inquiries and the accompanying media and political furore was that professionals, and social workers in particular, had intervened too little and too late to remove children from unsafe situations. As a result, managing risk came to dominate the professional and inter-professional discourse. This was reflected in the growth of specialist child protection teams and advisors, operating within an increasingly complex and prescriptive array of child protection administrative processes. These included what were often lengthy inter-agency child protection procedures, risk-assessment tools, child protection conferences, and the introduction of a child protection register.

From Paternalism to Partnership: The *Children Act 1989*

A sea change occurred in the summer of 1986 when over one hundred children living in Cleveland, in the northeast of England, were removed from home on suspicion of having been sexually abused. They were removed largely on the advice of a single pediatrician using a particular diagnostic procedure. The fact that many of these children were from middle-class homes and had to be placed in adult wards in hospitals resulted in a public backlash of unparalleled ferocity. Now the allegation was that doctors, as well as social workers, were intervening "too much and too soon." The resulting inquiry paved the way for new framework legislation, the 1989 *Children Act.*

This act signalled, in legislative terms, the move from paternalism to partnership. While it built on much good practice that had developed during the 1980s in terms of including parents in case conferences and planning meetings, the act formally recast the power balance between professionals and parents and children on a more equal and transparent footing. Although social services departments retained their duties to make inquiries about potential cases of significant harm (often referred to as "investigations"), the act established a range of checks and balances. These ensured that parents and children had a much earlier right to challenge such interventions. Crucially, the new term "parental responsibility" ensured that even when children had been removed from their family home and placed into local-authority care, parents retained parental responsibility, but they shared it with the local authority. Parental responsibility could now only be terminated if a child was adopted. Thus, the act provided the legislative basis for social services to work in partnership with parents even when the child was in care. The act also increased the court's role in managing statutory cases, especially with regards to arrangements for assessments, contact, and placement.

In addition, the act identified a new population of children for whom the local authority had a preventive duty, namely, "children in need." These are defined as children whose health and development are likely to be impaired if additional services are not provided. The term includes all disabled children as well as other children whom the local authority identifies as children in need. The preventive provision of the act allowed for considerable local interpretation and definition, which in turn made it vulnerable to local decisions about prioritization of resources. This vulnerability became all too apparent when research studies, in particular the *Messages from Research* (UK Department of Health, 1995), found that, despite the act's preventive intent, professionals continued to refer to children as child protection cases rather than as children in need in order to ensure a response and access to services. This feature of interdisciplinary practice reflects how difficult it can be to detach professionals of any discipline from the anxiety-driven habit of pressing the alarm bell in order to gain and guarantee another service's attention and resources.

Refocusing Child Protection: The Mid-1990s
One study (Gibbons, Conroy, and Bell, 1995) found that only one in every seven children referred for child protection got as far as being placed on a child protection register. Of the remaining six, who were all children in need, only three were likely to receive a family support service. In other words, according to this study, in three out of every seven cases where children in need were investigated for possible abuse, the child ended up receiving no supportive services. Thus, child protection continued to be the gateway for services. The impact of such studies triggered a professional movement to refocus child protection work by situating it within the broader concept of family support (NCH, 1996).

To underpin this paradigm shift, a new needs-based, multidisciplinary assessment framework was developed (UK Department of Health, 2000). *The Framework for the Assessment of Children in Need and Their Families* focuses on three main domains: the child's needs; the parents' capacities; and environmental factors. The holistic nature of the framework, which incorporates educational, health, and environmental factors in addition to traditional child protection factors, offers the possibility of building an interdisciplinary assessment process based on needs rather than risk.

New Labour and the Social Exclusion Agenda
The landslide election victory of the New Labour government in 1997 provided fresh impetus for a preventive approach to children's services. The government's social policy agenda sought to address a number of areas of critical importance to the welfare of children, including equality of opportunity, welfare reform, social exclusion, child poverty, and youth crime and its causes. In addition to important tax credit and other income-based interventions designed to reduce poverty, one of New Labour's principal vehicles to drive these changes was "joined-up government." This resulted in funding for a raft of new wraparound services, such as Surestart (www.surestart.gov.

uk) for children aged 0 to 5 years, to help children from vulnerable family backgrounds make a successful transition into school, and expanded child-care provision to assist mothers who were returning to work. As Prime Minister Tony Blair has repeated over and over, "education, education, education" is seen by New Labour as the principal route out of social exclusion.

Integrated Children's Services, 2002-6

By the early years of the new millennium, the pace of public sector reform meant the agencies that had formerly welcomed the opportunity to work across ministries to deal with complex social issues were suffering from "initiative paralysis." The range of acronyms describing these new collaborative structures – HAZ (health action zones), EAZ (education action zones), DVF (domestic violence forum), BEST (behavioural education support teams), and many more – became a source of ridicule as professionals struggled to remember what they all stood for.

At the same time, the central government's control of local authority work via target-driven funding streams, along with ever more powerful audit and inspection functions within each government department, were increasingly in conflict with the good, if somewhat mesmerizing, intentions of the new cross-cutting initiatives.

In child protection, these tensions emerged dramatically following the death of Victoria Climbié, a child in London (Laming, 2003). The case exposed not only a lack of front-line collaboration, knowledge, and capacity, but also, more seriously, a lack of senior management and political accountability for the most vulnerable children. Following a national multidisciplinary audit of child protection systems, the result was a major policy paper, *Every Child Matters* (UK Treasury, 2003), which proposed a range of measures to transform children's services.

Every Child Matters

At the heart of this policy paper was a new determination to ensure organizational accountability and collaboration for the work of safeguarding children across government departments and to create a coherent relationship between universal and targeted services based on a national outcomes framework for all children. It identified five overarching objectives, namely, that each child should:

- be healthy
- stay safe
- enjoy and achieve
- make a positive contribution
- achieve economic well-being.

Every Child Matters also formalized what had been a gradual process since 1995 of redefining the concept of "safeguarding" as an activity that had a much wider scope than traditional, forensically focused "child protection." In effect, it sought to create a new set of governance arrangements designed to remedy the organizational and inter-agency barriers that had frustrated achievement of the preventive aspirations of the *Children Act 1989*, at the same time as it addressed wider aspects of social exclusion. Thus, aspects of "staying safe" included both environmental and interpersonal dimensions. Children must be cared for, must have security and stability, and must be safe from:

- maltreatment, neglect, violence, and sexual exploitation (interpersonal harm)
- accidental injury and death
- bullying and discrimination
- crime and anti-social behaviour (environmental harm).

To support this new and widened agenda, the *Children Act 2004* established a legal framework for integrated children's services. At the local authority level, education and children's social services were merged into a single "children's services authority" under a director of children's services. Alongside this, health services, police, and other agencies came under a new statutory duty to "safeguard and promote the welfare of children." The act also provided for the establishment of cross-government inspection regimes and created statutory Local Safeguarding Children Boards in every local authority. These boards were charged with co-ordinating the work of agencies to ensure they were effectively safeguarding children. If the *Children Act 1989* had provided the case management framework for the shift from paternalism to partnership, the *Children Act 2004* and *Every Child Matters* provided the template for a shift from collaboration to integration (Howarth and Morrison, in press; Morrison and Lewis, 2005).

Every Child Matters provides a framework for a continuum of differential responses to children's needs, with high-quality universal services as the cornerstone. The concept of children's trusts, with inter-agency responsibility and accountability for commissioning and delivering children's services, will play a key role in developing a more integrated approach. At the ground level, there are an increasing number of co-located multidisciplinary teams delivering services. New practice tools are evolving to support inter-agency collaboration over a much broader range of children's needs. These tools include:

- a common assessment framework

- the role of a lead professional
- an information-sharing index
- common and core competencies for all practitioners working with children.

(Note: Readers who are interested in these provisions can download details of the outcomes and their indicators, the inspection arrangements, and all of the tools mentioned above from the Every Child Matters website: www.everychildmatters.gov.uk)

Current and Future Challenges

While the philosophy and direction of *Every Child Matters* have been broadly welcomed by practitioners across the interdisciplinary spectrum, many challenges lie ahead. The implementation of this complex matrix of organizational and practice innovation poses a formidable challenge in terms of change management. This challenge is increased by the fact that few additional resources have been offered. The message is that the changes can be achieved by reconfiguring, rather than expanding, current service provision. Moreover, while *Every Child Matters* recognized the problems arising from conflicting central government targets and funding streams, this continues to be a problem. For instance, a new *Education Act* that has recently increased the autonomy of individual schools directly conflicts with the movement toward integrated services. The result is to make it harder to engage education at a strategic local authority level. On the health side, recent financial crises in the National Health Service, combined with the drive to a mixed health economy with an increased private-sector role, have significantly depleted health providers' capacity to focus on children's issues.

At a more fundamental level, the merger of children's social services with education presents major political and cultural challenges in addition to the administrative and professional issues involved. At the political level, education is a far larger player in every way. In particular, it is, alongside health, the most significant public-sector battleground on which coming elections will be fought. Voter satisfaction is a major function of education policy in a way that rarely affects policy in children's social care. Thus, this merger may turn out to be more akin to a takeover.

At the cultural level, education and children's social care, while both focused at the broad level on children, follow differing paradigms. Where education focuses on the many, social services focus on the few; where education focuses on group and curriculum, social services focus on the individual and a care pathway; while education seeks to make compromises to address the needs of individual children, for social services, the needs of each child are paramount and cannot be limited by the needs of other children.

In a recent workshop, education and social services managers were asked to describe what "behaviour" meant to them. Whereas the social services professionals saw behaviour as a signal to be understood within a wider context, their education colleagues saw behaviour as a problem to be managed. This brief anecdote speaks volumes about the chasm of context and paradigm that must be bridged if the merger of education and children's social care is to be truly effective. One thing is clear: without detailed attention paid to these differences and without developmental work across the services, the merger will not work.

Beyond these challenges are the problems of recruitment and retention that beset many of the front-line services crucial to children. Although a comprehensive workforce reform program is underway, vacancy rates and the use of external agency/bank staff continue to undermine the quality and continuity not only of social work services, but also of child psychiatrists and pediatric services. In addition, issues related to asylum seekers, new immigrants, and people-trafficking present new and formidable challenges to our health, education, social services, and police systems. Indeed, Victoria Climbié was a case in point. There are significant professional challenges arising from the increasingly rich cultural and ethnic demography of our workforces. As research on culturally heterogeneous workgroups points out, the successful management of difference, emotions, and conflicts will require emotionally competent and thoughtful managers (Ayoko and Härtel, 2002).

In conclusion, the jury is still out on whether the transformational aspirations of *Every Child Matters* will be met. One thing is clear, however, and that is that the journey from paternalism to partnership is a long and complex one, requiring profound change at both practice and organizational levels. It also cannot be achieved without the continuity and quality of leadership that acts as the nexus around which cultural change can be a shared and valued goal for everyone involved.

References

Ayoko, O.B., and Härtel, C.E.J. (2002). The role of emotion and emotion management in destructive and productive conflict in culturally heterogeneous workgroups. In N.M. Ashkanasy, W.J. Zerbe, and C.E.J. Härtel (Eds.), *Managing emotions in the workplace* (pp. 77-97). New York: M.E. Sharpe.

Gibbons, J., Conroy, S., and Bell, C. (1995). *Operating the child protection system: A study of child protection practices in English local authorities.* London: Her Majesty's Stationery Office.

Howarth, J., and Morrison, T. (in press). Collaboration, integration and change in children's services: Critical issues and key ingredients. *Child Abuse and Neglect.*

Laming, Lord. (2003). *The Victoria Climbié Inquiry: Report of an inquiry by Lord Laming.* Norwich: The Stationery Office.

Morrison, T., and Lewis, D. (2005). Toolkit for assessing the readiness of Local Safeguarding Children Boards: Origins, ingredients and applications. *Child Abuse Review, 14*(5), 297-316.

NCH. (1996). *Children still in need: Refocusing child protection in the context of children in need.* London: NCH.

UK Department of Health. (1995). *Child protection: Messages from research.* London: Her Majesty's Stationery Office.

–. (2000). *Framework for the assessment of children in need and their families.* London: Her Majesty's Stationery Office.

UK Treasury. (2003). *Every child matters.* Norwich: The Stationery Office.

13
Final Thoughts
Brian Wharf

It is apparent, from the Chapter 12 review of reforms in England, that many of the recommendations outlined in Chapter 11 have been implemented in that country. Legislation has emphasized the importance of including parents in making plans for the future care of children; social services have been integrated with education in an effort to erode the stigma attached to "welfare," be it child welfare or income assistance; and the responsibility for providing services has been awarded to local authorities. Yet despite these efforts, child welfare in England remains a severely troubled enterprise. Local authorities have experienced difficulty in recruiting staff, and there is frequent turnover of front-line personnel. In addition, as Morrison points out, front-line staff are bewildered and discouraged by the frequency with which new initiatives and plans emanate from head office, often with little consultation, minimal time or thought for implementation, and insufficient funding.

Morrison's review raises a question: Is child welfare such a seriously stigmatized set of services that "solutions," such as devolution and integration, and plans imposed from head offices have little or no effect? We know from a number of sources (e.g., Community Panel Reports, 1992; Callahan, Brown, Mackenzie, and Whittington, 2004) that parents experiencing difficulties in caring for their children do not turn to the ministry for help: "Grandmothers in our study had a highly negative image of child welfare, one that is frequently shared by the public, and they clearly feared the power of child welfare workers" (Callahan et al., 2004, p. 72). Rather, the ministry is regarded with suspicion bordering on hostility – staff are seen as "social cops" and "child snatchers" and are to be avoided at all costs. Is it then time to leave child welfare in the residual mould that it has occupied for so long? Is it time to confine the ministry to the task of investigating complaints and forget about well-meaning attempts to change it into an agency devoted to supporting and helping families?

It is worth noting here that for several decades the literature has severely criticized the residual, investigative approach to child welfare for being intrusive and disrespectful to clients, for stripping professional skills from staff, and for being, as a consequence, ineffective. (For verification of this claim, see, among many other sources, Callahan and Lumb, 1995; Cameron and Vanderwoerd, 1997; deMontigny, 1995; Kufeldt and McKenzie, 2003; Levitt and Wharf, 1985; Prilleltensky, Nelson, and Peirson, 2001; Swift, 1995; Wharf, 1993, 2002). Yet the literature has had little or no effect on practice. It may well be that both policy makers and first-line staff are so immersed in their day-to-day responsibilities and frequent crises that they have no time or energy to read critical reviews of their work or, following judicial reviews or public inquiries, to engage in substantial reforms of practice unless compelled to do so.

The foregoing argument immediately calls into question where the responsibility for support services should be placed and, as a second and equally important issue, whether provincial governments should provide funding? Some neoconservative governments would doubtless argue that the responsibility to provide support to young parents appropriately belongs to grandparents, relatives, and churches. While some relatives have the resources and time to assist, the study by Callahan et al. makes it clear that many grandparents take on the task of caring for their grandchildren without sufficient money or time. Kinship support and care often requires some aid from the state (Callahan et al., 2004).

Other types of governments, particularly those committed to social democracy, may well accept that they have a moral obligation to fund supportive services, and there is the additional and powerful argument of cost-effectiveness – providing support will divert many families from the formal child welfare system, at perhaps a lesser cost than having them in care. One study has estimated the costs of child abuse in Canada are between $15 and $16 billion annually (Bowlus, McKenna, Day, and Wright, 2003). While they suffer from a chronic lack of funds, agencies that provide a range of preventive programs do exist in most urban communities. Neighbourhood houses, community schools, and family places come to mind. These agencies are located in neighbourhoods, are governed by residents, and welcome residents to be both a recipient of and contributor to the work of the agency. And while attention has rarely been paid to evaluation, some evidence of effectiveness is available. For example, the rigorously evaluated Highfields project in Toronto demonstrated that the programs provided through this project reduced the number of children placed in the care of the Toronto child welfare agencies (Pancer, et al., 2003). An earlier project in Winnipeg concluded that "the risk for child maltreatment in a community can be reduced by social network intervention" (Fuchs, 1995, p. 121).

We cannot emphasize too strongly that we are not recommending a return to previous patterns of privatization in which the ministry contracted with agencies to provide time-limited skill-training programs to clients selected by the ministry. Rather, we want to strengthen neighbourhood-based preventive programs that serve all residents of a community and enhance the capacity of families and communities. Seen in this light, the recommendation is all about community development.

This recommendation might require the establishment of a provincial office of community development that could allocate funds to neighbourhood houses, family places, and community schools that conform to the above description of neighbourhood-based and -governed agencies devoted to strengthening the capacity of communities.

Two exceptions should be noted. First Nation communities should be given the choice of assigning the tasks of investigation and apprehension to the ministry and concentrating on preventive work or taking on both responsibilities. In fact, many First Nation agencies have shown a remarkable ability to fuse both tasks (see, for example, Brown et al., 2002; McKenzie, 2002).

A second exception concerns rural communities where agencies like neighbourhood houses do not exist. Here, the challenge to the provincial office would be to locate suitable agencies, be they community schools, transition houses, First Nation agencies, or public health units. Indeed, some rural offices of the ministry have, in a most unheralded fashion, taken on the task of both investigation and prevention and have welded them together in a harmonious fashion (see, among other sources, Wharf, 2002). Such offices might well qualify for funding from the provincial office in order to continue and enhance their preventive work.

In recommending the ministry be confined to its residual role of investigation, we wish to make clear that investigations should not be conducted in an intrusive fashion. Rather, they should take the form of family action planning, with all involved assessing both the gravity of the family circumstances and the resources available (see Callahan et al., 1997; Weller and Wharf, 2002). In instances where serious injuries have occurred, parental involvement may not be possible nor indeed desirable.

While we recognize that the ministry does not have the mandate nor the resources to address the poverty that surrounds the lives of its clients, we believe it does have the responsibility to systematically record and report on these circumstances. Politicians, the press, and all citizens must be educated about the intimate connections between the welfare of children and poverty. Child neglect and abuse are related in large part to poverty, some of it intergenerational, and the attendant consequences of substandard housing, stress, and feelings of despair and hopelessness. The lack of awareness of the impact of poverty inhibits policy makers' ability to take action to combat this most serious of social issues.

To conclude, it is our view that the paths to reform charted in this chapter and in Chapter 11 would bring about substantial changes in the lives of clients and of staff. Transforming the ministry into an organization dedicated to community work and family support would be extremely difficult; hence, building the capacity of neighbourhoods might be the most feasible strategy. But to continue down the residual road will only serve to confirm the status of clients as failures and to deny them opportunities to become caring parents and responsible citizens.

References

Bowlus, A., McKenna, K., Day, T., and Wright, D. (2003). *The economic costs and consequences of child abuse in Canada: Report to the Law Commission of Canada.* Ottawa: Law Commission of Canada.

Brown, L., Haddock, L., and Kovach, M. (2002). Watching over our families and children: Lahum'utul'smun'een child and family services. In B. Wharf (Ed.), *Community work approaches to child welfare.* Peterborough: ON: Broadview Press.

Callahan, M., Brown, L., Mackenzie, P., and Whittington, B. (2004, Fall/Winter). Catch as catch can: Grandmothers raising their grandchildren and kinship policies. *Canadian Review of Social Policy, 54,* 58-78.

Callahan, M., Field, B., and Hubberstey, C. (1997). *Best practice in child welfare.* Victoria: University of Victoria School of Social Work.

Callahan, M., and Lumb, C. (1995). My cheque or my children. *Child Welfare, 74*(4), 796-820.

Cameron, G., and Vanderwoerd, J. (1997). *Promising programs and organizational realities.* New York: Aldine de Gruyter Press.

Community Panel on Family and Children's Services Legislation Review. (1992). *Making changes: A place to start.* Victoria: Ministry of Social Services.

deMontigny, G. (1995). *Social working: An ethnography of front line practice.* Toronto: University of Toronto Press.

Fuchs, D. (1995). Preserving and strengthening families and protecting children: Social network intervention; A balanced approach to the prevention of child maltreatment. In J. Hudson, and B. Galaway (Eds.), *Child welfare in Canada* (pp. 113-23). Toronto: Thompson Educational Publishing.

Kufeldt, K., and McKenzie, B. (Eds.). (2003). *Child welfare: Connecting research, policy and practice.* Waterloo, ON: Wilfrid Laurier University Press.

Levitt, K., and Wharf, B. (1985). *The challenge of child welfare.* Vancouver: UBC Press.

McKenzie, B. (2002). Building community in West Region Child and Family Services. In B. Wharf (Ed.), *Community work approaches to child welfare* (pp. 152-63). Peterborough, ON: Broadview Press.

Pancer, M., Nelson. G., Dearing. B., Dearing, S., Hayward, K., and Peters, R. (2003). Promoting wellness in families and children through community based interventions: The Highfields project. In K. Kufeldt and B. McKenzie (Eds.), *Child welfare: Connecting research, policy and practice.* Waterloo, ON: Wilfrid Laurier University Press.

Prilleltensky, I., Nelson, G., and Peirson, L. (2001). *Promoting family wellness and preventing child maltreatment.* Toronto: University of Toronto Press.

Swift, K. (1995). *Manufacturing bad mothers.* Toronto: University of Toronto Press.

Weller, F., and Wharf, B. (2002). Contradictions in child welfare. In M. Hayes and L.T. Foster (eds.), *Too small to see, too big to ignore: Child health and well-being in British Columbia.* Canadian Western Geographical Series 35. Victoria: Western Geographic Press.

Wharf, B. (1993). *Rethinking child welfare in Canada.* Toronto: McClelland and Stewart.

– (Ed.). (2002). *Community work approaches to child welfare.* Peterborough, ON: Broadview.

Appendix 1
Key Events in British Columbia Child Welfare, 1863 to May 2006

This appendix has been created as a summary or "snapshot" of major events that have affected and influenced child welfare decisions and policy-making in British Columbia over the last 140 years. As well as using material from chapters included in this book, a variety of different sources have been used. These include published annual and other reports of the Ministry of Children and Family Development and its predecessor ministries and departments; internal Ministry of Children and Family Development reports and documents held by the Health and Human Services Resource Centre of the BC Ministry of Health; the Gove Commission Report of 1995; an unpublished document, "A History of Child Welfare," created by Chris Welch, policy analyst in the Ministry of Children and Family Development, in 2004; an unpublished summary of key events in Aboriginal child welfare, created by H. Monty Montgomery of the School of Social Work at the University of Victoria; and other published and unpublished texts and papers noted at the end of the appendix.

Events	Significance
1863 First Indian residential school established	• St. Mary's School opens at Mission with over forty boys from the Sto:lo Nation. This is the first of sixteen residential schools to be established in the province.
1871 Order-in-council passed by Dominion of Canada respecting "Indians"	• The Dominion of Canada is granted "charge of Indians, and the trusteeship and management of lands reserved for their benefit" within BC.
1871 *Municipalities Act* passed	• Municipalities are given responsibility for "the relief of the poor."
1873 First BC orphanage opened	• Protestant Orphans Home is established in Victoria for Protestant children aged two to ten years who are homeless.

Events	*Significance*
1876 *An Act to Promote the Gradual Assimilation of the Indian Tribes of Canada*	• The Dominion of Canada passes legislation that formally introduces the residential school model as the vehicle for child welfare for indigenous peoples.
1880 Destitute, Poor and Sick Fund established	• Funds are provided by the provincial treasury for support in unorganized territories.
1890 Juvenile reformatory opened	• First BC reformatory comes into operation primarily to house youth suffering from "incorrigibility."
1891 *Act to Prohibit the Sale or Gift of Tobacco to Minors in Certain Cases*	• Cited as the *Minors' Protection Act*, it limits non-Aboriginal children's use of tobacco.
1892 Alexandra Orphanage established	• The orphanage is opened on Thanksgiving Day in Vancouver.
1895 First Friendly Aid Society founded	• The society is founded in Victoria to assist families in distress, establishing the friendly visitor tradition in BC.
1896 Vancouver Friendly Aid Society established	• BC's second society is established in the lower mainland in Vancouver.
1900 *An Act Respecting the Closing of Shops, and the Employment of Children and Young Persons Therein*	• The act regulates the employment of children under age sixteen in shops.
1901 The *Children's Protection Act* passed	• The act provides for the legal transfer of guardianship of orphaned or neglected children to the state or Children's Aid Society (CAS). • Superintendent of Neglected and Dependent Children to be appointed (voluntary).
1901 *An Act to Regulate Maternity Boarding Houses and for the Protection of Infant Children*	• The act requires all places caring for pregnant women and children to be inspected and registered with the municipality. No child under the age of one year is to be adopted without the consent of a children's aid society or superintendent of police.
1901 *An Act Respecting the Maintenance of Wives Deserted by their Husbands*	• A stipendary or police magistrate can order a husband to pay support.

Events	Significance
1901 Children's aid societies established	• First CASs incorporated in Vancouver and Victoria.
1903 *An Act Respecting the Support of Illegitimate Children*	• Establishes that the father of an illegitimate child is liable for the necessities of the child.
1905 Catholic Children's Aid Society established	• The third CAS is incorporated in Vancouver.
1905 Boys' Industrial School established	• A provincial school is opened in Vancouver on 1 February for custody and detention of boys under the *Juvenile Delinquents Act*.
1911 *Infants Act* passed	• The *Protection of Children's Act* is rolled into the *Infants Act*. Other legislation dealing with guardianship, apprenticeship of minors, infants contracts, settlements, illegitimate children's supports, and youthful offenders are also consolidated in this act.
1914 Girls' Industrial School established	• A provincial school is opened in Vancouver on 1 March for girls under the *Juvenile Delinquents Act*.
1914 *An Act to Make Provision for the Welfare and Protection of Women and Children Living under Communal Conditions*	• The act requires communes to register births, send children to school, and abide by the *Health Act*.
1919 Paid Superintendent of Neglected Children appointed	• D.B. Brankin is appointed superintendent and also superintendent of Boys' Industrial School (1920).
1920 *Mothers Pension Act* passed	• Administered by the Superintendent of Neglected Children under the Attorney General, the act provides a small pension for widowed/abandoned mothers with children under age sixteen.
1920 *Adoption Act* passed	• Provides legal framework for adoption. • Prior to this, children placed in a foster home were considered adopted if the family kept the child and did not return the child to the institution.

Events	*Significance*
1922 *Children of Unmarried Mothers Act* passed	• Allows for cash settlement from the "putative" father. • Administered by the Superintendent of Neglected Children.
1927 BC Child Welfare Survey	• There is a major reorganization and improved standards/professionalism of Vancouver CAS following review by Charlotte Whitton. • Social worker (Laura Holland) becomes director of CAS.
1927 Formal social work courses introduced	• Social work courses offered at UBC for the first time.
1930 School of Social Work established at UBC	• UBC opens its School of Social Work, the third such school in Canada.
1931 New superintendent model created	• Superintendent of Neglected Children combined with Superintendent of Welfare position (William Manson). • Director of Vancouver CAS is appointed deputy superintendent of neglected children.
1932 Child guidance clinic opened	• This specialized clinic, using psychiatrist, social worker, psychologist, and public health nurse resources, is established in Vancouver. • The clinic employs community resources to assist children who are "seriously maladjusted to their environment," as indicated through unhealthy habits, unacceptable behaviour, or an inability to cope with social and scholastic expectations.
1932 Survey of child welfare and mothers pension administration undertaken	• Charlotte Whitton undertakes the survey, which results in the decentralization of administration. Four offices are opened in Nanaimo, New Westminster, Nelson, and Kamloops.
1934 *Infants Act* amendment	• The amendment introduces preventative services to child welfare, making "ameliorating of family conditions that lead to the neglect of children" a CAS duty.
1935 Formal Child Welfare Division created	• Specific division is established under the Provincial Secretary, and a Welfare Field Service is established to cover twelve rural areas of the province.

Events	Significance
1937 *Mothers Allowance Act* passed	• *Mothers Pension Act* is replaced. Benefits are changed to an allowance rather than a perpetual pension. • The act also allowed a near female relative of a child to receive the allowance if she were acting as the child's foster parent.
1939 *Protection of Children Act* passed	• Replaces several parts of the 1911 *Infants Act*. Creates Superintendent of Child Welfare position. • Additional definitions of "neglected child" are added.
1942 Initiation of service amalgamation within government	• Child welfare section is amalgamated with other health and welfare sections, specifically Unemployment Relief Branch and mothers allowance under the Provincial Secretary. • Social Assistance Branch is created. • Five regions created to service the province through twelve district offices.
1944 An Act to Control the Employment of Children	• Prohibits employing children under the age of fifteen without written permission from the minister of labour.
1945 *Social Assistance Act* passed	• The act includes foster homes or boarding care as social services. • Provides funding for family counselling/preventive measures. • Much of the cost of services is borne by municipalities.
1946 Department of Health and Welfare created	• Separate cabinet portfolio created for Social Welfare Branch (which includes Child Welfare Division) and Health Branch, with two distinct deputy ministers appointed. • Start of decentralization of casework to the five regions on 1 October.
1947 Report of the Royal Commission on Provincial-Municipal Relations (the Goldenberg Report)	• Recommends province reimburse municipalities 80 percent of social aid cost, including foster home care for children under superintendent's permanent or temporary guardianship.
1950 Social Welfare Branch assumed responsibility for placing certain children	• The responsibility for children requiring care in municipalities surrounding Vancouver is taken over by the branch, which places them in their own municipalities rather than in Vancouver.

Events	Significance
1951 *Federal Indian Act* revised	• Section 88 is added to the legislation. • Provides for provincial legislation to apply on Indian reserves in the absence of federal laws. • Province becomes responsible for child welfare on Indian reserves. • This followed from a brief submitted by the Canadian Welfare Council and the Canadian Association of Social Workers to a Senate and House of Commons committee that was reviewing changes to the *Indian Act*.
1956 BC Association of Social Workers (BCASW) established	• BCASW is formed to create a professional association of social workers.
1958 Cost-sharing with municipalities changed	• The province increases its contribution to municipalities for child welfare costs to 90 percent from 80 percent on 1 September.
1959 *Department of Social Welfare Act* proclaimed	• Department of Health and Welfare is reorganized into two departments: Social Welfare and Health Services/ Hospital Insurance. • Wes Black is named minister.
1962 Battered child syndrome recognized	• Henry Kempe publishes groundbreaking article indicating many injuries to children are deliberately inflicted by parents.
1963 *Families and Children's Court Act* passed	• The act extends preventative services to families.
1964 Federal Treasury Board Minute Number 627879 established for on-reserve social services	• This minute indicates that provincial standards and procedures will apply in service delivery to BC First Nations. It essentially transfers much authority for on-reserve social services from the federal government to the province.
1966 Federal Canada Assistance Plan passed	• Legislation provides for federal government to pay 50 percent of basic social service costs, including child welfare and family counselling and preventive services.
1967 *Protection of Children Act* amended	• Amendment requires anyone *suspecting* maltreatment of a child to report their concerns. • Categories of "temporary" and "permanent" wards are established. The former offers temporary care for the child where planning indicates that the natural parents could be helped to become good parents.

Events	Significance
1968 Further amendments to *Protection of Children* *Act* passed	• Amendments allowed superintendent to permit adoption of permanent wards. • They also brought about closure of institution- alized care, including industrial schools.
1969 First full-time minister for social welfare appointed	• Phil Gaglardi is appointed to standalone social welfare portfolio.
1970 Department of Rehabili- tation and Social Improvement created	• Premier W.A.C. Bennett indicates name change from Social Welfare to reflect Social Credit government's social policies.
1973 Department of Human Resources created	• The name of the department is changed again by the newly elected New Democratic Party (NDP) government.
1973 Royal Commission on Family and Children's Law established	• Mr. Justice Thomas Berger is appointed to review all provincial laws related to children and families.
1974 *Community Resources* *Board Act* passed	• The act allows for the integration and decentralization of services, community participation, and local accountability. • CASs to be eliminated.
1974 Indian Homemakers Association of BC resolution	• This resolution called upon the federal government to recognize indigenous peoples' jurisdiction in the area of child welfare.
1975 Vancouver Resource Board created	• The board assumes responsibilities of Vancouver CASs and city welfare department, with power to provide statutory services, including child protection and guardianship.
1976 GAIN introduced	• Services to children were included on a discretionary basis under this program.
1976 Ministry of Human Resources created	• All departments are renamed ministries in the fall of 1976.
1977 *Community Resources* *Board Amendment Act* passed	• Vancouver Resource Board is eliminated, along with other community resource boards. Services are consolidated and centralized under Ministry of Human Resources.

Events	*Significance*
1978 Draft *Family and Child Service Act* released for public discussion	• The draft act emphasizes the role of the family in caring for children and also the government's role to provide the family with support services to carry out this responsibility.
1981 The *Family and Child Service Act* implemented	• Replaces 1939 *Protection of Children Act* after public review. • Grounds for child apprehension are reduced. • The definition of child is redefined to under age nineteen (previously under age seventeen). • Allows for greater supports to families to prevent children coming into care. • Provides for joint planning between social workers and Native bands regarding child welfare for Status children.
1981 Formal agreement signed between Spallumcheen band and federal government	• Federal government signs agreement with Spallumcheen band, giving it responsibility for the welfare of its children and child protection.
1983 Major provincial budget restraint program introduced by the province	• Social Credit government introduces a major restraint program following election win. • Includes a major staffing reduction for family support workers. • Start of major contracting-out of social services.
1984 Last Indian residential school closes	• Last residential school in BC, at Mission, closes, ending over 120 years of such schools operating in BC.
1984 Badgley Report is released	• Federal report identifies nature and extent of child sexual abuse in Canada.
1985 Nuu-chah-nulth tribal council agreements	• Agreement between the council and federal government for funding child welfare. • Agreement with the provincial government for delegation of provincial child welfare functions to the council. This is the first of twenty-four such agreements between the province and Aboriginal communities to be signed by May 2006.
1986 Moratorium on further transfers of First Nations child and family service	• Federal government imposes this moratorium while an assessment of current programs is undertaken.
1986 Ministry of Social Services and Housing created	• Ministry of Human Resources replaced by new ministry.

Events	Significance
1988 Major ministry reorganization	• Integrated offices in urban areas are changed to separate offices to deliver income assistance; family and children services; and services for people with mental handicaps.
1989 United Nations Convention on the Rights of the Child adopted	• Total of 54 articles in this convention approved in November. • Convention ratified by Canada and BC. • Convention's articles influence future child welfare legislation.
1990 Native and Family and Family Services Unit created	• On 19 March 1990, the province establishes this unit in Vancouver to focus on urban Aboriginal services.
1990 BC Ombudsman Report No. 22	• Report deals with the need for a single authority within government to oversee public services to children, youth, and their families.
1991 Ministry of Social Services created	• Ministry shortens title with the election of the new NDP government. • Major child care program is moved to a new Ministry of Women's Equality.
1991 Community panels established	• New NDP minister Joan Smallwood appoints community panel and separate Aboriginal community panel to review child welfare issues throughout the province.
1991 Federal Treasury Board Directive 20-1 adopted for Aboriginal child welfare	• Following the federal review initiated in 1986, this directive requires that First Nations have delegated authority from the province in order to receive federal funding for child welfare.
1992 Moratorium on adoption for Aboriginal children in care	• Restrictions on non-Aboriginal families adopting Aboriginal children are introduced.
1992 Community panels reports released	• Reports of the two community panels are released publicly. • *Making Changes: A Place to Start* contains over 160 separate recommendations. • *Liberating Our Children, Liberating Our Nations* contains 102 recommendations for Aboriginal child welfare.
1993 Korbin Commission report	• Recommends moving from a contracting relationship to a partnership relationship between government and funded agencies.

Events	Significance
1993 Province and Union of British Columbia Indian Chiefs sign Memorandum of Understanding (MOU)	• MOU signatories agree that protection and support services for First Nations children and families are the sole responsibility of First Nations. • They also agree that provincial jurisdiction will be withdrawn from the field of child welfare and family services as First Nations assume jurisdiction in these areas.
1993 *Making Changes: Next Steps* released	• Minister Smallwood releases White Paper on the *Child, Family and Community Service Act.* • Proposed legislation will continue to protect children, but will focus on supporting families as the best first step. • It will also place greater emphasis on the role of extended family and community members.
1994 Gove Commission created	• Judge Thomas Gove appointed to review the 1992 death of Matthew Vaudreuil.
1994 *Child, Family and Community Service Act* passed	• This legislation replaces the 1981 child protection legislation. • Implementation is delayed while the Gove Inquiry is underway.
1994 *Child, Youth and Family Advocacy Act*	• Joyce Preston becomes province's first independent advocate in 1996 when the legislation is finally implemented.
1995 *Child, Family and Community Service Act* amended	• The yet-to-be-implemented legislation is modified to take into account Gove's suggestions that the "safety and well-being of children" be listed as the "paramount considerations."
1995 Royal Commission on Aboriginal Peoples report is issued	• Volume three of this report, titled *Gathering Strength,* includes many recommendations related to Aboriginal child welfare being governed by Aboriginal peoples.
1995 Gove Report	• Gove Commission is completed in November and makes 118 recommendations to improve the child welfare system.
1996 *Child, Family and Community Service Act* implemented	• New legislation finally replaces 1981 *Family and Child Service Act.* • Expands definition of child in need of protection to include emotional abuse. • Emphasizes preservation of Aboriginal culture.
1996 New *Adoption Act* passed	• This act recognizes Aboriginal custom adoption.

Events	Significance
1996 Transition Commission created	• Cynthia Morton becomes Transition Commissioner to oversee implementation of Gove Report recommendations.
1996 New Ministry for Children and Families (MCF) created	• New ministry is created to integrate children and family services from five separate ministries following report from the Transition Commissioner. Child care program is reunited with child welfare, but income assistance program goes to a new ministry. • Twenty regions established to coincide with boundaries of health units.
1997 Children's Commission created	• Cynthia Morton becomes first Children's Commissioner, reporting to the Attorney General. • Commission made responsible for child death reviews.
1998 Child care program removed from ministry	• Child care is the first of several programs to be removed from MCF over the next several years.
1999 Major regional reorganization of Ministry for Children and Families	• The number of regions is reduced from twenty to eleven to save money.
1999 Nisga'a Treaty signed	• This is the first modern-day Indian treaty signed. • New Nisga'a Lisims government is given the right to make laws with respect to children and family services on Nisga'a lands.
1999 Amendments to *Child, Family and Community Service Act* passed	• The amendments allow social workers to supervise a child without having to remove him or her from the family.
1999 Strategic Plan for Aboriginal Services	• The underlying principle of this plan reflects a desire to have Aboriginal peoples involved in the delivery of services for children and families, either through consultations or through delegated service delivery agencies contracted with the province.
2001 Agreement signed by province and key Aboriginal leaders	• Agreement on moving control of Aboriginal child welfare to Aboriginal groups is signed with Aboriginal political and service groups.

Events	*Significance*
2001 Ministry of Children and Family Development (MCFD) created	• New Liberal administration makes major changes to the Ministry for Children and Families. • Some programs are transferred to other ministries. • Linda Reid becomes first ever Canadian minister of state for early childhood development.
2001 Core review	• All ministries are asked to review programs. • Core review for MCFD identifies six strategic shifts, including building capacity with Aboriginal communities to deliver a full range of services, with emphasis on early childhood and family development. • Cabinet approves the establishment of regional authorities to administer child welfare.
2002 Budget restraint	• In January, MCFD is instructed by Treasury Board to reduce budget by 23 percent and staffing by 22 percent over three years.
2002 Tsawwassen Accord	• Key Aboriginal groups (United Native Nations, First Nations Summit, Union of British Columbia Indian Chiefs, and the Métis Provincial Council of BC) agree to put past differences aside to take control of Aboriginal child welfare. • Memorandum of Understanding for Aboriginal Children is signed by the four Aboriginal groups, nine Aboriginal service organizations, the premier, and the ministers of MCFD and the Ministry of Community, Aboriginal and Women's Services. All agree on the need to reduce the number of Aboriginal children in care and to return them to their communities where appropriate. • The need for separate Aboriginal authorities for child and family services is recognized.
2002 New governance authorities concept approved by cabinet	• Ministry announces plans to create five independent regional authorities for family and children, with a similar number for Aboriginal services. • Regional planning committees are established.
2003 New Children and Youth Officer created	• Jane Morley is appointed to this position, which combines some of the functions of the Child, Youth and Family Advocate and the Children's Commissioner, which were both eliminated following Jane Morley's recommendation under the core review.

Events	Significance
2003 New fiscal plan for MCFD approved by Treasury Board	• Ministry undertakes a mid-term review because of concerns about its ability to meet its reduced budget target. • Ministry's budget changed to 11 percent reduction rather than 23 percent reduction.
2004 Minister resigns	• Gordon Hogg resigns to ensure public confidence in the office following concerns over alleged financial and other irregularities. Christy Clark becomes new minister.
2004 Introduction of new governance authorities postponed	• New regional authorities postponed until 2006-7. • Non-Aboriginal regional planning committees are disbanded. Aboriginal planning committees continue but with a lower level of funding.
2004 Minister resigns	• Minister and Deputy Premier Christy Clark announces her resignation and retirement from politics. • Stan Hagen is appointed as the new minister.
2005 New relationship developed between province and First Nations	• The premier's office works behind the scenes with the Attorney General and First Nations groups to develop a new relationship for revenue sharing to improve First Nations health and welfare.
2005 Ministry of Aboriginal Relations and Recon- ciliation created	• Liberal government creates new ministry to help work out the "New Relationship" framework.
2005 Controversy develops over the death of young Aboriginal child	• Numerous reviews (ten) are established to examine aspects of the death, which occurred while the child was cared for under a "kith and kin" agreement.
2005 BC Children and Youth Review established under the direction of the Honourable Ted Hughes	• This is the key review coming out of the above-mentioned child death. • The review is later requested to investigate why over seven hundred child death records were never reviewed. They were placed in a warehouse following the elimination of the Children's Commissioner's Office.
2006 Report of the BC Children and Youth Review is released	• The review provides sixty-two separate recommendations to improve the child protection system and to implement formal child death reviews of children "known to the ministry."

Events	Significance
	• A major recommendation is to establish a new position, Representative for Children and Youth, which will be an independent Officer of the Legislature.
2006 Legislation introduced and passed to create the Representative for Children and Youth as recommended by Hughes	• This legislation is approved unanimously by the legislature. • An all-party search committee is established. • An all-party Select Standing Committee on Children and Youth is established, to be chaired by Gordon Hogg, previous minister of MCFD. The representative will report to this committee.

Information Sources

Aboriginal Committee of the Community Panel on Family and Children's Services Legislation Review. (1992). *Liberating our children, liberating our nations.* Victoria: Ministry of Social Services.

Allen, D. (1998). *Contract and program restructuring review: Report to the Honourable Lois Boone.* Victoria: Ministry for Children and Families.

Armitage, A. (1993). Family and child welfare in First Nation communities. In·B. Wharf (Ed.), *Rethinking child welfare in Canada* (pp. 131-71). Toronto: McClelland and Stewart.

–. (1998, Summer). Lost vision: Children and the Ministry for Children and Families. *BC Studies, 118,* 93-108.

Clague, M., Dill, R., Seebaran, R., and Wharf, B. (1984). *Reforming human services: The experience of the community resource boards in B.C.* Vancouver: UBC Press.

Community Panel on Family and Children's Services Legislation Review. (1992). *Making changes: A place to start.* Victoria: Ministry of Social Services.

Cruickshank, D.A. (1985). The Berger Commission report on the protection of children: The impact on prevention of child abuse and neglect. In K.L. Levitt and B. Wharf (Eds.), *The challenge of child welfare* (2nd ed., pp. 182-200). Vancouver: UBC Press.

DiGeorgio, J.-A.L. (n.d.). *Child welfare history.* Unpublished background notes. Victoria: Ministry of Children and Family Development.

Foster, L.T., and Wright, M. (2002). Patterns and trends in children in the care of the province of British Columbia: Ecological, policy and cultural perspectives. In M.V. Hayes and L.T. Foster (Eds.), *Too small to see, too big to ignore: Child health and well-being in British Columbia* (pp. 103-40). Canadian Western Geographical Series, Vol. 35. Victoria: Western Geographical Press.

Gove, T. (1995). *Report of the Gove Inquiry into Child Protection in BC. Vol. 2. Matthew's legacy.* Victoria: Ministry of Attorney General.

Hughes, E.N. (2006). *BC children and youth review: An independent review of BC's child protection system.* Victoria: Ministry of Children and Family Development.

Johnston, P. (1983). *Native children and the child welfare system.* Canadian Council on Social Development. Toronto: Canadian Council on Social Development in association with James Lorimer.

Kempe, C.H., Silverman, F.N., Steele, B.F., Droegemueller, W., and Silver, H.K. (1962). The battered child syndrome. *Journal of the American Medical Association, 181,* 17-24.

Lundy, C.W. (1948). A historic review of the social services of the government of British Columbia. In R. MacKay (Ed.), *Annual report of the Social Welfare Branch of the Department of Health and Welfare* (pp. 7-31). Victoria: King's Printer.

MacDonald, J.A. (1985). The child welfare programme of the Spallumcheen Indian band in British Columbia. In K.L. Levitt and B. Wharf (Eds.), *The challenge of child welfare* (2nd ed., pp. 253-65). Vancouver: UBC Press.

MacKay, R. (Ed.). (1948). *Annual report of the Social Welfare Branch of the Department of Health and Welfare.* Victoria: King's Printer.

McKenzie, B., and Hudson, P. (1985). Native children, child welfare, and the colonization of Native people. In K.L. Levitt and B. Wharf (Eds.), *The challenge of child welfare* (2nd ed., pp. 125-41). Vancouver: UBC Press.

Ministry of Aboriginal Relations and Reconciliation. (2005). *The new relationship.* Victoria: Author. Retrieved 21 August 2005 from www.gov.bc.ca/arr/popt/the_new_relationship.htm

Ministry of Children and Family Development. (2002). *Memorandum of Understanding for Aboriginal Children.* Retrieved 21 August 2005 from www.mcf.gov.bc.ca/about_us/aboriginal/mou.htm

Montgomery, H.M. (n.d.). *First Nations child welfare: Background and historical context.* Unpublished fact sheet. Victoria: University of Victoria, School of Social Work.

Morgan, J. (1987). *Native Indian autonomy: Historical overview, emerging trends and implications for the Ministry of Social Services and Housing.* Victoria: Ministry of Social Services and Housing, Corporate Services Division.

Morton, C. (1996). *Morton report: British Columbia's child, youth and family serving system; Recommendations for change. Report to Premier Glen Clark.* Victoria: Transition Commissioner for Child and Youth Services.

Nelson, L.M. (1934). *Vancouver's early days and the development of the social services.* Vancouver: Social Workers Club.

Royal Commission on Aboriginal Peoples. (1996). *Report of the Royal Commission on Aboriginal Peoples. Vol. 3. Gathering strength.* Ottawa: Minister of Supply and Services.

Walkem, A., and Bruce, H. (2002). *Calling forth our future: Options for the exercise of indigenous peoples' authority in child welfare.* Vancouver: Union of British Columbia Indian Chiefs.

Welch, C. (2004). *A history of child welfare.* Unpublished report. Victoria: Ministry of Children and Family Development.

Appendix 2
Key Government Decision Makers in British Columbia Child Welfare, 1947 to May 2006

As government became more involved in the direct delivery of child welfare services, the role of political decision makers and public servants became increasingly important in child welfare policy, practice, and decision making. The table on the following pages lists the key individuals in government responsible for child welfare over the last six decades.

The minister is generally responsible for political direction and policy. The deputy minister has responsibility for the operations of the ministry, while the superintendent (whose title changed to director in 1996) has responsibility for child welfare practice issues.

Year	Government ministry/department	Minister responsible	Deputy minister	Superintendent/Director
1947	Department of Health and Welfare	George Pearson (Liberal)	E.W. Griffith	Ruby McKay
1950		A.D. Turnbull (Liberal)		
1953		Eric Martin (Social Credit)		
1955			C.W. Lundy	
1956			E.R. Rickinson	
1959	Department of Social Welfare	Wes Black (Social Credit)		
1961				Mary King
1965				T.D. Bingham
1967		D.R.J. Campbell (Social Credit)		
1969	Department of Rehabilitation and Social Improvement	Phil Gaglardi (Social Credit)		Vic Belknap
1972		Norm Levi (NDP)		
1973	Department of Human Resources			
1975		Bill Vander Zalm (Social Credit)		
1976	Ministry of Human Resources		John Noble	
1977		Grace McCarthy (Social Credit)		
1979				John Noble
1986		Jim Nielsen (Social Credit)		
1986	Ministry of Social Services and Housing	Claude Richmond (Social Credit)		
1987			Jim Carter	Andrew Armitage
			Isabel Kelly	Leslie Arnold
1988			Dick Butler	
1989		Peter Dueck (Social Credit)		
1990		Norm Jacobsen (Social Credit)		
1991	Ministry of Social Services	Joan Smallwood (NDP)	Lynn Langford	
1992			Bob Cronin	Joyce Rigaux

Year	Government ministry/department	Minister responsible	Deputy minister	Superintendent/Director
1993		Joy MacPhail (NDP)	Sheila Wynn	Bernd Walter
1994				
1995				Chris Haynes
1996	Ministry for Children and Families	Dennis Streifel (NDP)	Brenda Eaton	Ross Dawson
1996		Penny Priddy (NDP)	Bob Plecas	
1998		Lois Boone (NDP)	Mike Corbeil	
2000		Gretchen Mann Brewin (NDP)	Sharon Manson Singer	
		Edward John (NDP but unelected)		
2001	Ministry of Children and Family Development	Gordon Hogg (Liberal)	Chris Haynes	Wayne Matheson
		Linda Reid, Minister of State for Early Childhood Development (Liberal)		David Young
2002				In addition to David Young: Elaine Murray (Headquarters; revoked in 2003) Jane Cowell (Vancouver Island) Fred Milowsky (Vancouver Coastal) Les Boon (Fraser) Rick Childerhose (Interior) Doug Hayman (Northern)

Year	Minister	Deputy Minister	
2003			Linda O'Brien (replaces Fred Milowsky in Vancouver Coastal) Jeremy Berland (replaces David Young in HQ)
2004	Christy Clark (Liberal) Stan Hagen (Liberal)	Alison MacPhail	Bruce McNeill (replaces Les Boon in Fraser) Tom Webber (replaces Jane Cowell in Vancouver Island)
2005	Stan Hagen (Liberal) Linda Reid, Minister of State for Child Care (Liberal)	Arn van Iersel (Associate Deputy Minister)	Robert Watts (replaces Doug Hayman in Northern) Jean Macdonald (appointed to cover Community Living BC children)
2006		Arn van Iersel (Acting Deputy Minister) Beth James (Acting Associate Deputy Minister) Lesley du Toit	Mark Sieben (replaces Jeremy Berland in HQ as Acting Director)
2006			

Sources: Ministry of Children and Family Development and predecessor ministries and departments annual reports and press releases; Welch, C. (2004), *A history of child welfare*, unpublished report, Victoria: Ministry of Children and Family Development.

Appendix 3
Delegated Aboriginal Child and Family Service Agencies' Status, May 2006

Delegation agreements give legal authority to Aboriginal agencies and their employees to undertake administration of all, or specific parts, of the *Child, Family and Community Service Act (CFCSA)*. After the provincial Ministry of Children and Family Development, the federal Department of Indian and Northern Affairs, and the Aboriginal community served by the agency have negotiated the delegation enabling agreement, the agency is in start-up mode. The agency moves from one delegation level to another following readiness assessment conducted by the director of the *CFCSA*.

At the end of May 2006, the delegation status for agencies was as follows: seven agencies had the appropriate delegation to provide full child protection services as well as voluntary and guardianship services (Level 15); ten agencies could provide guardianship services and approve foster homes for children in continuing care (Level 13); and four agencies could provide limited services related to voluntary services and the recruitment and approval of foster homes (Level 12). Three more agencies were in start-up mode, for a total of twenty-four active agencies. Five agencies were in the planning stages for obtaining delegation to provide particular services.

Three agencies – Vancouver Aboriginal Child and Family Services, Métis Family Services in Surrey, and Surrounded by Cedar Child and Family Services in Victoria – provide services in urban areas. These urban agencies are funded by the provincial government. The remaining agencies are all First Nations agencies providing on-reserve services, though some provide off-reserve services as well. All First Nations agencies are accountable to their communities, the federal government, and the Ministry of Children and Family Development. The table below provides a summary of the levels of delegation and status for twenty-nine agencies.

The editors acknowledge the assistance provided by Julie Dawson, Director of Aboriginal Services, MCFD, in compiling this appendix.

Service Agency	Communities		Children in care
	Name	Band no.	

Operational level 15/C6

Lalum'utul Smun'eem Child and Family Services *Initial Agreement:* 22 January 1993	Cowichan	642	57
Knucwentwecw Society *Initial Agreement:* 13 October 1995	Canim Lake Canoe Creek Soda Creek Williams Lake	713 723 716 719	29
Ktunaxa-Kinbasket Family and Child Services *Initial Agreement:* 27 July 1999	Columbia Lake Lower Kootenay Shuswap St. Mary's Tobacco Plains	604 606 605 602 603	48
Nlha'7kapmx Child and Family Services *Initial Agreement:* 22 September 1994	Cook's Ferry Kanaka Bar Lytton Nicomen Siska Skuppah	694 704 705 696 706 707	11
Scw'exmx Child and Family Services *Initial Agreement:* 31 May 1994	Coldwater Lower Nicola Nooaitch Shackan Upper Nicola	693 695 699 698 697	34
Usma Nuu-chah-nulth Community and Human Services *Initial Agreement:* 12 February 1987	Ahousat Ditidaht Ehattesaht Hesquiaht Huu-ay-aht Ka:'yu:k't'h'/ Che:K:tles7et'h Mowachaht/ Muchalaht Hupacasath Nuchatlaht Tla-o-qui-aht Toquaht Tseshaht Uchucklesaht Ucluelet	659 662 634 661 663 638 630 664 639 660 666 665 667 668	130

| Service Agency | Communities | | Children |
	Name	Band no.	in care
Xyolhemeylh Program Sto:lo	Aitchelitz	558	324
Health and Family Services	Chawathil	583	
Initial Agreement:	Cheam	584	
26 November 1993	Kwantlen	564	
	Kwaw Kwaw Apilt	580	
	Lakahahmen	579	
	Matsqui	565	
	Peters	586	
	Popkum	585	
	Scowlitz	568	
	Seabird Island	581	
	Shxw'ow'hamel	587	
	Skawahlook	582	
	Skowkale	571	
	Skwah	573	
	Skway	570	
	Soowahlie	572	
	Squiala	574	
	Sumas	578	
	Tzeachten	575	
	Union Bar	588	
	Yakweakwioose	576	
	Yale	589	

Operational level 13/C4

Service Agency	Name	Band no.	Children in care
Ayas Men Men Child and Family Services	Squamish	555	46
Initial Agreement:			
28 April 1993			
Carrier Sekani Family	Burns Lake	619	42
Services	Cheslatta	620	
Initial Agreement:	Lake Babine	607	
29 January 1998	Nadleh Whut'en	612	
	Stella'ten	613	
	Saik'uz	615	
	Takla Lake	608	
	Wet'suwet'en	725	
	Yekooche	728	
Gitxsan Child and Family Services	Gitanmaax	531	4
Society	Gitanyow	537	
Initial Agreement:	Gitsegukla	535	
3 June 1999	Gitwangak	536	
DCA signed:	Glen Vowell	533	
28 September 2004	Kispiox	532	

Service Agency	Communities		Children in care
	Name	*Band no.*	
Kwumut Lelum Central Island Child and Family Services *Initial Agreement:* *8 December 1997*	Chemainus	641	59
	Halalt	645	
	Lake Cowichan	643	
	Lyackson	646	
	Malahat	647	
	Nanoose	649	
	Penelakut	650	
	Qualicum	651	
	Snuneymuxw	648	
Métis Family Services *Initial Agreement:* *11 April 2001*	Métis (Simon Fraser/ South Fraser)		111
Nisga'a Family and Child Services *Treaty Initial Agreement:* *5 May 1997*	Citizens of the Nisga'a Lisims government, including villages of:		22
	Gingolx/Kincolith	671	
	Gitlakdamix	677	
	Lakalzap	678	
	Gitwinksihlkw	679	
Northwest Inter-Nation Family Services Society *Initial Agreement:* *8 February 1999*	Hartley Bay	675	14
	Iskut	683	
	Kitamaat	676	
	Kitkatla	672	
	Kitselas	680	
	Kitsumkalum	681	
	Lax-kw'alaams	674	
	Metlakatla	673	
	Tahltan	682	
Sechelt Child and Family Services *Initial Agreement:* *28 April 1993*	Sechelt	551	12
Secwepemc Child and Family Services *Initial Agreement:* *6 March 2000*	Adams Lake	684	71
	Bonaparte	686	
	Kamloops	688	
	Neskonlith	690	
	North Thompson	691	
	Skeetchestn	687	
	Whispering Pines	702	

| Service Agency | Communities | | Children |
	Name	Band no.	in care
Vancouver Aboriginal Child and Family Services Society (VACFSS) *Initial Agreement:* *20 September 2001*	Vancouver Urban (Vancouver/ Richmond)		323

Operational level 12/C3

Heiltsuk Kaxla Child and Family Service Program *Initial Agreement:* *31 March 2000*	Heiltsuk	538	
Nil/tu'o Child and Family Services *Initial Agreement:* *5 March 1999*	Beecher Bay Pauquachin Songhees Tsartlip Tsawout T'sou-ke	640 652 656 653 654 657	
K'wak'walat'si First Nations Child and Family Services ('Namgis) *Initial Agreement:* *28 January 2005*	'Namgis	631	
Surrounded by Cedar Child and Family Services *Initial Agreement:* *24 May 2005*	Victoria Urban		

Start-up operational level

Desniqi Services Society *Initial Agreement:* *23 June 2005*	Alexandria Alexis Creek (Tsi Del Del) Anaham (Tl'etinqox) Nemiah (Xeni Gwet'in) Stone (Yunesit'in) Toosey (Tl'esqotin)	709 710 712 714 717 718	
Haida Child and Family Services *Initial Agreement:* *1 April 2006*	Old Masset Village Council Skidegate Band	669 670	
Nezul Be Hunuyeh Child and Family Services *Initial Agreement:* *31 July 2002*	Nak'azdli Tl'azt'en	614 617	

| Service Agency | Communities | | Children |
	Name	Band no.	in care
Planning stage			
Dlugwe Che-Chuy Family and	Campbell River	622	
Child Services Society	Cape Mudge	623	
	Comox	624	
	Homalco	552	
	Klahoose	553	
	Kwiakah	628	
	Mammalilikulla-		
	Qwe'Qwa'Sot'Em	629	
Northeast First Nations Child	Blueberry River	547	
and Family Services	Doig River	548	
and	Fort Nelson	543	
South Peace Aboriginal Council	Halfway River	546	
Child and FamilyServices	Prophet River (Dene		
(SPAC)	Tsaa Tse K'nai)	544	
	Salteaux	542	
	West Moberly, including		
	communities of:		
	Dawson Creek		
	Pouce Coupe		
	Kelly Lake	545	
Okanagan Nation	Lower Similkameen	598	
	Okanagan	616	
	Osoyoos	596	
	Penticton	597	
	Upper Nicola	697	
	Upper Similkameen	599	
Stl'atl'lmx Nation	Bridge River	590	
	Cayoose Creek	591	
	Douglas	561	
	Fountain (Xaxli'p)	592	
	Mount Currie	557	
	N'Quatqua	556	
	Samahquam	567	
	Seton Lake	595	
	Skookumchuk	562	
	T'it'kit	593	
	Ts'kw'aylaxw (Pavilion)	594	
Wetsuwet'en Nation	Moricetown	530	
Child and Family	Hagwilget	534	
Services			

Source: Ministry of Children and Family Development, Aboriginal Services Branch.

Contributors

Andrew Armitage is professor emeritus at the School of Social Work, University of Victoria; author of *Social Welfare in Canada*; and a former BC assistant deputy minister and Superintendent of Child Welfare.

Leslie Brown is the director of the School of Social Work, University of Victoria, and is currently engaged in several research projects examining such subjects as grandmothers caring for grandchildren, fathering in child welfare, and supporting Aboriginal people with disabilities. She recently co-edited *Research as Resistance: Critical, Indigenous and Anti-Oppressive Approaches* (2005).

Marilyn Callahan is professor emeritus at the School of Social Work, University of Victoria. She has written extensively on women and child welfare and is currently working with colleagues on projects examining the role of grandmothers raising grandchildren, the voice of fathers, and risk assessment in child welfare.

John Cossom is professor emeritus at the School of Social Work, University of Victoria. He also taught at the universities of Regina and Waterloo and at Wilfrid Laurier University. He practised in child welfare, family service, and corrections.

Leslie T. Foster is adjunct professor in the faculties of Child and Youth Care and Geography at the University of Victoria. He was assistant deputy minister in the provincial ministries of health, social services, and children and family development, and has written extensively on these policy issues. His latest co-edited book is *The Youth of British Columbia: Their Past and Their Future* (2005).

Jacquie Green is currently an assistant professor in the School of Social Work, University of Victoria. Her traditional name is Kundoque, which originates from the Tsimshian peoples in northwestern BC. She is Kemano on her father's side and Kitselas on her mother's side. Within these two traditional places, she is Haisla and was born and raised in this territory.

Riley Hern is a retired Ministry of Children and Family Development team leader. Having worked in child welfare for forty years, he believes that practice improvement can be achieved only through research collaboration between government, local universities, and local communities.

Maggie Kovach is an assistant professor at the School of Social Work, University of Victoria. She is of Plains Cree and Saulteaux ancestry. Her scholarship includes indigenous research methodologies and First Nations curriculum development. As a First Nations social worker, Maggie has worked with First Nations communities in the area of child and family services training for several years.

H. Monty Montgomery teaches in the School of Social Work, University of Victoria. He is of Micmac ancestry and is a graduate of the University of Victoria Bachelor and Master of Social Work by distance program.

Tony Morrison is an independent child welfare trainer and consultant in Rochdale, U.K. He works with staff in social services, health, and other agencies on management development, interagency collaboration, staff supervision, and workforce development. His publications include *Staff Supervision in Social Care,* 3rd edition (2005) and *Strength to Strength* (2005). He has delivered training in BC and Manitoba, and is a visiting research fellow at the University of Huddersfield in England.

Elaine Murray has more than thirty-five years' operational experience serving families and children throughout British Columbia. She retired in 2003 as assistant deputy minister with the Ministry of Child and Family Development and is currently the director of organizational development for Community Living BC, a provincial Crown agency established to provide services to families and persons with developmental disabilities.

Sandra Scarth is a social worker who has authored reviews of child welfare services across Canada and advocated for over forty years for the rights of children in child welfare to permanent family and cultural connections. She is also a founding member of the Child Welfare League of Canada.

Richard Sullivan is associate professor in the University of British Columbia School of Social Work and Family Studies. With thirty years' experience in social work with children and families, Dr. Sullivan teaches courses in child development and child welfare policy and practice as well as in family policy and the theoretical foundations of social welfare.

Karen Swift is associate professor and former director of the School of Social Work at York University. Her book *Manufacturing Bad Mothers* reveals the everyday practices of child welfare that perpetuate the struggles of women and children. She also does research and publishes on Canadian social policy. Dr. Swift is studying risk assessment in child welfare, funded by the Social Sciences and Humanities Research Council.

Deryck Thomson is a retired social worker. For twenty years he served as executive director of the Family Service Centres of Greater Vancouver, and he held a similar post with the G.R. Pearkes Centre for Children in Victoria for nine years. In 2004, he received the Distinguished Service Award from the Canadian Association of Social Workers for contributions to his profession and community during the past fifty years.

Christopher Walmsley is the chair of the Bachelor of Social Work Program at Thompson Rivers University. He is the author of *Protecting Aboriginal Children* (2005) and co-editor of *Child and Family Welfare in British Columbia: A History* (2005). Dr. Walmsley is currently involved in research projects exploring fathering within child welfare and social action in small cities.

Brian Wharf is professor emeritus at the School of Social Work, University of Victoria, and the author/editor of a number of books, including, most recently, *Community Work Approaches to Child Welfare* (2002).

Index

The letter (t) following a page number denotes a table, the letter (f), a figure.